The Arch and the Path

THE LIFE OF LEADING GREATLY

BY MICHAEL H. SHENKMAN, PH.D.

TABLE OF CONTENTS

ACKNOWLEDGMENTS

This book was possible because of the courageous openness with which my clients engaged in the mentoring work. All of the stories told in this book are theirs, though their actual identities have been withheld. I want to thank each and every one of them for making leader mentoring the most exciting work I have ever done. Also, the real people behind the CEO characters, whom I have named "Harry Kaufman," "Brian Thomas," and "Howard Keats," have been willing to invest in outstanding new leaders. To them, and the other organizational leaders who have done this work, for caring to develop new leaders, we all owe our thanks.

EXPLORE THYSELF.

HEREIN ARE DEMANDED THE EYE AND THE NERVE.

—*HENRY DAVID THOREAU*

DEDICATION

This book is dedicated to Carol, my loving wife and inspirational companion on this journey of wondrous discovery.

Introduction

Think about the leaders who have touched your life in important ways. What made these leaders "great" in your eyes? Did they have a vision? With these leaders, did you learn more about yourself than you ever had before? Did these leaders have a way that made the impossible seem possible, and so you didn't mind the pains along the way?

My answer is this: Great leaders inspire success by shaping their lives in dedication to a vision they offer to others, in the spirit of collaboration and mutual aspiration.

"So," you might ask, "how do they do that?"

This question launches us into The Arch and the Path: The Life of Leading Greatly.

When great leaders attempt to reveal their "secrets" in speeches on the rubber chicken circuit, or in hagiographic autobiographies, they offer this typical advice: "Find the best people and let them do their work." Well, how do you know in advance who the best people are? Once you have them in your organization, then what? Answers like these just show that leaders themselves may be the worst people to ask about their secrets.

So they certainly aren't telling the pundits the real secrets. A major focus of the pundit's approach to the question is to characterize a successful leader's style. But if you ask one of these experts to enumerate which aspects of a leader's style makes for success, the answers sound like something out of LaoTsu. "Be yourself," they say. Good. True. But what does that advice do for you when you are struggling to get a handle on who you are as a leader in the first place?

Another approach is overkill. A recent issue of a business magazine I subscribe to was devoted to leadership. In that twenty-page issue (that is merely twenty pages), I counted up ninety-five major bits of advice, to which were added forty-five minor and supporting bits of advice. That means in twenty pages, aspiring leaders were given 140 bits of advice to follow in order to succeed. In addition to it being completely impossible for anyone to remember 140 bits of advice, no less follow them (no matter how good they are), I know of no successful leader that uses a cheat sheet of behaviors to check off in order to determine if they are leading well, properly, excellently, or greatly. Even with that cheat sheet in hand, which bit of advice are you going to follow today, young leader?

THE REAL ANSWERS

Aspiring leaders really want to ask great leaders: "What is it that you seem to know, intuitively or consciously, what wisdom do you use every day, all the time, in every leader engagement you undertake, that helps you most? How do you inspire others to overcome their fears and habits in order to succeed? How do you act with such ease, in the face of such daunting challenges? Can we do that?"

Why can't we get answers to these questions? On one level, leaders just want to get the interview done with and get out the door. But a deeper reason is that the real answers to these questions are contained in nothing less than *life practices that leaders engage in, as a matter of course, in response to what they deeply care about.*

To answer those questions, leaders would have to describe the everyday activities they "religiously" engage in, so as to be able to offer wisdom, patience, insight, humility, and courage to their followers. They would have to catalogue the habits of study and observation that they use to grasp the brute essence of a situation; explain the need leaders feel to keep up current with trends and ideas; describe their practices of keeping fit and shepherding energy; enumerate the time and money spent on courses that help them hone their skills of expression; and so on. And, sadly, in all probability, most people, especially the interviewing pundit, wouldn't see the connection between all of these "activities" and that leader's "charisma."

The premise of this book is that there are certain patterns or *"practices" of living—thinking, feeling, behaving—that are conducive to leading greatly; and some people, and not others, engage in those activities with the express purpose of being fit, ready, and able to lead.* In other words, there are certain ways of living—there is an "ethic" so to speak—that leaders subscribe to and that others don't subscribe to. *These "practices," or ingrained patterns of feeling, thinking, and behaving, result in a particular quality of engagement with the world such that they create followers who, together, strive to succeed in accomplishing large collaborative endeavors.*

CREATIVE LEADING

Now another question arises: What do we mean by leading? Does anyone who gains power or attains authority, wins an election, or is appointed by a designated process, qualify as being a leader? I don't think so. I doubt that you would answer the question, what makes a leader great by saying, "Gee, this boss of mine could really cut costs"? Greatness isn't attributed to people because they design efficient production processes that get good results. Neither does greatness follow on from an outsized "Iacocca" personality or a "Six Sigma," Jack Welch mentality.

To make matters even murkier, not all those who are acknowledged as leaders are people whom we would want in such positions. One need only think of Adolph Hitler. He was supremely capable of rousing the energies of his people. And he led them, along with the rest of the world, into hell. He and his ilk are *not* the kind of leaders we want, no less help others become. So, just because someone is in a position of authority, reaching that office by whatever means, does not mean they are leaders as we understand the term. Throughout this book, we are envisioning a kind of leading that excludes all of those deficient or daemonic expressions of persuasion, coercion, or power that has been called leading.

Our aim is to help readers foster the attitudes, behaviors, and ethic of "*Creative Leading.*" First, there are some qualities that don't meet our criteria. Undertaking a leader role for the purposes of ego gratification, self-aggrandizement and personal enrichment, especially at the expense of others, does not meet our criteria. Destructive (sectarian, racist, territorial, power-hungry) attitudes, such as arrogance, control (for its own sake), antisocial aggressiveness for the sake of gaining and maintaining one's power, are antithetical to what we mean by creative leading.[1]

When we think of "creative leading," we envision how so many of our clients work hard and conscientiously to:

➤ *Touch many people, really changing their lives, for the better.*

➤ *Demonstrate qualities of friendliness, respect, and appreciation for other people's accomplishments in both successes and failures.*

➤ *Enable people to envision and then fulfill their own aspirations while fulfilling the mission at hand.*

➤ *Accomplish goals that to others genuinely seemed impossible—from turning around failing companies to creating new technologies or changing whole societies.*

➤ *Willingly mentor others so as to pass the torch to the next generation of leaders.*

➤ *Actively seek out potential leaders and nurture their talents.*

So, putting these observations together, we offer a definition of creative leading:

[1] In fact, we wish people would start to form crisper, more refined descriptions of the people in power. They may be officers, authorities, executives, officials, administrative heads, bosses; but because people occupy positions of authority or act in dominating, controlling, or power-wielding ways, this does not qualify them for the mantle of being considered what we call a leader. Eskimos have scores of terms for snow, reflecting the quality of attention Eskimos pay to that fluffy white stuff. I wish we'd pay the same attention to the way we differentiate leading from other forms of exerting authority or power. There would be far fewer people whom we would name as being leaders, or we'd find ourselves in really important discussions as to whether or not a given authority figure is a leader.

Creative leading is one of the roles² to which some people commit their lives, laboring in and with organizations, in order to take what was once merely a vision of new, more expansive and encompassing possibilities into actual products, services, relationships, and actions that people experience in their everyday lives. They do so by creating followers—informed and capable people who freely and consciously devote their individual talents and energies in collaborative endeavors—and then guiding their experiences as they strive toward their goals.

If we look at that definition more closely, we can make these points about the endeavor of being a creative leader:

"Commit their lives." Creative leading is a lifetime commitment, not a nine-to-five job. Those leading in this way do not leave the job at the office. They think and work on the issues of the endeavor all the time, with much, but not all, of their energies.

"A vision of new, more expansive and encompassing possibilities into actual products, services, relationships and actions that people can experience in their everyday lives." Creative leading is not about incremental process improvements. It comprises actions dedicated to change—changing attitudes, behaviors, living conditions, people's sense of capability and well-being—in the real world. Creative leaders want the world to be different. But they want it to be different in a specific way. They want

---

[2] There are four transformational roles: mystic, artist, prophet, and leader. All of these roles entail being called to discern and craft a life that is in tune with deeper and/or more transcendent currents of life. Mystics shape their individual existences to be a solitary instrument for experiencing those energies and attesting to their reality. Prophets translate these messages into insights and lessons that carry urgency, sufficient to stimulate others' new thoughts and actions. Artists feel these currents and translate them into a form of expression that others can see or hear. Leaders take these insights into practical action that entails collaboration and sustained effort.

All of these roles are necessary for the kind of meaningful, expansive, and encompassing change we envision taking place. Leading-organized action is actually the last step in a succession of psychic, intellectual, and emotional changes that transformation entails.

For more discussion on the four transformational roles go to our website, www.archofleadership.com.

nothing less than *transformations*—large scale, sustainable changes in whole ways of engaging our lives—that enable more people to be more able to express their own talents and energies; they want to nurture diversity in the world—within the human community and between the human and nonhuman worlds; they want to support actions (including some limitations) that foster the next generation of leaders, who, in turn, will foster diversity themselves. These leaders do not need enemies to establish themselves as worthy of leading and do not need to abuse instruments of power and/or office to accomplish their vision.

"By creating followers—informed and capable people who freely and consciously devote their individual talents and energies in collaborative endeavor."[3] The followers upon which creative leaders rely are not sycophants, or blindly obedient knaves. They are not fearfully responding to bravado in the face of real or hyped-up dangers; they are not sadly dispirited people who are grasping at illusions for hope; they are not ignorant conformists looking for a mob to join or a guru who will ply them with pat solutions. *They are people who decide to devote their talents and energies to the endeavor and open themselves to the risks and learning that will be put upon them.* Future leaders emerge out of the group of those who have followed and now see how they too can be creative leaders.

"Guiding their experiences as they strive toward their goals." Creative leading does not only entail "getting results" or "getting the job done." The people who undertake this endeavor realize that failure does happen. The outcomes of their efforts may not be predictable. But people will be affected by the effort. They will have experiences in which their aspirations are informed and made more palpably real. Everyone affected by the effort will feel more alive for having participated.

---

[3] We will have a great deal to say about followers in chapter 3, so I will be brief here.

CAN CREATIVE LEADING BE TAUGHT?

The first step into leading begins as though one were *called.* This call manifests itself in many ways. Some people just find themselves being asked to lead, or that it is already assumed that they are the leaders. Others find themselves caring so much about certain situations; they really want to do something about it. No one asks them to lead, but their internally driven need to do something proves to be too irrepressible to deny. Or, for those who are asked, the invitation itself is a surprise. Other people just feel the need to engage the world in the company of others. They feel the need to take on endeavors of such a scale that they cannot do it by themselves. These people find themselves leading, almost whether they want to lead or not. For many, leading a large-scale collaborative endeavor is just the perfect thing to do; for others, leading is a responsibility of weight and difficulty, but no less compelling for those travails.

The call can be easily missed however. So, usually the call also comes with a *mentor*—someone who helps potential leaders sort out all the signals and realize that the unrest they feel is the call to lead. Another reason mentors are important is that getting the call is only the beginning. Because some people suddenly and unexpectedly find themselves leading does not mean they will subsequently (when they realize what they have gotten themselves into) and consciously *decide* to shape their lives as leaders. They are, actually, more likely to get the hell out—retire, or become a consultant—than take on the next, larger, more encompassing challenge. Mentors help potential leaders step into the role and actually lead. Mentors then help leaders become great leaders. Finally, mentors help to keep great leaders in the game.

Then, once the call is accepted, leaders need to learn certain skills.

Accordingly, the purpose of this book is to foster that learning, to act as a surrogate mentor. We provide a guide, a companion for those who have been thrown into the experience of leading, by helping them to focus energies and attention on the inner experiences and relationship skills that guide creative and effective leading. This is what we have called the "path" for developing one's self in a way that is appropriate and constructive for becoming a leader.

THE PATH

As in many mythical stories or fairy tales of self-actualization, we follow a sojourner, an aspiring leader, through many years, as she passes through successively more difficult challenges. It seems that however vast the range of the leader's experiences, there are always higher hurdles to vault, forcing the leader to decide whether or not to take on the next challenge. The young novitiate needs to consider how to respond to the discovery of a talent and ability to lead. For the experienced CEO, a different level of learning is going on. This leader has to decide whether or not this is the kind of life he wants at all.

To depict the outline of the journey undertaken by the creative leaders, and the path on which their learning takes place, we offer two characters: an imaginary leader whom we call Beth and a fictional mentor, Matt, in whom she confides. Beth's story spans many more years than we have spent with any one client. But because we have worked with so many different leaders, at all stages of their careers, Beth represents the common threads of a story we have seen played out by many leaders, as their story in leading unfolds. And then, by combining the work done by myself and the other mentors in our firm, our fictional mentor can be portrayed as a resource to Beth over the span of her entire career.

THE IMAGE OF THE ARCH[4]

The idea of leading conjures up vivid images: the commander up in front of the troops beckoning them to follow; the figure atop the pyramid, elevated above all the others on a platform, glorified in lights, and dignified with trappings of office is another. Creative leaders need a different image in order to conceive and picture the relationships they project and coordinate. To meet this need, we created the image of the "Arch of Leadership."

The arch symbolizes a structure of all the energies, talents, and knowledge the leader calls upon in order to lead. Thus the spires, the keystone at the top of the arch, and the space defined by the arch combine into a picture of the leader's psyche.[5] We envision a leader as one who guides certain experiences of competent people (who hardly need an authority figure to make their lives worthwhile). The leader is thus not an august figure above and beyond followers, but rather exerts structured, focused energies into a defined area, in which there are others as well as the leader, in order to provide a place apart, a place in which those special things, once only dreamed of, can take shape into collaborative actions.

---

[4] A full explanation of the arch and its development during the course of our journey can be found in the appendix.

[5] "Psyche" is a word I use to designate the physical, mental, and emotional activities our bodies undertake in order to coalesce all the factors in play, at any given moment, to arrive at a coherent decision and/or course of action.

11

THE ARCH OF LEADERSHIP:

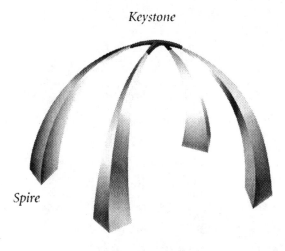

Keystone

Spire

THE STRUCTURE

With its four vaulting spires and binding keystone, the arch is self-supporting. There is no need for mortar; no fasteners hold the structure together. Each of the spires stands upright, their weight anchoring them into the earth, the keystone breaking their propensity to topple over. The keystone is held in its lofty position by the vaulting strength of the spires. Energy from each spire comes to rest and is stabilized by transferring into the mass of the keystone. This is where the energies of the arch converge and are integrated into a single structure. The *spires* thus represent specific structural elements of the leader's psyche that must be present for the arch to be an enduring presence amidst the larger, already established environment. The *keystone* symbolizes the leader's binding and unifying strength that give the arch its coherence and integrity and thus represents that dimension of self that anyone who leads must have—and must have in a highly developed form that is easily accessed. All the energy people within the arch feel from a leader emanates from the integrating element represented by the keystone.

The *interior* of the arch also symbolizes how the leader's energy and spirit mark out a special place in the world where the energies of the leaders and followers interact. Within the arch's area flow energies of interconnecting communication, information sharing, and focused attention generated by the leader's character and the followers' enthusiasm as they collaborate in pursuing the goals of the endeavor.

OPEN STRUCTURE

The arch remains open to the outside world so everyone within the arch remains connected to the influences and events occurring beyond its perimeter. Even with its openness, however, the arch marks off a *defined space* such that there is a difference between the interior it demarcates and the larger world in which it is situated. Within the space marked off by the arch, *leader and followers are connected by a binding energy not present (in concentrated form) in the general environment that surrounds them.* Within the arch, the leader's energies are directly experienced as being ordered and structured. Outside the arch, well, anything goes.

At this point, it is enough to say that the whole purpose of the arch and each of its components is to produce this energy for others. The arch is not a symbol of self-consciousness or of one's isolation from the world. It is an open structure, gathering energy and information from its open spaces as well as from the ground on which the spires stand and from which they draw their energies.

It is a structure that channels, forms, and structures life energies so as to help others move into new actions and uncharted territories.

The arch's open structure also signifies the *completely voluntary and free-flowing nature of followists*. A leader creates followers, who, in our definition, are always in the act of choosing to be a part of that relationship. There is no coercion—whether that be a matter of political force or the threat of withdrawing wages—in the leader-follower relationship as we envision it. It is a mutually propagated relationship that is, at all times, of mutual and holistic benefit, or it withers and dies. Followers choose to enter the arch, and so long as there is energy from which they draw sustenance to act and risk and move into the unknown, they will stay—and no longer.

OVERVIEW

The book thus envisions the unfolding of the story by which people who are leaders become great leaders. The story has four parts. Each of these parts constitutes a learning moment, an occasion for pausing and reflecting, as we journey on the path to great leading. During these moments, we check in with Beth and reflect on the experience that is bringing her to a point of needing new realizations. Then we discuss what those realizations spark in terms of new insights and new openings into the practices that enable great leading to take shape.

At each of these pauses on the path, we find a marker that helps us sort out what is occurring for Beth at this time and place. The markers take the form of the arches. The components of each of the arches remain the same—four spires and a keystone—but at each point in the journey, what those components represent evolves. They have to evolve because each of these occasions makes an occasion during which the leader realizes new dimensions of herself and of the endeavor. The lessons learned at the previous arches are retained and are actually expanded and enriched. Thus at any point in the journey, the leader is learning at most five (not 140) lessons. After the third arch, we might imagine, the leader can venture forth with no need of any learning device, any "arch," at all.

PART 1, the "Arch of Effectiveness," describes the unexpected turn of attention that the decision to lead entails. If our clients choose to step on to the leader path, they are surprised to find that rather than focus on job skills, they develop "Skills of Character" and "Self-Trust." We introduce the idea of "Leader Brand"—the special relationship in which followers have a reliable gauge of their leaders' expectations, and in which leaders are appropriately available to meet followers' needs.

PART 2 introduces the second arch, the "Arch of Vision and Organization." The impetus to lead begins with a vision of what can be different, better, more expansive and inclusive for others. The leader's unique qualification as a transforming agent is that he takes the vision into the form of an organized, collaborative effort to change interactions among people, rather than into an art object or a pronouncement of some prophetic or mystical sort.

In this section, we also consider a whole new way of looking at organization under the rubric of "Complexity Theory" or "self-organizing systems." This new view of organizations envisions open systems, in which leaders capture *emergent* possibilities and formulate *attractors* that gather energies and organize them into living entities. This science, in our view, gives us a way to treat leading concretely and dispel some of the unhelpfully mysterious qualities that are ascribed to it.

IN PART 3, we talk about leading greatly. In the "Arch of the Leader's Ethic," we introduce the notions of how leaders learn about themselves and the world at the most basic and profound levels, raising themselves to the levels of challenge they and their followers take on. We introduce terms such as "Moral Learning" and "Moral Imagination," and we see how the leader's decisions comprise the guiding dialogues and narratives that constitute the vision as a shared and lived occasion for everyone in the organization (and arch).

IN PART 4, we conclude our use of the Arch of the Leader's Ethic by considering its keystone, symbolizing the leader's ethic, which we call the ethic of "Attentive Responsibility." Here, we find that the leader's practices take on the characteristics of humility and humanity, engagement, challenge, growth, alertness, and vitality. In this context, we introduce the fourth spire: "Flow," a special quality of the learning experience, which both is produced by and engenders support for the leader's practice.

PART ONE

Entering Onto the Path

INTRODUCTION

Matt met Beth when she strode into the small meeting room. She bound through the door, pulled out a chair with great energy, sat down, opened a notebook, and looked up. "I am Beth. You must be Matt," she asserted. She carried herself in a way that conveyed the message, "What we do matters and merits your attention." Her back was always firmly erect, and she held her shoulders straight. Always neatly dressed in square-shoulder suits, she never slouched or slumped into her chair. In her mentoring sessions, sitting at the conference table with Matt, she was clear eyed, articulate, yet sparing in her words, always getting right to the point. Small talk wasn't her strong suit.

All Matt had been told was that Beth was an up-and-coming executive prospect in the midsized corporation that had retained him as mentor. At the time, Matt was working with eight of this company's young executives, and Beth stood out as a particularly promising creative-leading prospect.

By the time of their third session, it was September. Her current project was to determine strategy and pricing for the company's launch of its new Christmas products—on which the company depended for nearly 20 percent of its revenues and 50 percent of its fourth-quarter profits. You could count the number of weeks until launch on a single hand. She had started building her team in May, picking for her group the best talent in finance, advertising and promotion, operations, general marketing. She established close ties with the field sales organization, keeping them apprised of the group's thinking and incorporating their expertise into the mix.

She was doing all the right things, managerially; she was sure of that. To say she was daunted by the challenge would be going too far, but she definitely felt uneasy. She had been promoted many times in her three years with the company. When she joined the company after completing her MBA, she had been promised that she would be put on the fast track, and her bosses kept their word. Now in her late twenties, she was a director in the Marketing Department.

In the course of the mentoring, Beth opened up to Matt: "I'd never say this to my boss, but sometimes I just wonder, well, whether I shouldn't be doing more. And what bothers me is that I don't know what it would be. It's nothing about the job, or the people on my team or my boss. I have nothing to complain about. So what could it be? It's driving me crazy. My grandfather would say, 'Snap out of it. What's your problem?' But that advice just doesn't help me right now. In fact, not much of my grandfather's advice is much help. But that's another story."

"Is the project going all right?" Matt asked. "Are you hearing rumbles of complaints, or are you getting the preshow jitters, as some actors do?"

"From a management perspective, the project is going fine. I am sure of that. No, what I am sensing is hard to explain. It's more of a quality thing. It's as though there are times in my work when I feel I should say things to people, or jump in to their problems in ways that I never felt before, offer them some kind of personal advice or something. But then I'll ignore the feeling, pat them on the back, tell them they're doing a great job and go back to my work."

Matt then asked, "Do you think of yourself as a leader?"

She didn't respond right away. She thought about it. "Well, this may sound strange, but I've never asked myself that question before. I know that's what we're here to discuss—you being a leader's mentor. But, honestly? I don't know. I guess others have thought of me as a leader—my bosses have put me in charge of this big project and I run a major department in this company. The people that report to me always respond well to me. But I never thought about it. I never asked myself that question. In grad school, they always talk about us being business leaders, but I just pictured myself as a high-up executive, a 'super-manager' really. I never thought about much else."

She paused. "Am I a leader? How would I know that?"

"Do you have followers?" Matt asked.

"What do you mean?"

"Followers: people who would go with you if you changed jobs; people who have told you that you made a big difference in your life."

"I don't know. Is that important? The people that report to me respect me. They ask for my opinion, and they trust me. So are they followers?"

"What do you think about this idea: managers are needed by their bosses, while leaders are needed by their followers?" Matt responded.

After a long pause, once again, she replied, "That says to me that managers get things done so their bosses look good, whereas leaders provide some kind of special relationship that is really important in the lives of their followers."

Matt continued to dig at this question. "So, do you provide some kind of special relationship? Do you put something special in the lives of the people who report to you?"

"I don't know," Beth responded, in a surprisingly tentative voice. "I never thought about having an effect on people in a way that would make them followers. Could having that effect be what's missing? Creating followers. Is that the 'something else' I'm missing? I would have thought it would be 'vision,'" she continued, "that you'd be asking me about. Or am I passionate about my work? Lots of people ask me that question, for some reason. Followers? I don't know. I guess I thought that considering someone to be a follower was kind of putting them down. You are saying that to be a leader I have to have followers? I don't know about that."

And at this doubting juncture, Matt's true mentoring, our journey with Beth begins.

ARCH OF EFFECTIVENESS

Beth arrives at the first arch by feeling a chasm between what she is able to do and what she is able to offer others of herself. The first arch gives us a picture of what Beth must understand about herself in order to bring others into her arch, potentially as followers. I call this the Arch of Effectiveness because its components deal with the most basic skills by which leaders establish themselves.

SKILLS OF CHARACTER AND SELF-TRUST

First, Beth needs the Skills of Character, which we discuss in chapter 2. We define this first arch's four spires as Drive, Self-Awareness, People Skills, and Practical Insight. Then, these skills need to be melded into a unified, coherent, understandable and "attractive" (charismatic) personality. So, the keystone of the Arch of Effectiveness represents Self-Trust—that special quality of resolve that leaders convey in getting the endeavor off the dime and moving. As Matt noticed, Beth seemed to exude a quality of Self-Trust, in her bearing and seriousness, and didn't know it. Matt's job was to get Beth to realize just what she brought to the table in terms of these skills and Self-Trust, so she could bring the full force of her leading persona into action.

LEADER BRAND

But Beth was confused by another crucial aspect of leading: her relationship to followers. In our egalitarian society, the idea of having followers or being a follower makes us nervous. So Beth is not alone.

Still, Matt had to help Beth find a way to accept that she leads others who follow—at least on this occasion, creating followers is exactly what she is being asked to. She has to realize—no followers, no leader. Our way of looking at the relationship is discussed in chapter 3, under the title "Leader Brand."

CHAPTER ONE

Experiencing Leaders

HE WAS ALREADY FEELING THE FIRST VAGUE
STIRRINGS OF THAT MYSTERIOUS IMPULSION,
FOUND IN ALL EVENTUAL MORAL-HEROIC
FIGURES, TO GIVE ONESELF OVER TO SOME
LARGER TRUTH AND PURPOSE AND MEANING,
'TO SOMETHING THAT TRANSCENDS OUR
INDIVIDUAL LIVES,' SO ENLARGING ONE'S
OWN LIFE TO THE HISTORIC DIMENSION OF
THAT GRANDER REALITY.

—*MICHAEL FRADY*[1]

ON *MARTIN LUTHER KING JR.*

[1] *Martin Luther King Jr.* (New York, 2002), p. 18.

THE EXPERIENCE OF LEADERS IN OUR LIVES

We often feel ambivalence toward the leaders who have affected our lives. Some probably left you cold, made you angry, hardly left you feeling like a valued team member. Then there are times when a leader spurred you to enter life-altering experiences. And even in those affirming circumstances, your experience of leaders may have brought you many moments of hurt, disappointment, and self-doubt. Maybe, in some ways, you felt close to the leader; you were uplifted and inspired, but there were also times when that same leader infuriated you, even left you feeling betrayed, left you feeling that you weren't even given a shot at that responsibility you wanted. While leaders don't necessarily create "feel good" experiences when they are engaged in making something happen, the experiences they engender are, certainly, vivid.

How do we judge whether or not a leader has been "successful"? Some criteria are fairly easy to apply, i.e., did the dream come true? Were the goals (qualitative and quantitative) met? Did the leader deliver the goods, so to speak? But those are also very limiting criteria by which to judge whether or not someone has acted as a leader in your life. Actually, many endeavors undertaken by leaders fail. For instance, according to estimates of the Desmond Consulting Group, 80 percent of businesses fail. Then, how many efforts at social reform have we seen to have dissipated and are overwhelmed by the status quo? Racial disparities still exist, gender inequalities are perpetuated, despite a much heralded "War on Poverty" in the seventies and eighties; a Census Bureau report shows that the number of Americans living below poverty line increased by more than 1.3 million in 2002, to 34.8 million.[2]

[2] *New York Times* (September 3, 2003), p. 16. Also, according to Lynnley Browning of the *New York Times* (September 25, 2003), p. C2, the gap between the rich and the poor doubled from 1979 to 2000 such that "the richest 1 percent of Americans in 2000 had more money to spend after taxes than the bottom 40 percent." And this was before Bush's tax cuts in 2002 and 2003. This constitutes "the greatest economic disparity between rich and poor for any year since 1979, the year the budget office began collecting this data."

Is everyone who failed at an attempted endeavor—at starting a business or alleviating racism or poverty—unworthy of being called a leader? Some who attempted to lead failed and yet were experienced by their followers as being true leaders. For instance, did Martin Luther King Jr. fail as a leader in our lives because racial injustices prevail? No matter what, he created a new gold standard for understanding ourselves and experiencing each other. He was a leader because of the fact that by experiencing his leadership, we were moved into a new experience of our own lives. What does dissecting a leader's operational success tell us about the quality, effect, and experience of that person's leading? Past successes may get an erstwhile leader the benefit of the doubt for the "honeymoon" period. From these past successes, some legitimacy may rub off onto this executive's persona for a while. Yesterday's success will buy some legitimacy in terms of that leader meriting my compliance, but not for long. In the final analysis, I have too many choices in my life, too many good opportunities for making my energies and talents amount to something, to hang around waiting for an erstwhile leader to prove himself. Right?

Why do I say that someone has been a leader in my life, while others, who are in positions of even greater authority, have not? *The leader succeeds by, first, imparting to us an ability to envision and then make real something that makes a difference, for the better, in this world; and secondly, by displaying, exemplifying, and imparting to us the ability to grow into larger, more encompassing, inclusive, and expansive visions of our own lives.*

WHAT IS THAT FEELING WE GET AROUND LEADERS?

Leaders evoke feelings that make them seem to be "from us and for us, but not of us." Leaders emerge from out of the midst of our community of interests—our professional domains, our cultures, and our worlds. They are instantly recognizable to us as being from the worlds we share. And they are for us. They are interested in us, pay attention to us, understand us, and see things for us. *But these people are not of us.* These leaders are different, cut from a different cloth; they have a different weave and texture to their personalities. They are not "superior" people; they are not necessarily smarter or more heroic. In their leader roles, however, they just seem to stand apart.

I think of the difference between leaders and nonleaders as being analogous to the eye of a hurricane that resides amidst the winds and rain that swirl around it. The eye is different from the rest of the hurricane. There would be no eye without all the activity around it; and the eye is *for* the hurricane, since without the eye, the winds and rain would dissipate into oblivion. Yet the eye is different than the rest of the storm. Around the eye, the beclouded, churning motions of the winds and rain swirl ferociously. It is from and by the wind and rain that the eye forms; but in the context of the whole hurricane, the whole system, the eye has neither wind nor rain in it. It is a calm, eerily serene center. The hurricane cannot exist without this eye; and the characteristics of the eye (its pressure level, size, shape) determine the strength of the hurricane.

We experience leaders in ways that resemble the way the eye of the hurricane works. Leaders attract us; they pull us into their vortices. We feel that from being in proximity to them, we gain a strength and energy of some sort. It is our own energy; yet it is somehow dependent on this different energy conveyed to us by the leader, indeed projected by the leader onto, into, and through us. Leaders experience the same situations as we do, but out of that common material, they create a different kind of self. Leaders are affected by the same things nonleaders are, but live in that experience differently; they draw different conclusions from the experience than do nonleaders, and using the same data, they take different actions in response to the situation than nonleaders do.

THE MARKS OF THE LEADER DIFFERENCE

I see five drivers—orientations to how leaders live within the situation, their own lives and other people—that generate this difference: (1) they just love to organize people into collaborative endeavors; (2) they do not relate to just the facts of a situation; (3) they seem to actually live out of the future; (4) they are always seeking ways to raise the bar; (5) they develop a habit of changing, not only external situations, but themselves. Let's look at each of these drivers in detail.

LEADERS LOVE TO ORGANIZE

What else can I say? Some people love to play music or write a poem. Some love to skateboard. Leaders love to organize. Some people just seem to have a deft touch with organizations. They seem to be able to get people to respond effectively, and they are able to help these people identify and capitalize on every opportunity to thrive amidst challenge. The secret to that touch is in realizing that they, as leaders, do not create the change that the endeavor aims at. Followers create that change. Organization happens when energy within a focused and clearly identified endeavor is channeled through many people. This energy is multiplied exponentially, as these people identify the myriad ways to address the guiding issue.

The leader brings a special realization to this process. By recognizing the efforts of these people, by providing an opportunity for their efforts to have import and meaning, by guiding their experiences of collaboration into real accomplishment, magic happens. First, this recognition fuels collaboration; then this collaboration breeds communication and connection; and third, through this structuring of energies, people take on specific roles and responsibilities in order to assure the success of the endeavor as a whole. One person, whom we will follow periodically throughout this book and who exemplifies this proclivity to organize, is Brian Thomas (fictitious name), the "Serial Entrepreneur."

Brian is a local business star, a poster child for having taken a technology out of a government R&D lab environment and successfully launched a commercial company from it. His career is in many ways unique. Even though he made his mark at some of the country's leading technology labs, he doesn't have a PhD. Much of his training is in biology, but he made his mark in physics. And for all of this, you'd hardly know that Brian was a technology geek at all. He's actually more like a "creative type," more typically found in marketing, or even in an ad agency than a scientist; in many ways he is more like an artist, or maybe a professor of religion, or even a mystic aspirant, than someone you'd expect to find driving a start-up into becoming a successful business.

Brian deeply believes in alchemy—in taking raw, simple, unrefined nature, mixing it with the right people, the right processes, the right intelligence, and coming out with gold.

He likes to do what, to others, seems to be impossible. He constantly asks questions. He questions himself; he questions any conclusions arrived at through a process of dialogue or speculation. He constantly envisions possibilities and he hates the constraints of tradition or what has already been done. For Brian, there has to be more to it. He settles into a decision only when the expectations of those around him cluster together into a compelling necessity to put something out there.

When hired by Brian to be his mentor, I did some discovery interviews with others in the company to get a sense of his impact. The building was brand new; only three of the twenty or so people in the company were on board for more than a couple of months. The other three had known Brian for a long time and came out of the lab or came over from another tech company because of the lure of working with Brian. One of them had been with Brian on several projects over many years.

"To make this work," I heard commonly, "is a long shot. But I am here because I believe Brian can do it."

As we shall see, as we unfold more about Brian, he wasn't so sure. This was his first venture out of the labs and into business. He wasn't very happy with many aspects of the corporate strings that came along with funding his venture. He wasn't really sure he could lead a business. He wasn't so sure that these people were the right ones to get this job done. He questioned his commitment, his ability, his values—am I selling out? he wondered. It wasn't until months later that he began to crystallize a new picture of himself as a leader and business as a place where alchemy could really take place.

NOT JUST THE FACTS

Leaders approach situations with the specific intent of having an effect on whatever is happening at the moment. At a minimum, a leader approaches a project with the expectation that, by virtue of his presence, something is going to happen. And there is no shrinking from whatever that "something" may be.

Most of us approach situations with pretty modest intentions. We are content to approach a new situation so as to get through it without embarrassment; and we operate proficiently enough to hold our own and maintain a modicum of dignity in the process. To do that, we try to reduce what we know about the environment; we constrict our awareness to the things we already understand and can deal with.

This reduction also forecloses on my being a leader in the situation. It dissipates the "aliveness" of the situation, that is, the situation's potential for creating novelty in my experience, for stimulating a wider range of sensory and emotive awareness, for demanding a higher and more energetic quality of engagement in the situation. In contrast to this, when a leader walks into a room, we can see that he is not just taking in who is there, what is appropriate to talk about, who the hosts are, who the must-see guests are. To be sure, the facts are there, salient and significant. But the leader sees these facts in their fluidity, as mere grist for his irrepressible will, as raw material for his engagement.

Thus their perspectives on situations remain vitally alive. What they know emanates from their intimate distillation of their experiences. It is personal, immediate, engaged knowledge. Their knowledge of a situation is not merely a matter of what is functional, correct, and verifiable, but rather what is palpably alive and thus possible in it. By seeing the world through the eyes of leaders we get a sense of their irrepressible agency.

Leaders envelop facts—they don't just know them—into a field of discernment, understanding, recollection, and determination.

A real-life leader whom I have worked with and exemplifies this aspect of leading is Howard Keats. We'll study in detail how he had to grow into his own repressible agency in chapter 5. But let's meet him briefly here now. Here is "Howard, the Irrepressible":

You would pass Howard on the street a hundred times and probably not remember him, so unexceptional is he in appearance and demeanor. But as soon as you start to talk to him, he becomes unforgettable. His voice is sandy and high pitched; his eyes are big and blue, and as he makes points that excite, they open wider, their sparkle becoming a cascade of energy that excites you. He has a way of saying, "Yeah," that is magnetic. The pitch of his voice starts out in a high range and then musically descends a scale in an unnamable key. The music of it pulls you into the oracular energy.

"I break myths," Howard says of his leadership. He means that he doesn't see the need to do things in ways that old habits and customs have declared as the norm. He is able to envision different ways to do things and make them work.

He never tires of telling the story about the string of experiences that led him to break this myth. It starts with the birth of his son who has Down syndrome. His own myths had to be broken at this point. His life would not be lived in some kind of Norman Rockwell ideal; his family would need to address someone special, different. Every day, his capacity to reach someone with life's lessons would be stretched, and he'd have to work just that much harder to create a picture of what makes sense to his son. He became a teacher and explainer extraordinaire. In the process, he would discover that many things we take for granted couldn't be explained because, in fact, they don't make sense. He learned how some myths need to be broken, not explained. When you talk to Howard, you feel the patience in listening that he must have developed; you feel from him the eagerness to engage with you in a conversation of challenge and envisioning.

Somehow, to settle into the assumed and accepted won't do in this conversation. If you want the "Yeaaaaahs" from Howard, and you do because they feel so good, you have to go beyond the easy stuff and get into what just might be possible if you put in a little effort.

LIVING OUT OF THE FUTURE

Another way leaders are different is that they do not live so absolutely and completely in the present. Instead, they live their lives in the manner in which they literally embody the conduct and presence they expect will be called for when the processes in which they are engaged are fulfilled. They embody that *endpoint* rather than live within the ebb and flow of the current circumstances.

I have seen the difference between a nonleader who reacts to a situation on the spot, erupting with full emotional ammunition deployed for all to see, versus the leader whose powder is always dry, ready to be fired if necessary, but is always held in reserve until it is tactically expedient to be fired. The difference between the two is a person who needs to make feelings known, on the spot, versus someone who is envisioning and embodying longer-term outcomes that need to be brought to life regardless of the difficulties of the present, incomplete, status of things. The leader lives in a mindset in which, irrespective of present difficulties, he feels the need to remind people of the larger picture, the greater effort, the more worthy future. This makes the leader seem to be "elegant," as one of my clients put it.

A sterling case that illustrates this point at the highest level of human aspiration is the conduct of Nelson Mandela while he was imprisoned for more than twenty years by the racist apartheid regime. From the superb biography by Anthony Sampson, it is clear that

Mandela carried into his daily prison life a concrete vision of how a multiracial nation's paramount leader must behave. But what makes the Mandela story so compelling on this point is that he acted this way while imprisoned for twenty-seven years.

As Sampson points out, in 1981, after Mandela had been in prison on the brutal Robben Island facility for eighteen years, the Afrikaner minister of justice, Kobie Coetsee, received a report on Mandela's background and mental state. I quote it at length as an example of how the leader lives in the present in a way that befits the envisioned future.

> *"He adopts a persistent attitude by making repeated representations about conditions, but in a way that no steps can be taken against him. But this should not be seen as good behavior [says his jailors]: he gives the orders and then withdraws to regard his actions from a distance. Mandela sticks to his chosen course and influences everyone with him not to deviate from this . . . . It is clear that Mandela has in no way changed his position and that imprisonment so far has had no positive [sic] effect on him."*

The report then goes on to make these eleven points:

> ➤ *Mandela is exceptionally motivated and maintains a strong idealistic approach.*

> ➤ *He maintains outstanding personal relations, is particularly jovial, and always behaves in a friendly and respectful ways toward figures of authority.*

> ➤ *He is manipulative, but nevertheless not tactless or provocative.*

> ➤ *There are no visible signs of bitterness towards whites, although this may be a fine game of bluff on his part.*

34

➤ *He acknowledges his own shortcomings, but nevertheless believes in himself.*

➤ *He is a practical and pragmatic thinker who can arrive at a workable solution on a philosophical basis.*

➤ *He has the capacity for integrated and creative thought.*

➤ *He has an unbelievable memory, to reproduce things in the finest detail.*

➤ *He has an unflinching belief in his cause and in the eventual triumph of African nationalism.*

➤ *He regards himself as called to the task and this elevates him above the average white who, according to him, has apparently lost his idealism.*

➤ *He believes self-discipline and continually taking the initiative to be the prerequisites for success.*

"There exists no doubt," the document continues, *"that Mandela commands all the qualities to be the Number One black leader in South Africa. His period in prison has caused his psycho-political posture to increase rather than decrease, and with this he now has acquired the characteristic prison charisma of the contemporary liberation leader."*[3]

And remember, these comments were made by Mandela's *jailors, while he was under their collective thumb,* in prison. The comments illustrate graphically how different the creative leader is from others. Who among us can assume that we would behave this way under the

[3] Sampson, *Mandela: The Authorized Biography* (New York, 1999), pp. 294-5.

35

stresses and degradation of prison? Mandela, according to Sampson, always acted in prison as the conciliator, keeping in mind that all of the groups there in that vicious microcosm would have to learn to live together in the multiracial South Africa he envisioned. He wrote in an unpublished prison essay, "Today South Africa has almost three million Afrikaners who will no longer be oppressors after liberation but a powerful minority of ordinary citizens, whose cooperation and goodwill will be required in the reconstruction of the country."[4]

But what about leaders who work at more mundane levels of creating new businesses, or turning around faltering ones, do they possess this same kind of capacity to live out of the future? Most definitely. The same skill that Mandela exhibited of living his life, under the most extreme duress, as though his dream of a multiracial society was already established, is a critical component of how leaders create an experience that impels followers into a future now only envisioned.

ALWAYS RAISING THE BAR

Leaders I have experienced turn whatever they are doing into a contest, a challenge. They are not content to just get something done, in the mode of the manager, but insist on using the occasion to make a difference, go to another level, both in terms of what the outcomes will be, and, for our immediate attention, go to another level in their own abilities, competence, and capabilities.

A leader I have known and worked with for many years, who exemplifies this, is Harry Kaufman, the "Impresario Executive."

[4] Ibid., p. 293.

Tall, handsome, graying, you could easily say that Harry looks like a CEO. When he starts talking, it is clear that he is knowledgeable about his industry; he is confident in his role; he seems very soft spoken, personable; he makes you feel at home. He is passionately competitive about whatever he does. When it comes to business and the companies he runs, that competitiveness shows up as an insistence to win, and the irrepressible insistence on winning right away.

Twelve years ago, when I met Harry as part of a three-person consulting team, he signaled most emphatically that he was going to be a tough customer. He was serious. And he tested us in every way he could: Were we up to the task? What were our values? What did we know about running a company? His questioning was clearly intended to determine many things: Were we smart? Could we take criticism? Were we observant? Did we have a sense of humor? And did we get his sense of humor? He wasn't rude or aggressive. He had expectations, standards, a very short time line, limited resources, tight budgets, and then more expectations. That impression has stood me in good stead since I have worked with Harry in four different turnaround situations.

His way of operating has been consistent over the years.

He drives to simplify. He won't hear from anyone that the issue is "complicated." If an operation is complicated, then, in Harry's view, it isn't being done properly. Period. Find another way that is simple, that makes sense to anyone who hears it, on hearing it the first time around. Then, he understates. He asks, politely, if you had some time to look into something, or do something for him. A seemingly open, low-key request. However, he fully expects that the request is interpreted as a command.

When he says "if you have the time," he means "make time." If he asks you get back to him, he means get it to him ASAP. In my years of working with him, his direct reports, especially new ones, often miss these nuances and suffer the consequences that result.

While Harry's humor bubbles up as soon as business matters are appropriately cleared away, he can be devastating when he expresses dissatisfaction. A young executive he worked with had been reduced to tears because Harry chastised her for not returning a phone call from him promptly enough. "He didn't raise his voice; he wasn't rude. It was in the tone. I had crossed some kind of line that I had never encountered before. I don't even know why it was so devastating. But it was. I'm still on edge with him now." In a way, encountering that withering tone is a rite of passage in being on his team. It's going to happen some day, about some issue. You don't know when. But it's worse to not experience that moment at some juncture, because that means he isn't counting on you.

When Harry is in charge, he expects certain things will happen. When he starts out to turn a company around, he is never satisfied with just doing business differently or more effectively. There will be improved results to be sure, but there will also be changes in what people understand about their work; changes in what people accepted as being satisfactory; changes in the way people view what the company stands for and what the company can accomplish. In the inner circle, in other words, Harry expects that "his people" will put into reality what he already sees.

Leaders, like Brian Thomas or Harry Kaufman move from one start-up situation to the next, or from one turnaround to the next, because they only feel fully alive when they challenged by making a successful company out of only the slightest wisps of ideas. They don't want to just keep reinventing companies though. *They actually need and thus seek out more and more demanding situations in order to lead at higher levels.*

It is like a drug. In order to get the flow geared up, it takes more and more strident challenges. When others are anxious or fearful, leaders see opportunity for excitement and stimulation. Leaders push others way beyond their comfort zones because leaders seek challenge. A follower may fall by the wayside as the challenges get more difficult. But those that remain do so because they know the leader is seeing what can be done in the situation. Therefore the followers can learn what can be done in these situations. These followers often become a new generation of leaders.

A HABIT OF CHANGE

By this oxymoron, I want to point out how leaders thrive on different psychological and spiritual experiences than do nonleaders. Leaders *thrive on the process of having to change themselves* at different stages of an evolution of an effort. Any stop along the way causes frustration; completion brings on boredom. People can become "addicted" to continually seek out opportunities that engender the experience of change and growth. Creative leaders seek out situations in which they can experience those challenges. Some, occasional leaders, will grudgingly respond when a situation is forced on them, and some will grow into it; most will try to winnow the situation down to what they can handle. Most of us, in the meantime, avoid those situations altogether and get on with our normal lives. The leader uses the changing sensations, feelings and emotions generated by a situation as a stimulus for raising their level of growth and learning, and they are more than willing, in the meantime, to incite others to reach that state of being as well.

After years of behaving this way, leaders change their "hard wiring." The very way they experience the world around them seems to be different than others. We have alluded to that difference above. Creative leaders look at whatever is occurring as an occasion during which to identify what can be done better. And that expression is not made in the manner of the detached experimenter, who artificially sparks a change and then stands back to watch the events unfold. They stay fully engaged in the unfolding events, evincing irrevocable concern that events tilt toward an envisioned outcome.

Most of us just don't like the feelings our bodies and minds register when these situations arise. We like the positive emotions, like happiness—when our bodies loosen, our minds are alert, but we open to the outside influences and let ourselves go. We seem to absorb energy from the outside with ease and we feel enlarged, generous, showered in light.

But leaders have a different take on their feelings. To a much greater extent than the rest of us, they actually welcome assaults of experiences on their settled, already assembled, selves. Instead of separating the emotions of fear from those of happiness, they seem to gain happiness from embracing the experiences of fear, anxiety, and unease and then overcoming them. These experiences give them more material to work with, so to speak. Since they can react with joy to challenge and threat, they are able to convey to others the fact that the situation need not result in paralyzing fear. "We have nothing to fear but fear itself," Franklin Delano Roosevelt said in his speech accepting the nomination of the Democratic Party in 1932. This is the archetypal leader saying to his people, yes, there is fear, but there can also be other emotions you can bring to bear on this situation. He feels these other emotions and so gives others the ability, the opening to summon up their own fear-countering emotions as well.

Leaders are wired differently in that they have developed extremely fluid senses of their selves; they have the ability to accept an extremely wide range of experiences and allow themselves to change, to learn, from these experiences. Leaders have developed the propensity to actively seek out experiences, which act upon, change and challenge the range of ways they characterize themselves and are conscious of themselves. Leaders, in other words, seek out situations that enable them to validate or change their identity, which enables them to expand the compass of experience, which their "selves" can accommodate.

A SPECIAL LEADER BIOGRAPHY

How does this happen? How do some people develop that wiring, while others do not? People, with the will and drive to do so, change and grow all their lives. Recent work in neuroscience at Princeton University has discovered, for instance, that active brains (and not ones that are dormant or remain locked in habituated patterns) produce new cells, neurons, and thus connections that enrich experience, throughout life. For people such as leaders, and for others who are "called," there is no such thing as "human nature," that is defined, fixed, and unalterable. We are creatures that can grow, and leaders show us how to do this. Still, we might ask, is there some kind of foundation, in early childhood experience maybe, that predisposes a person to be able to aggressively attack any settling of the self into contented habituation? Cognitive psychologists, such as Howard Gardner, for instance, do see vague traces of possible patterns that are conducive to fostering continual learning and leading.

41

One model of the leader's biography has a leader growing up in a situation in which one parent creates insecurity (is stern, is an unpredictable alcoholic, dies when the person is young, creating a sense of abandonment) while the other is supportive, loving, and generous in praise. The image that emerges from this scenario is one in which a person's psyche expects turmoil and suffering and also expects to be praised and affirmed in their responses to those adversities. They are used to both experiencing extreme changes (and the feelings that accompany them), and they develop the means to link their sufferings with actions that generate praise and support. This creates a story that is not merely one of suffering, but of suffering and then, by dint of their own actions, overcoming and triumphing. Their feelings of being alive, successful, and whole depend on the complete cycle of suffering, acting, and receiving praise for succeeding. Normal, low-feeling, shallow, and quotidian living won't do for these people.

Whether or not this is a necessary biographical life path for the creating of leaders, most of the people I mentor emerge from their difficult circumstances with a greater ability to reflect on their lives and their capabilities as leaders. They have considered their situations and come to some kind of peace or arrived at some kind of strategy in order to deal with the situation by a long process of reflection, decision, and resolution. Whether or not all of these people seek out suffering in seeking out their challenges I do not know, but many, the creative leaders among them, do.

These leaders actually crave experiences in which they consciously work their way through their sadness and fear. The scope of a leader's reach depends on how large a challenge they are able to accommodate. Those who cannot tolerate insults to their accepted and settled self-images will take on roles that promise only to affirm their egos. But for those few who are willing to recreate themselves, and expand (not diminish or harden) their senses of themselves as the endeavor grows, with all its surprises and difficulties, there is no limit to the scope of their leading. The lives of people such as Jesus, the Buddha, Nelson Mandela, and Lincoln are all stories of leaders who always were able to surpass any small sense of themselves in order to raise their autobiographies to the level of the greatest human endeavors.

MENTORING: THE SINE QUA NON

One aspect of the leader's biography I have personally witnessed and hold to be necessary is this: people are mentored into the leading role. *All the leaders I know, who identify themselves as leaders and have consciously decided to enter this role, have had a mentor who put them on this path.*

Yes, leading is a calling, but is it one that can easily be missed? For instance, are Beth's musings about "doing more" indications of the calling to lead, or the insecurities of struggling manager? Her mentor, in this case, the professional, Matt, suspected that it was the former. If someone didn't suspect that her concerns emanated from the disquiet that leaders feel, from a need to bring something of their deeply held values into the world, would those anxieties have been directed toward leading? If her boss had been strictly bottom-line oriented, or was a hard-driving "macho" executive, wouldn't these concerns have been taken for female "softness"?

We have a great deal more to say about mentoring throughout our story. We offer our story of Beth in order to depict the slow, careful nurturing, and the special awareness it takes to mentor prospective leaders; and we show the kinds of special attention leaders must bring to their own lives in order to sustain themselves

43

in this arduous role. I see the presence of the mentor as the sine qua non of the creative leader's biography. No mentor, no leader— period. And thus, the most important aspect of all the leaders' responsibility is to be a mentor, and enter into the biographies of those who dare to enter creative leading.

CHAPTER TWO

Skills of Character

In a traditional Zen Buddhist story, a novice asks his master,
"Master, what is the goal of all learning?"
"Wisdom," replies the master.
"What is wisdom?" asks the novice.
"Good judgment," replies the master.
"How do you get good judgment?" the novice persists.
"Experience."
"How do you get experience?" asks the novice.
"Bad judgment," the master replies.

ENTERING ONTO THE PATH OF LEADING

The questions that really disturb young leaders, that undermine their effectiveness, are rarely those of process. These leaders organize, monitor, coach, and drive for results quite well, thank you. No, the questions that disturb them are ones like these: "So, how do I know if I am leading?" "What do I have to do differently?" "What am I leading towards?" or "What is my leadership creating?" Or, "Do I really believe this is the right way to go?"

Where do the answers to those questions come from? No leadership book, no efficiency study, no amount of factual data will provide them. Books about leadership are written as though all leaders need to know is what behaviors to exhibit and demeanors to adopt, and they will be effective and acknowledged as leaders. Often, when they try on those new behaviors, young leaders feel like they are faking it. It turns out the new traits provide no cover for their insecurities and doubts. Instead of these superficial affectations, they want their leading not only to appear to be effective; they want it to feel "natural," and they want their leading to be authentically their own.

THE TURN

Our clients make *leading* the main trajectory of their path of personal development. We help them along this path by enabling them to make a "turn," to rotate the direction of their attention 180 degrees. We first help them to pry their attention away from their extroverted and process-oriented (managerial) concerns; and then we turn their attention around, so they begin to comprehend themselves. We want them to be able to see the hows, the wheres, and the whys of the decisions they make. If their decisions seem worthy such that they will result in learning and deeper understanding, we also want them to cultivate the ability to accept those decisions and carry them forward.

This event, deciding to take the turn, marks the first stop on path of creative leading. The first of the three arches we will encounter in our journey marks this decision.

SPIRES OF THE ARCH OF EFFECTIVENESS[1]

KEYSTONE: SELF-TRUST
INTERIOR SPACE: LEADER BRAND

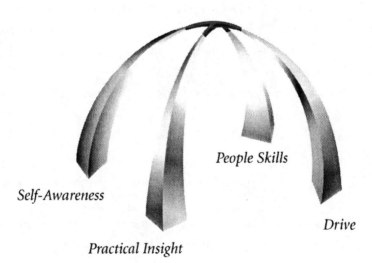

People Skills

Self-Awareness

Drive

Practical Insight

[1] See the appendix for the full explication of the development of the arch through its three phases.

SKILLS OF CHARACTER

The Arch of Effectiveness depicts the "Skills of Character" the leader must draw on every day in the course of leading.

We all understand what we mean by "skills" when the term applies to our interactions with things in the world. It takes skill, acquired through instruction and practice, to drive a car safely, or especially to parallel park it. It takes skill to write well or to read with understanding. Skills, in other words, are activities on which we concentrate attention and energy in order to gain a specific result. We learn these skills through instruction and repetition; and we offer the attention to being instructed, and we take the time to repeat the actions involved because we regard the skill as being important for accomplishing our life ends.

Skills of Character call upon certain aspects of our psyches in order to create certain kinds of relationships. In leading, we call upon Self-Awareness, People Skills, Practical Insight, and Drive. Leaders have to direct their attention inward, to how they are thinking, feeling, valuing, evoking the right behaviors in a given situation. They do so in order to calibrate how they will present the choices to be considered, or to offer people an appropriate focus for the feelings that a situation is engendering or will engender as it unfolds.

We have many character traits: temperaments, preferences, and tastes—habits can all be considered character traits. What we highlight here are those aspects of one's character (the behaviors, attitudes, expressed emotions, etc. people come to know as being "you") that leaders need to have practiced, ready to hand, in order to fulfill the demands of their role.

SELF-AWARENESS

Self-Awareness comprises the psychic sources of emotions, feelings, beliefs, knowledge frameworks, and values that impel leaders toward certain decisions.

Challenging endeavors force even the most extroverted, outwardly focused of leaders to become more familiar with the sources of their psychic development. At a minimum, they want to see more clearly how their past experiences relate to what they are asking others to do in the present. We spend a great deal of time helping leaders retrieve the important stories of their lives. Telling one's stories to those in the endeavor conveys what the effort means for the leader—where it fits in his life. From this account, others in the endeavor can decide for themselves what means for them so that everyone in the endeavor is more able to decide about their level of commitment to the effort.

By knowing and offering one's stories, leaders create a more relaxed and flowing relationship within the organization. Correlatively, when leaders are a mystery to others, when they seem to be inscrutable to others, they set up tensions that squander valuable energy in the organization. Leaders are often surprised to find how interested people are in their stories. Well, when people know their leader, they get to know themselves, and so are able to freely offer what they can to the effort's success.

Knowing their own stories enables leaders to fully enrich life of the organization, imbuing it with the same energy and significance attached to other parts of people's lives. Unfortunately, when managerially oriented executives don't offer their stories they produce a truncated range of life in the organization. When this happens, no matter how noble the organization's intent, people end up distrusting the organization as being politically manipulative, even aggressively destructive to all concerned. Organizations are emptied of their vitality; they are reduced to using values of the lowest common denominator.

DRIVE: ENERGY AND WILL

Leaders seem to draw on inexhaustible wells of energy—up before daylight to do a physical workout, attend a breakfast meeting, put in a full day's work at the office, and finally head off to the charity banquet or dinner to play politics with a disgruntled board member. A sixteen-hour workday is not unusual. Just observing the energy levels of these leaders exhausts me.

I am reminded, for instance, that I just don't have Harry Kaufman's energy. Day after day, he keeps his daunting schedule. No matter how early I arrive at the office, he is already there. Instead of getting tired, the schedule seems to pump him up. He's constantly in motion, continually working with his followers, creating followers or alienating some who will never be followers. All these activities light him up. He might complain if he gets only five hours of sleep a night for a couple of months in a row. However, he complains most loudly when he is on vacation—sleeping as long as he wishes—and is not inundated by business demands (to the chagrin of his family that is accompanying him).

Then there's the leader's tenacity. Can leaders be effective if they don't have the will to see things through to the end? We often see how young leaders are so intent on meeting their goals, that they push people to the point of breaking. They apply their abundant energy and drive, working seven days a week for months on end, pushing and cajoling everyone else to do the same. Often these leaders hear the criticism that they don't listen well, and they act erratically. We see hard-driving leaders get irritable when confronting what they perceive as a painfully slow pace of change, or they "lose it" when they see a loss of focus or when processes break down and stop progress. These behavioral tendencies go hand in glove with the leader's energy. But they are also tendencies that a more mature leader learns how to moderate.

Top leaders take care of their energy, keeping it vibrant and affecting by staying in good physical shape. They regulate their diets within a relatively healthy range—despite lunches of quick food takeout and dinners accompanied by wine and single malt scotches. They maintain relatively consistent—if brief—sleeping schedules and learn how to manage themselves when dealing with jet lag from extensive travel. They soak up all kinds of materials in the self-help literature and experiment with regimens so as to find what works for them. Mentors, such as myself, as well as psychologists, nutritionists, physical trainers, have whole careers based on providing assistance to executives in nurturing and sustaining their Drive.

PEOPLE SKILLS

Leaders always work with other people and do so under challenging circumstances. If they didn't want to work with people, they'd be artists or mystics. Managers may not need People Skills in their efforts to improve processes and increase output, but leaders, who affect people's lives, do need them.

Daniel Goleman says that a key element of People Skills is based on empathy, which he describes as "sensing others' feelings and perspectives, and taking an active interest in their concerns."[2] He goes on to point out that in the leadership arena, the empathy is not

[2] Daniel Goleman, *Working with Emotional Intelligence* (New York, 1998), p. 138.

an equally traveled two-way street. He says, "Those with little power are typically expected to sense the feelings of those who hold power, while those in power feel less obligation to be sensitive in return. In other words, the studied lack of empathy is a way power holders can tacitly assert their authority."[3]

We feel that empathy doesn't lessen as a leader moves to higher levels, but the focus of that empathy does change. As we said above, the leader is responsible for creating change while keeping the organization whole. *The strategic and visionary leader's empathy is thus not lessened; it is just directed at the whole organization, rather than its parts, or at any single individual.* A production level leader can be content with one-on-one empathy. But when leaders take on whole organizations, big companies or political representation, that one-on-one empathy fades. My answer to Goleman is that the more encompassing the whole for which the leader is responsible, the more remote from empathy for individuals he may seem. But this is not the same as a leader lacking empathy or substituting power for empathy.

PRACTICAL INSIGHT

Practical Insight names the Skill of Character by which leaders are constantly able to see things anew.

Our society divides up its diverse activities into "domains" in which certain competencies are perfected and then offered for others' use and benefit. Every organization offers to its constituents or customers a particular expertise, skill set, talent, or product. A nonprofit service organization meets some specific social, health, or educational need that a particular kind of specialty can provide. Considered as a

---

[3] Ibid., p. 144.

small organization, the family is a domain as well, since keeping it together and having it perform its function optimally require specialized skills and knowledge. So every organization works within its domain and is based on an area of knowledge and expertise. Academic, professional, technical, corporate management domains also have a recognized means of progression through the ranks of their hierarchies.

Practical Insight is the skill that translates knowledge within a particular domain—such as engineering or marketing or human services—into new imperatives. Creative leaders, more than "officials" who are placed in already designated roles, rely on this skill. It is the initial source of their "legitimacy." For instance, in many of the companies I work with, some technical knowledge is imperative. There is no way Brian could lead a technical start-up if his credentials weren't up to snuff. When Harry left his "home" industry and went into an allied field, he knew he had to take on a steep learning curve.

Creative leaders have to establish their legitimacy by exhibiting prowess in their domain before they can claim authority. So, while some kind of domain knowledge is a bottom-line necessity, still, it is only a start. Their legitimacy is based on their understandings of the domain, but what establishes their authority (and whatever power she is granted) as a creative leader is *the ability to see new possibilities, or to grasp them when they are offered, so that the organization carves out a distinctive niche or role in that domain.*

Leaders are eminently practical in this regard. The insight has to be feasible, an "adjacent possible."[4] Thus, unlike the mystic or the prophet or artist, the leader has to not only envision an innovation but also discern how people can collaboratively work on it, in the here and now,

---

[4] These are the words of Stuart Kauffman (real name), one of the architects of self-organization and complexity study. C.f.: Investigations.

bring it to fruition and, finally, spur a positive response within their domains in real time, limited by real resources and competitors.

THE KEYSTONE: SELF-TRUST AND CHARISMA[5]

Like the keystone in the architectural structure, *Self-Trust is that dimension of our lives that binds our many and disparate abilities, skills of character, into an integrated constellation.*

A DEFINITION OF SELF-TRUST

Self-Trust is a psychic state in which one arrives at "resolve" in the face of pressing demands that call for a decision and/or action. It is reached by a leader through a more or less conscious process of connection, with a recollection of experiences, values and knowledge, that results in an acceptance by the leader, of that decision being worthy of her time and attention and is also worthy of the actions and attentions of others.

To understand this critical idea, we will look at each component of the definition.

ARRIVAL

Self-Trust feels as though one has arrived somewhere, a place where one had not been before. The moment of "arrival" is a fleeting experience, often signified by first "taking a deep breath" and then jumping off into the future. But the sense of difference, that there is a "before" and an "after" to that moment, lingers.

---

[5] The identifying of this dimension of the leader's psyche and its naming owes a great deal to Keith Lehrer, *Self-Trust: A Study of Reason, Knowledge, and Autonomy.*

It is "existential" because the experience actually changes the flow of that person's existence. It transforms a struggle into a guided and informed "life."

Thus, "Self-Trust" is a concrete, conscious experience, in which one summons up one's memories, values, aspirations, and knowledge, in order to answer a call into the future. Once answering that call, it may or may not be necessary to continue to evoke one's Self-Trust continuously. Still, it begins in that moment of taking a deep breath, arriving at that resolution, and then, with one's life reconfigured by that recollection, moving forward into an as-yet-uncharted future.

RESOLVE

Self-Trust is not a feeling of being "confident." By "confident," I mean that stance of surety people take when setting out to prove something. There is within "confidence" a sense of showing something to someone, or even one's self. Confidence pushes other kinds of responses to the situation aside so as to distinguish and distance itself from the intrusion of doubts or fears.

There is plenty of room for doubt in Self-Trust, but not paralysis. The leader fully incorporates the new lessons and moves on to learn other things. There lingers a sense of the vulnerability to failure, but not vacillation in the ability to learn from those failures. Thus Self-Trust feels less like confidence and more like a gritty determination to move forward, out of the morass of doubt.

The best way to actually describe the feeling that leaders have with regard to Self-Trust is that of "resolve." It is a feeling of inner conflict falling away of a softening, a dissolving (not a steeling of one's courage or "conviction") of what once seemed like a hard and immovable barrier.

The energy doesn't go away; it is just not running against the tide any longer. The barrier changes its character also. It is no longer an unassailable, impenetrable wall. It is now a soft, pliable, semipermeable membrane.

CONNECTION

One of the great strengths of Self-Trust is that it is not necessarily an "insight" or "revelation" that comes in the night. To be sure, it can come that way, and often does. But that unexpected quality of the artistic insight, so to speak, is not necessary in this case. Self-Trust often comes through dialogue, discussion, and fully awake, aware, conscious, and concentrated thinking. Neither is Self-Trust an abstract idea that is available only in times of quiet reflection. It is experienced in a concrete, visceral, intimate, immediate connection with what is pressing, cries out for attention, decision, and action. It is an experience that can be summoned at will, whenever, and in whatever are the circumstances.

Leaders are intensely engaged and connected with the situation at hand, in all its complexity and nuance. They relate to their own lives in the same way. They are connected to what has happened to them in their lives. They remember incidents, events, and lessons and recount those things vividly. They recount these experiences vividly because they are vivid in the leader's psyche. When a situation arises that creates a feeling, that feeling is usually associated with some concrete event, and that event is easily recalled. That information—the event, how it unfolded, meeting or confounding expectations, the consequences to people, plans, hopes, and dreams, and the emotions brought up at that time—is used by the leader to guide people in the organization toward a decision.

So leaders are deeply connected with their experience. Experience, someone once said, is not what happened to you, but what you realize happened to you. Leaders let things happen to them, and they pay attention, not merely observing process and outcomes, but letting the experience affect them, register its impact and allow learning to transpire. They put themselves into positions where things happen to them. They are not sheltered by other's opinions, or blinded by prejudices. They are living at the edge, between what is known, certain and set, and what is not any of those things. Then they hold on to what happens out there. They remember the facts and the incidents. They remember the feelings brought up within themselves and for others. All of these coalesce into the leader's experience of what happened.

RECOLLECTION

Leaders are always recollecting their experiences. As much as leaders live their lives forward, leaning into the future, they look back as well. A daredevil may be willing to rush headlong into a chasm of danger, but leaders, who are responsible for the careers, livelihoods, and maybe lives of others, do not do so. Leaders' actions are richly endowed with recollection.

Recollection is an important dimension of all self-development processes. Humans are not machines that improve by adding enhancements, or enlarging the power train. Humans develop by deepening and broadening their capacity to learn. Humans have a choice about learning. Another saying that I like is, "We learn, not from our experience, but from our capacity to experience." In other words, we comprehend not only what is happening to us, but we can learn from what is happening to us. We do that by comparing that information we had, and the lessons we had learned from that information, to new circumstances. We then decide whether or not to alter their conclusions from that past lesson and create a new conclusion. Or we can take lessons learned from totally different situations and apply them, in an analogous or metaphoric way to the new situation. Our "capacity to experience," in that saying then, is another way of saying that we learn from our capacity to bring forward, to recollect, our experiences and make them active and alive in the present.

Leaders' recollections are not limited to the dimensions of psychic development, which are drawn largely from the "Self-Awareness" spire. Leaders also recollect experiences, energy, information, and images drawn from the other spires as well. Practical Insight will come into play, often as a "feeling" of what is right for that industry, company, or market. Certainly empathy for others and ability to read into how others can and will react to a challenge inform Self-Trust. We are not limiting recollection to a recalling of facts or incidents. In moving toward a decision, leaders draw on all the spires in the arch, all the reservoirs that comprise their Skills of Character.

ACCEPTANCE

One of the things we do not do very well in our perfectionist Judeo-Christian-Islamic culture is allow for acceptance. We have a culture based on the drive toward perfection. Many of us accept ideas such as these: perfection is what is closest to God; perfection is the standard by means of which we judge our achievement; to give 100 percent or more, that is the standard. To accept our contribution as being sufficient, adequate for the situation, is foreign. "Necessary, but not sufficient," we say. How can a leader accept what is not perfect and still lay claim to being a leader?

We offer just the opposite perspective: leaders find ways to reach an attitude of acceptance, of moving forward on the basis of what can be real and effective, even if that is not perfect. A guru or an artist can afford to strive for perfection because they are accountable only to their beliefs. Leaders work in real time, under real circumstances of the need to decide, to act, and to produce a viable next step. Leaders, therefore, know how to accept what is able to be accomplished and train themselves to be able to recognize when that point has been reached.

This ability to reach attitudes of resolution and acceptance is what others experience as a leader's "charisma." *Webster's New World Dictionary* defines "charisma" as a special quality of leading that captures the popular imagination and inspires allegiance and devotion. But its other meaning is "to show favor to; a divinely inspired gift, grace or talent." Another meaning is "the endowment of grace." Clearly, charisma's effect is that of inspiring others, but its source is that of receiving a gift. To receive a gift, one must accept it. To receive the gift referred to in the notion of charisma is to receive and accept a divine gift. That means, at a minimum, accepting a gift touches one at the deepest levels and then unfolds to command a sense of one's wholeness. To the extent that one is able to accept a gift of a deep and significant magnitude, and then is able to have it to be received by one's whole being, one will have charisma. All of that energy is available to the followers within the arch as the illumination that spurs action and decision.

WORTHY

Self-Trust opens up through the growing realization that good things happen in response to one's actions. This is not a naïve belief or blind assumption. Self-Trust happens over time, and with the application of a self-conscious process of connecting the accumulation of one's experiences, remembering what had occurred in those experiences, correlating those experiences with a grounded sense of how one's decisions played or did not play in that experience.

Self-Trust includes the acceptance of the "worthiness" (not perfection) of what one is putting forward. This is a point so often forgotten by leaders as they criticize themselves for a failure or see the discouragement in the eyes of followers. Creative leaders just reach a point in their lives when they realize how with each disappointment some kind of learning takes place that moves the endeavor along. And with this realization comes a kind of peace.

It is a state of grace, and nothing less. (Charisma, as this state of grace, emanates from this acceptance of the worthiness of the effort.) Creative leaders express gratitude far more than they strut around exuding heroic bravado. There is no need to defend or exude confidence. There is just going ahead, learning as we go, experiencing what happens with openness and acceptance, adjusting and moving ahead again. No leader that inspires success can be frantic and panicked at the passage of the unexpected or at the encounter with disappointment.

Thus Self-Trust brings all of the dynamics of the spires to bear in order to encompass the space in which the events unfold that will make or break the endeavor. What the followers within the arch see is that driving energy, offered with humility, humor (words derived from the Latin *humus*, meaning earth) that enables all concerned to take that next step, experience what comes to be, and then go on, increasing self-awareness, fostering the shared experiences that build esprit and collaboration. It is because of Self-Trust that a forceful leader's driving energy doesn't bowl people over and crush them, but instead, inspires them to take the next steps, and in so doing, firm resolve and ignite action in others.

Now we turn to talking about just that energy that, emitted from the keystone, makes all of this possible. It is the incarnation of charisma that we call "Leader Brand."

CHAPTER THREE

The Leader's Brand

LET'S GO.

—*ALBERT JONES, QUOTED BY ROBERT COLES*[1]

[1] Robert Coles, *Lives of Moral Leadership* (New York, 2001), p. 208.

THE LEADER'S ENERGY

It takes energy to break us out of our comfort zones.

Most of us keep ourselves happy by remaining safely within the boundaries of our busy, automated lives, performing our daily tasks, meeting our obligations. Our duties and our enjoyments are ordered, sequenced, and justified down to the smallest detail. We are most skillful at preventing anything from breaking those routines. The habits and routines people build for themselves become protected psychic realms. But judging from the problems of drinking, addiction, behavioral and psychically based compulsions that we see all around us, we know that such confinement, even when self-imposed, does not make us happy.

Creative leaders enable change. How do they do that? How do they get us to break out of our self-imposed confinement or (even more difficult) to break through of our self-imposed contentment?

Facts, even the overwhelming weight of an accumulation of facts, won't induce us to jump. A plan or a strategy won't inspire us to leap over the walls either. For the conservative soul, no plan or a strategy provides a sufficient map of ensuing events.

This state of affairs will never be acceptable to creative leaders. These people have devoted their lives to new possibilities. They unsettle our comforts and dare us to adopt new mindsets, activities, and patterns in order to make those possibilities real. In a business, when the CEO is mandating changes, most employees just go along, modifying their tasks as requested, all the while protecting their old habits, mindsets, and worldviews. As anyone who has led a turnaround will tell you, most employees go along to get along.

But if the CEO is a creative leader, a person who emits self-trusting energy from the keystone of her arch, another scenario is possible.

Some people will pick up on that energy—just that pure energy itself. They will not only get that they have to do their tasks differently, or that there will be new things to do, but those people will feel that special energy and use it to grow and change.

These are the people creative leaders have converted into being their followers. "Convert?" you ask. Is that an appropriate way to think of the leader's task? Doesn't "conversion" carry religious connotations that are markedly out of place in the work environment? The answer to both questions is yes. We see the leader's task to be converting employees into followers. And we feel that such a "spiritual" connotation is unavoidable here.

Here's why. When a new leader comes on to the scene, she typically finds employees' attentions functioning at a low level. At best, employees' attentions are dispersed, task-oriented, self-involved, and self-interested. The new leader needs these people's attention to be focused and directed, needs these employees to willingly displace some of their personal concerns for the strenuous collaboration that is required. Thus, the leader must initiate a process in which these employees, of their own volition, look to the leader. In exchange for this attention, the leader has to offer these employees something that is worthy of their heightened, newly directed and concentrated attention. The leader expects her offering to be accepted and her efforts reciprocated—completely willingly and generously—by these employees. She is thus asking of the employees in her group that they "turn" (Latin: *vertere*) "together" (Latin: *con*) toward each other. In short, she is asking these people to undertake a self-guided conversion.

So how does a leader inspire the willingness in people to undertake change? The energy leaders emit from their Self-Trust affects these employees. Employees experience the quality of resolve, acceptance, and agree with the worthiness of the propositions the leaders offer. From this experience the converts contemplate whether or not they will feel compelled to vault over their walls of complacency or fear. *Only when the connection is made between a leader's energy and the dormant energies of potential followers do these people propel themselves beyond confinement within their walls of habit and comfort.*

In our depiction of the arch, the leader's energy streams out of the keystone of Self-Trust and is experienced by receptive followers as a guiding light. The image symbolizes how energy released from the keystone forms a special field in which new possibilities are illuminated. In this light, people are stirred to offer their focused collaboration. We call this energy that is available to others who decide to participate in a change effort a "Leader's Brand." It describes the firm foundation on which a relationship between leaders and followers develop. The brand expresses Self-Trust and the passion about a possible future that the leader accepts as necessary and as requiring his active agency in bringing about.

The Leader's Brand thus expresses the set of enduring expectations, aspirations, and commitments that she projects, out of Self-Trust, in order to create, qualify, recognize, and reward followers. From the standpoint of followers, the Leader's Brand summarizes indefinable qualities capable of converting them into followers. It is the expression—the words, deeds, demeanor, empathy, and determination—that some call "charisma" and which others are content to enjoy and not name at all as they move forward. It is this energy that propels them out of their conforming habits into new worlds, with all their danger, excitement and promise.

WHY "BRAND"?

BRAND

In the world of business marketing, the idea that a company must have a clearly identifiable "brand" forms the bedrock of marketing dogma. A recognizable brand distinguishes the company from the pack. The company gets to create immediate and topical advertising messages that can leverage off a stable platform of consumer knowledge. In essence, when a company has a brand, people can form a relationship with that company. This differentiation can command higher prices against the "commodity" or "discount" producers.

On the other side of the brand equation, customers demand high levels of performance from that company: they have definite expectations as to what its logo looks like; what its products are; what its pricing means; how it can be accessed; how the company will stand behind that product and back it up with a satisfaction guarantee. If the company violates those expectations, those customers will act on their anger and will likely go elsewhere. Knowing that, branded companies will exert exceptional energies and will expend vast sums of money to keep the trust of their customers.

One need only recall the Tylenol scare of November 12, 1982. In that case, a few bottles of Tylenol in the Philadelphia area were laced with poison. Johnson and Johnson took full responsibility for assuring that their brand represented safety and life-enhancing products, not life-threatening ones. In response to the scare, they pulled all Tylenol off the shelves of pharmacies nationwide and immediately added safety seals to the packaging of the product that they put back on the shelves.

A LEADER'S BRAND?

The idea of a "Leader Brand" distinguishes our concept from that of a leader's "style." A "style" refers to a collection of personality traits that are exhibited when leaders deal with others and issues. We have already discussed "style" when we talked about the Skill of Character we called "Drive," the spire of the arch that incorporates with how people self-consciously channel their energies. In that context we were concerned with the impact a leader's energy had on others and how others experienced the leader's personality.

LEADER BRAND:
The energy that flows out from the keystone and down into the arch.

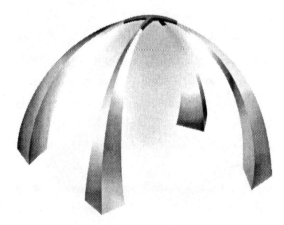

In offering the idea of "Leader Brand," we are talking about a dimension of leading that goes beyond anyone's personality. *"Brand" characterizes the way a leader acts, day in, day out, in all kinds of situations, while on the job, so as to create followers.* The brand will determine if the leader has followers (and not merely occupy a position or office), and it will also determine what kind of followers they will be. The brand considers the expectations leaders and followers have of each other and how each meets the other's needs in the course of meeting the challenges of the endeavor. When successfully negotiated, the relationship builds the bond of trust so essential in accomplishing anything of importance in our lives.

FOLLOWERSHIP

That said, we have to take a step back for a moment and consider this whole idea of "followers." The notion of "having followers" is a difficult one for some aspiring leaders to swallow. In their egalitarian humility, the idea of "having followers" seems to be egotistical, self-aggrandizing, inappropriately elevating them over and above other very good people. It seems to place leaders on a "higher plane" than followers.

While I sympathize with these concerns, this kind of thinking drives potentially effective leaders to take refuge in their managerial roles, to concentrate on tasks and processes, and thus to abrogate their responsibilities as leaders. I now tell my clients that followership is an idea that must be incorporated into their self-trusting acceptance of their roles as leaders.

One client ably expressed the reluctance to accept the idea that people could accept the role of being a follower. "No one tells his or her child to grow up and be a follower," he said to me. "Can you imagine a scene in which you, as a parent, take your child on your knee, tell them to do good, and be a good follower?"

He is so right. An advertisement that sells 2003 Audi's bombards the viewer with flashing images of glamorous youths doing stylish consumerist things and then ends with the tag line "Never Follow" (as though you can do anything else in this mass consumerist culture). But my point flies in the face of this stereotype: this attitude is not only inappropriate; it is harmful and socially destructive. We hold in esteem many kinds of follower behaviors. We teach our children to listen to us as parents, listen to teachers, and to be law-abiding and good citizens. Some teach their children to obey the tenets of their religions. Many of us adhere to and/or enforce, the standards and practices of our professions. These are the behaviors of people that follow.

A DANGEROUS ATTITUDE

I believe this attitude is dangerous for several reasons. First, the attitude leads to cynicism, isolation, and despair—all of which are in ample evidence in our society today. How so? Following is the action that precedes our being able to connect with others, with other worlds. It is from this connection that we are able to envision possibilities and have hopes for ourselves. *When we follow, we declare our ability and desire to connect with others so that they too, and we altogether, can realize new possibilities.*

By denigrating the notion of being able to follow, we undermine our abilities to lead. So far we have said that leading is about bringing to the fore all the lessons we have garnered in our lives and arriving at a point of Self-Trust in regard to them. Here's another way to describe this experience: a leader is one who has learned how to follow what life needs in order to be better for all, whether others behave or believe this way or not. Self-Trust is another form of following, a self-following in which our own lives and experiences act as our guide.

In this sense, the leader is the paramount follower: the "follower on steroids," as a client of mine said. *Followers have the living, flesh-and-blood leader to follow, while leaders follow something that doesn't exist yet.*

Gandhi, for instance, regarded himself as a threefold follower: first of his religious convictions, then of the personal vows he made about his stance and conduct in the world, and finally to the political aspirations of his people. The leader accepts that these life experiences, vows, and beliefs have yielded guidance for decisions that they must follow or face at the peril of losing their way.

"FOLLOWISTS"

For all of these reasons, I feel the need to clarify our thinking about the followership that engages with creative leaders from the denigrated and degraded connotations the word typically entails elsewhere. I hate to do this, but to help make this distinction, I am going to coin a term. That term is "followist." While leaders of all kinds create followers, that special class of creative leaders we are addressing, create followists. We will use this term only in this chapter in order to emphasize our point about the character of followers creative leaders cultivate. Then, in subsequent chapters, we will return to the standard term, "follower," but with new insights as to what we mean by the term.

Followists are autonomous, mature people who want to accomplish something significant in their lives, on a large scale, within a certain time span. They work with the leader because that person shows a way, clears a path, sorts out extraneous energies, puts them with like-minded and hearted people, so that this kind of accomplishment is possible. Followists want to do something themselves, not have something done for them. Followists don't expect miracles to be done for them, but you can bet that together, they want to see miracles happen because of what they have done.

For the reminder of this chapter (only) I will be using the terminology precisely. When I am speaking of any leader's efforts, I will use the word, "follower." When I am speaking specifically of people who collaborate with creative leaders I will use the term "followist."

STEPPING INTO FOLLOWERSHIP

Some call the act of becoming a follower one of "enrollment." I don't accept that idea. The idea of enrollment connotes passivity. It is as though the "cause" is there; people just have to be persuaded to sign up, and everything proceeds on in its way from there on in. In our understanding, creative leading brings about something or does something that others have not formerly engaged in, proposes new insights and so changes the habits and practices of everyone the endeavor touches. At a minimum, this endeavor entails creating a new relationship, in a person's life, one that a person did not have before and did not necessarily ever expect to have. And followists, even more than leaders, have to *create a new relationship*. The new followists had not, previously, been moved to act in these ways or envision these possibilities. They are, as we have said, "converting" to something that had not previously appeared on their radar.

This is no mere "enrollment," as the coaching community likes to call it. Creating this new relationship is hard, deliberate work on the part of the followists. To do this work, people shed old habits and patterns, expose themselves to things they have never done before and so risk failure, often on a grand scale. And unlike a course or a class in which you enroll, to learn what you have already decided you want to learn, becoming a followist has no agenda attached to it. There is no telling what you are heading for or what you will have to do. Followists are the first to experience this. Indeed they are the ones who, more than the leaders, suffer first through the mistakes, mishaps, misunderstandings, and bruised feelings that go along with creating new relationships to others and the world.

RECIPROCITY

The relationship between creative leaders and followists is marked by reciprocity. Each gives to the other, uses the other, and makes certain things possible for the other that would not otherwise be possible for either if they continued in their solitary lives.

Followists certainly use leaders. As a followist, I may not be able to devote my full-time energies to the endeavor. That is one of the limitations on my life that I accept in becoming a followist. I have other things to do, a family to raise (and lead), a skill to learn, an emotional battle to resolve. So I use the leader to help me sort out extraneous information and focus on what matters right now. Since I am a bit distracted, the leader helps me to keep the end in sight and reminds me that there is an end—so keep at it. That we are really accomplishing something—highlighted by the leader's recognition and recitation of the milestones we have passed—she energizes, excites, and inspires me.

And the creative leader reminds me of my own aspirations. In those moments when I fall into my chair, exhausted, anxious, discouraged, the leader reminds me of why, how, and the occasion during which I got into this thing in the first place. These are, after all, my aspirations. The greatest compensation, after all, is not what we are paid, but what we become. And by pursuing these aspirations, this is what we can make the world to be. For some, in our history—such as the Freedom Riders in the sixties, who rode on buses through the south in an effort to overcome segregated terminals, their following of the call of many leaders (Martin Luther King Jr., Bayard Rustin, James Farmer)—this aspiration for what we needed to be as a nation acted as an imperative that was larger than the confines of their individual, private lives.

And then leaders use their followists in important, emotionally stabilizing and enriching ways. I don't endorse the oft-cited Gandhi quote, "There go my people. I must follow them, for I am their leader," but there is in that idea an important kernel of truth: To assure that the leader is doing the job, followists demand stringent performance from leaders. They keep the leader in touch with what is happening on the ground, in real time. They keep the leader in touch with the humanity and the high aspirations that brought them to their decisions to become followists in the first place. And in so doing, followists encounter risk.

When a leader is too far out in front, imbued with her "high purpose" and "high Self-Trust," she can veer off track. She can mistake her commitment for entitlement; she can mistake her role with followists for license. In these circumstances, the best followists "manage up," realizing fully well that that offering a corrective suggestion to the leader could result in ostracism or even termination. The fate of whistle blowers in our culture is not one to be wished on anyone. When a followist takes on this responsibility, he absorbs a deep sense of personal risk. Many followists I know have chosen to take that risk. Some have been rewarded; others have been made to pay the price.

When leaders veer off track, they cause pain, loss, and despair for the followist and failure for the whole endeavor. The leader that disappoints engenders feelings of nothing less than betrayal. It is not a matter of mere failure or foible. The notion of a brand, after all, is that it is a relationship laced through and through with expectations—mutual expectations—that are met through the open offering of trust. A follower who disappoints can likely be replaced, with some loss, of course, but the endeavor goes on, another follower may rise unexpectedly to the occasion. But when the leader disappoints, there is often nowhere for followers to go. When high-power executives—such as those we saw in the corporate criminal parade of 2002-3, featuring the likes of Skilling of Enron, or Ebbers of Worldcom, or Koslowski of Tyco—despoil the aspirations of people who build their companies, the loss is permanent. Followers may be powerless to upbraid the leader and exact consequences for his actions, but they can check out and heap derision on that leader.

Followists put leaders in the position to do their best. Leaders have the most to live up to. What must they do to meet the demands of followists? Make good decisions that advance them toward a goal. Provide the structure, clarity, and constancy of vision that will keep the endeavor together and on track. Create a path and milestones along the way that followists can navigate together.

CREATING A LEADER BRAND

But when all is said and done, whether or not an erstwhile leader will have a chance to create followists depends on the leader's brand ringing true. We now have to turn our attention to actually creating that brand. First, let us make clear what this idea does not include. A Leader Brand is not an advertising slogan accompanied by fantastic images, fanfare, or pageantry. The brands of creative leaders express their heartfelt will to offer something of themselves, something important and vital to others. *The idea summarizes, therefore, a leader's sense that the endeavor is worthy of the attention and effort of others, and accordingly, to engage in that effort entails meeting certain requirements and needs.* These are not met by the leader alone but are met through the collaboratively developed trust all participants in the endeavor offer each other.

Think of the image of the arch for a moment. In that image energy is emitted from the keystone, from the leader's Self-Trust. We name this energy, pouring down into the arch, the Leader's Brand. That energy is available to cascade down into the space opened by the arch due to a simple act: acceptance. When the leader has achieved the acceptance that characterizes Self-Trust, all kinds of energy-absorbing conflicts and egotisms (within the internal psyche of the leader) disappear. The energy doesn't go away, only the junk and noise that absorb and disperse that driving energy go away.

CHARISMA

This radiating out of the keystone of the energy released by Self-Trust is how we understand the leader's "charisma." Charisma is defined as a gift of grace, a gift of energizing spirit that seems to come only from God or some higher spirit. The leader's charisma clearly emanates from a more earthly source, that person's Self-Trust, but it is so purposeful, liberating, and joyful that it too has that inspirational quality. So when we describe Leader Brand, we are talking about providing a prescription for crafting a portrayal of charisma. A leader's brand portrays the natural, relaxed, seemingly unperturbed energy that flows from the creative leader's Self-Trust. Because Self-Trust emanates from the leader's real, lived experience, from the keystone of Self-Trust, charisma is experienced as that aspect of the leader's authentic character, which truly welcomes others.

The most potent example of what I mean by the charisma of a Leader Brand expressing genuine, imperturbable Self-Trust, I think of the miracle in Nelson Mandela's story. The miracle is that during his twenty-seven years in prison, Mandela's stature grew from that of being a functionary in a political faction to that of national, international, and spiritual leader.

Mandela's message of universal change and transformation of South African society was intended to affect everyone in that country, not just the "enemy," defenders of apartheid. Mandela insisted that the oppressed change also. Mandela asked his people to think not just about redressing their oppression; he asked them to open their hearts and minds to universal equality, freedom, and responsibility. That message actually took twenty-seven years to sink in, mature (like a fine wine) and become acceptable to all of those affected by the struggle.

It worked because his brand was clear: the new nation must transcend apartheid; it must be multiracial not a reverse apartheid in which the roles are turned on their heads—blacks oppressing whites. Mandela portrayed the brand with consistent respect for his jailors, including learning the Afrikaner language, with uncompromising adherence to his principles of universal human dignity. He demonstrated his authentic adherence to the brand by refusing to be released from prison until it was agreed that apartheid was to be dismantled. He refused any privilege from apartheid so as to demonstrate, to portray his brand, that his life was devoted to only one principle. Rather than being a waste, these twenty-seven years enabled Mandela to prove the authenticity of his brand, work it on a small scale and show its power. Imprisonment kept him from the petty squabbles and confrontations that might have diluted his brand. Imprisonment actually became part of the process of people forming a relationship to Mandela.[2]

THE WAY FOR THE REST OF US

But while there are many creative leaders among us, most of us are not Mandelas. And we don't have to spend twenty-seven years in prison to create followists. There are ways, short of his trials, to create an effective

[2] To get a fully developed picture of just how miraculous a story this is, please read Anthony Sampson's *Mandela: The Authorized Biography*.

Leader Brand. These are the questions we have our clients ask themselves in order to help them convert mere employees or acquaintances into potential followists:

1. How are you needed by your followists? Creative leaders are needed on many levels. A creative leader provides a constant presence that reshapes followists' mindsets, values, and worldviews, collectively and individually. Intelligent, capable people become followists because the leader puts a new perspective, a new opportunity, a new worldview into people's lives. None of that would be present without the leader.

This is a role that transcends any facts that are presented and goes beyond justifying or explaining any actions that need to be done. I say to people that leaders are needed by followers, managers are needed by bosses. A creative leader is needed by followists because she has made something possible for them that no one else has. Followists, especially in the beginning, cannot imagine things unfolding as they do without the efficacy of that leader.

A manager has subordinates. The manager oversees people doing things they, to some extent, know how to do. The manager enforces standards, demands certain behaviors. A different manager would do things differently, and that is of no particular concern to the subordinates involved. Fine, they'll do it that way. No big deal. When a leader has put something into place, however, those things do matter to followists. They have taken it upon themselves to change and move out of their protective shells into new territory. They can take this giant step because they are not alone, and because a leader is there to point the way.

Nelson Mandela fully realized in what ways his followists needed him. He was needed, to be sure, to represent the need for freedom to the apartheid regime and to the world. But he was needed also to move followists out of being fixated merely on a local, enemy-dependent rebellion to a creative vision of a new and greater world.

This aspect of creating a brand is crucial for the leader as well. I believe that the leader's reward is being needed. No pay sufficiently compensates the creative leader (as opposed to the people who occupy positions of power for the sake of their egos or accumulation of wealth or fame) for the risk and the pain of failure. The creative leader is primarily rewarded by successfully responding to others' needs. Leaders can claim legitimacy only when others need them. They have no offices to ascend to or trappings of power to display. As such, they do not give up being needed in certain ways (as we will see shortly) easily. They want to be needed for what they bring to the situation.

But let's also understand that the followists' need of the leader is not one of "codependence," as the psychologists say. Creative leaders do not create cults around themselves. The last thing they want in the endeavor is people who have such weak identities that they passively adopt that of the leader. No autonomy is taken from the followists. In fact, a great leader inspires autonomy. Followists need leaders to help spur them to create comprehending connections to a situation so they can envision new worlds and appropriate ranges of possible actions with which they can succeed. So, in creating a Leader Brand with our clients we ask them these questions: How do your employees (potential followists who are just waiting to be converted) need you? What do they need from you if they are to be able to rise to meet the demands of the endeavor? If you were gone tomorrow, what would they miss? What difference do you make in their lives?

2. What are you willing to be needed for? The fact is that leaders are needed for every reason one human can need another, and there is no way a leader can respond to all of those needs. Furthermore, in no way does it aid the cause if a leader responds to inappropriate needs. Nelson Mandela would not respond to his constituents' (legitimate) need for revenge.

On a more mundane level, a CEO I work with demonstrated how clearly he knew this aspect of his brand. We were talking about one of his direct reports and a follower who had left her previous job to join him on a new assignment. This person was "high maintenance," according to the CEO. I offered that if he provided more of an occasionally positive message to this person, she would probably not be so needy. "I am not here to baby-sit my senior staff," he averred. It was clear. There were certain kinds of needs he would not accept. Good. Done.

So ask yourself, what are you willing to be needed for? What needs of your followists do you have to meet on a regular basis in order to accomplish what you have set out as the goal and vision? If you will not meet those needs, what will you put in place so that your followers' fears or lacks in development won't get in the way? Or, alternatively, are you willing to wait (vis-à-vis Mandela) for them to get it, or are you willing to lose people who aren't ready to make the leap?

3. *What are your expectations of your followists?* Next, in order to create followers, your expectations of them must be clear. "Ask not what your country can do for you, but what you can do for your country" or "I have a dream today" are two of the most famous statements of expectations of great leaders in my generation's experience.

Followists want those expectations laid out before them with clarity and forcefulness. Your expectations as a leader lay out a path on which they can chart their aspirations. They also need those expectations to distinguish between themselves and others who are not yet part of the endeavor. Or, what actually comes first, they need those expectations as markers that tell them how far they have come in taking this step into the arch, into the movement toward what is next.

Meeting challenging expectations comprise the personal milestones by which a followist will measure the robustness of the leader's vision. A followist, after all, has many choices in his life. If the leader's expectations are smaller than the followist's own vision, the followist may demand more of that leader, or he may move on to become a leader or may find a more demanding one. If the expectations are daunting and yet inviting, unsettling yet justified, fresh yet sensible, the followist will remain in the fold.

The expectations are the other side of a *quid pro quo* implied in the leader's effort to meet followist's needs. For meeting these needs of yours, this is what I expect from you, the leader rationalizes. Then the leader's job is to provide ample opportunities and occasions on which he acknowledges that these expectations have been met, and by doing so, the endeavor is furthered, the bond strengthened and enriched.

4. What stories of yours demonstrate that this is your wall? Because a leader operates out of Self-Trust, she inhabits a story she must fulfill. All leaders aspire to fulfill a story that has become urgent in their lives. It is often a story that they stumble into, seemingly by accident, as they feel themselves being pulled to go in a certain direction. Only on reflection did they realize what had been happening. The world they experienced before this moment is somehow incomplete, or things in that world are not done in a way that gives that person satisfaction/confidence. They turn to a set of actions that allows them to fill that space.

These stories convey far more than facts. People respond to the hidden themes of leaders. Long after the overt actions and day-to-day utterances go by, people respond to the feeling for what living in the envisioned world would be like. Either you pick up on the undertones, and so decide whether or not to follow, or you don't, and you will remain oblivious to what is happening.

Stories create a texture of undertone and nuance. They convey the message that this world the leader is creating comes from hard-won realizations. And these realizations are now the only world the leader lives in. The message to the followist is clear: you are in my arch or you are not.

Are these stories always true? In some sense, a leader, in portraying a brand, is not recounting a set of experiences that are cast in stone or are captured permanently by a dispassionate, photographic lens. The stories are "myths." By "myth" we don't mean fabricated fables, but *stories that reveal a core of the leader's psychic truth at this particular point in time.* These stories are constantly recalled and relived. When they are reconnected with new events and stages of life, they change in nuance and emphasis, if not in actual sequence or population. They are told again and again, retaining a core of stability, but they are also often surrounded by a penumbra of loose, vaporlike factuality.

The stories actually may not be true in a journalistic or scientific sense. Ronald Reagan was famous for telling stories that purported to be about himself but that actually came from roles he had played in movies or that came from movies he had seen. His biographer even had to insert a fictional character into Reagan's story in order to give the book heft. When one of Lyndon Johnson's biographers went out to research many of Johnson's stories, he found many of them to be complete fictions. Yet these stories were completely, authentically internalized by these men as illustrating why they were leading as they were. These were stories that were offered as sincere, if somewhat manipulative, invitations to followists. They were offered as means to grasp the larger picture that these leaders were painting.

We ask our clients to begin the process of recovering their stories in the course of realizing their Self-Trust. And we carry that exercise forward here. We ask them to reflect on these questions: What is your story? What is the story you are acting out? What is the question or the problem that you keep seeing everywhere that leaves you dissatisfied?

Or, what is your "gift"—a talent, insight, concern, or passion you feel so strongly each and every day that you have to offer it, freely and without qualification—to others? Does it involve other people at the core? Does it entail affecting the lives of many other people? What are the stories you draw on to help your followists intimately connect with those expectations? What stories can you tell to make it vividly clear that your expectations are a wall beyond which they cannot retreat (or they will not be followists of yours)?

THE LEADER BRAND SPEECH

As a concluding exercise to our conferences and our individual mentoring, we ask our participants to create a Leader Brand speech. This is a ten-minute address imagined as being given to whomever it is the client is seeking to lead.

I love this part of the program. One of my most memorable engagements around this exercise happened at a conference we gave for an educational organization. Remarkably, many of these educators (academic deans and administrative department heads) resisted the idea of having to give a speech. I know that for some—when asked what they fear most in life, like Woody Allen—death comes in second, behind public speaking. But still, I didn't expect educators to be so reticent. One person wrote us a note, "It is disappointing that while you are offering such an innovative approach to leadership, and yet you are falling back on that old technique of giving speeches." The note was anonymous.

As we progressed through the program, we put people in situations in which they explore how their lives were worthy of being accepted as a basis for leading, how their lives were worthy of Self-Trust. People became more and more open to each other and saw how their stories moved and motivated others and brought others closer to them, even to the point of overcoming prior disagreements. The last night of the program, we had people retire to their rooms to prepare their speeches. The next morning the group of fifty broke into smaller audiences of seven each (plus one). Seven speeches were to be selected and presented to the whole group.

People couldn't decide which speeches not to choose, so instead of following our instructions, spontaneously, without consultation, each group chose two people to present. Since we were now going to hear fourteen speeches, we were clearly going to run past our appointed ending time; but no one cared. They wanted these speeches to be heard, and they wanted to hear these speeches. One of the people chosen to give a speech to the whole group owned up to having sent us the protesting note and expressed utter amazement that she had been chosen to speak. In fact, her speech was so good, so uplifting, that the metaphor she used to focus her speech was adopted as the rallying call for this group when they went back to work.

The others' speeches, from some very shy and introverted people, were so moving that there was not a dry eye in the house. Over the nearly two hours it took to hear all the speeches, no one asked for a break or left the room. They were truly authentic, real accounts of people coming to points of realization in their lives, and they offered an invitation to change that everyone in the room could not deny. These changes were within their power; these were the people, their own colleagues, who had the passion and ability to affect those changes.

THE LEADER BRAND SPEECH OUTLINE

Here is the outline we use in helping people prepare their speeches. Are you ready to create your speech now? Try giving it at the next meeting. Read it to your spouse or family. Keep it in front of you to remind you of what it is you are creating in your life, by the agency of your leadership.

> ➤ *Your expectations of your followists: "These are the kinds of people that accomplish what we have set out to do. I expect you are that kind of person, and I will treat you in a manner that anticipates that you are that kind of person.*

> ➤ *What you will give your followists: "Day in, day out, this is how I will show up for this job, and you can count on me for..."*

> ➤ *Where the journey goes: " I've seen lots of things happen to people on this journey. Some of you will...; others will...; but in the end, this is what each and every one of you will have accomplished:..."*

> ➤ *Statement of understanding: "I understand what you will be going through... [story that demonstrates understanding].*

> ➤ *What's in it for them: "Is it going to be worth it? You have to answer that question. But I'll tell you this: you will be a different person when we reach our goal. You will know this about yourself..."*

> ➤ *Endorsement of their aspiration: "And when you are done with this, you will reach new heights..."*

> ➤ *Personal stories that back up each element: "How do I know this. When I was..."*

> ➤ *A central, unifying, compelling metaphor: "I have been to the mountaintop..."*

> ➤ *Action statement: "Now it's your turn..."*

AN EXAMPLE OF THE LEADER BRAND SPEECH

One leader with whom I have worked put her brand speech into the form of a poem. I have her permission to offer it to you.

> *I draw from the inside. And mark the far site.*
>
> *You entrust me and provide the might.*
>
> *Both burden and joy. This mantle brings,*
>
> *And creates the space. For even greater things.*
>
> *Confident in attempt. With the will to succeed,*
>
> *Your trust is the power. By which I lead.*
>
> —*Deborah Perry, June 18, 2003*

PART TWO

Realizing the Vision

INTRODUCTION

A year and a half after Matt began his mentoring, Beth was promoted. As assistant vice president in Strategic Marketing, she managed a small group of planners who charted the company's products two years out. She enjoyed the work and stayed in the position for two years. When she was passed over for a promotion to the VP of Marketing slot, however, she felt the writing was on the wall, and Beth wasn't one to wait for the axe to drop.

After a few months of casual looking around and talking to friends, she was hired by an investment group to be the chief marketing officer of a high-tech start-up. A CEO and a CFO were also hired by the investors. Beth's assignment was to build a company capable of turning a promising technology developed by a group of university researchers into a viable commercial product. As part of her employment agreement, the investors agreed to pay for Beth working with Matt once again as her mentor.

They met in her new locale. No fancy offices and glass towers for Zee-Tech. Located in a park of similar small industrial firms, no one had enclosed offices, and there was only one small conference room. The rather spartan surroundings didn't bother Beth.

"What excites you about this position?" Matt asked in their first get-reacquainted meeting.

"Oh, that's easy," Beth answered. "I do it all myself. I mean creating the team, surveying the market, dealing with customers, really turning the technology into a product. That's all exciting to me. I knew the scientists from my last job, and I was interested in what they were doing then. I had no idea I'd be working with them, but here I am."

The excitement was obvious. And there was something else Matt noticed about Beth. She was dressed in jeans and a sweater, and the stiffness in her demeanor seemed to be gone. She had a spring in her step and any sense of unease was gone. She was on a roll.

"Besides the politics in the old firm, what made you jump ship?" Matt asked.

"Let me tell you a story," Beth said.

"Go for it," Matt replied.

"You remember how we talked about my grandfather," Beth said.

"The rather tyrannical, old-school male chauvinist?" Matt joked. They both laughed. "Well, let's not be too hard on him," Beth said. "Not that he doesn't deserve those descriptions."

Beth had told Matt how her grandfather lived with her family for a few years when she was between the ages of four and seven. All during that time, he strongly favored her older brother. From her grandfather, she would hear, "Your brother will be a great success in life." And when she asked him for his opinion about her, he would answer, "Women belong in the home. That's where you belong."

Those were fighting words to Beth. She had decided at that young age to prove her grandfather completely wrong.

"That's what my early career was all about. Proving him wrong. Then, when my father died, and I attended his funeral, I realized something."

"You never talked very much about your father," Matt noted.

"I know. I think I always took him and Mom for granted, I hate to say. Dad never made it big in a corporation, and I never knew why. His little accounting practice supported the family, but it never grew into a big firm. I never thought about those things before. He was always a wonderful father, but I don't think I understood what his life was about, until, I hate to say it, his funeral two years ago.

"There were hundreds of people at the funeral. I was shocked. I wondered where all these people came from. After the funeral, people kept coming up to me," she said, her voice wavering a bit, "Some were people from his corporate days. Others were his more recent clients. They all told me how much my *father had meant to them. And there was a common theme. At the corporation, he often stood up for people, resisted layoffs or helped people advance and improve their wages. Many of these people were immigrants, saying people like my father helped make this country great.*

"*Then his clients told me how they had lost someone they could absolutely trust. How he was a person who was not afraid of giving them bad news, but always helped them out of a jam—including forgiving his fee, or part of it—no wonder the firm never grew. And he have them great advice to protect their families or grow their businesses. They counted him as a friend, and not just an accountant.*

"*I was amazed. I didn't know he had stood up for people who needed it. That's probably why he didn't advance very high. I didn't know how much he cared for other people. And I began to wonder what I would have done if I were in his shoes. I can't say I was pleased at the answers I gave to myself. I was, after all, an executive on the rise; I was proving my grandfather wrong. And I was alone, not married, now without a father, and I was not so sure I was on the right track anymore. It was a real shock.*"

"*Are you saying your values changed as a result of this?*" Matt asked.

"*Maybe. I think 'changed' is too strong a word. I don't think I was ever unkind or was politically underhanded. I think I worked hard to get my position at my former firm, and I came to care much more for the people on my team—thanks in no small way to my conversations with you. So I think his caring values were there, but they weren't first and foremost. That's the change: now those values of really thinking about others—their aspirations, as you talked about, for instance—really are in the forefront of my attention.*"

"*That's what I want you to help me with,*" she instructed. "*How do I put those values into action?*"

And with that question, Beth had entered the second arch on the path of creative leading, the "Arch of Vision and Organization." She has reached a point at which she did not merely use her Skills of Character to advance some purpose that was given to her. As a creative leader, she sought out an opportunity in which she could put her own sense of what is important, her own values, into action.

She has set foot into the endeavor of transformation, the terrain of creative leading. Most people, even erstwhile leaders, don't take this step. In business, it is the entrepreneurs that take it; in social and service organizations, it is the reformers or radicals that take it. Beth has taken it because, at this stage of creative leading, she doesn't even think twice about the fact that these values must be real and viable. And she feels she is the one to do it, at least in this sector of the world she knows well.

THE SECOND ARCH: THE ARCH OF VISION AND ORGANIZATION

In chapter 4, Beth enters the second arch along her path to leading greatly. It might seem strange that the arch's components develop into organizational terms such as Values, Mission, Strategy, and Culture, and a keystone we name Signature Behavior. You might object, "I thought the arch symbolized the leader's mind, not the organization." That is the right question.

You've heard the expression, "Walking the talk." That's what we are getting at here: *the Arch of Vision and Organization symbolizes those aspects of organizational life that leaders need to embody in their attitudes, speech, and behavior.* When a leader strides into the room, people snap to what this leader's brand is about, as we said in the last chapter. In this section, we use the arch to symbolize the factors in the leader's psyche that ensures such a "snap" to the brand will happen.

Our train of thought goes this way: Beth wants to assure that certain values are effective and pervasive in her little part of the world; her organization has to behave and act in certain ways if that is to come to pass; she translates that behavior into a single, distinctive way the organization will present itself in and to the world such that it can establish a niche for itself; this is what we call the organization's "Signature Behavior." As of this moment, those specific "values guided behaviors" exist nowhere in the world, except in Beth's head. How will people in the organization (in the arch) know how to act if that behavior isn't modeled for them? That behavior is described and elaborated on by the information contained in the spires—Values, Mission, Strategy, Culture; but it is really learned and internalized by the employees and followers when they see it in the flesh, in the life of the leader.

Thus this arch is a construct of the leader's mind, in the sense that *the components represent the dimensions of the organization's character that the leader has to embody.* Just as an actor has to make sure certain aspects of a character's personality come to the fore, the leader here has to make sure that these values are portrayed. So, in a way, this arch provides the script Beth has to follow in order to assure that the organization truly does make her values come alive.

CHAPTER FOUR

Vision and the Creative Process

THE REAL ACT OF DISCOVERY CONSISTS

NOT IN DISCOVERING NEW LANDS,

BUT IN SEEING WITH NEW EYES.

—*MARCEL PROUST*[1]

[1] Lewis and Regine, *Complexity* (New York, 2000), p. 31.

VISION

We set a high bar for the ideas and inspirations we count as "visions." We have every right to be demanding toward these ideas. After all, we know the significance leaders' visions can have in our lives. Our concerns about the world, when coupled with the will and ability to act, can force us to commit ourselves to something. At a minimum, visions can unsettle even the most entrenched of lives. They uproot us out of our comfort and contentment, propelling us out of our accustomed routines and familiar abodes. Visions obligate us; they make us put demands on ourselves; they make us realize how, if we do act, we just might accomplish. That's a heavy burden. It makes sense to approach these attempts at disruption carefully.

Leaders share our reticence. Rarely do I hear leaders themselves claim that they have vision. Even people who occupy positions in which leading is offered—executive positions, titled positions of authority— are accustomed to downplaying "the vision thing." Yet, when you ask their followers why they participated with these leaders, the first thing they cite is leaders' vision. Whence the disconnect? For one, opportunities to recognize a "vision" occur rarely. So we get out of practice. For another, we have loaded the term up with so many mythic trappings of grandeur and "genius," a vision seems out of reach for us mortals. As a result, many important and worthy ideas are allowed to dissipate into thin air.

Visions may indeed be grand. Gandhi, King, Mandela, or Lincoln envisioned ways to reconstitute their whole societies such that greater freedom and dignity would be available to all. Or the vision may encompass a smaller scale. A local official solves a difficult zoning issue to the satisfaction of all; an organizational leader institutes a self-managing system that lowers costs and more widely distributes responsibility and recognition in a department. The scale or scope of the idea does not determine whether or not a leader offers a vision.

A creative leader's vision offers people a way to engage their worlds more effectively and inclusively at whatever scale is called for.

A "VISION" DEFINED

A creative leader's vision sees how new possibilities can arise out of seemingly stale circumstances—through a collaborative group effort—in such a way that more people derive greater benefit from resources and opportunities.

The ideas that gel into visions do not usually arrive out of the blue, in an instant of a falling apple striking the head of the leader. Visions come as a result of an internal life process the leader undergoes, sometimes over the span of years. In other words, visions do not take hold on unprepared ground. They take root in the psyches and lives of leaders who ardently and passionately consider situations—from a long perspective of experiences and deeply considered values—they deem to be far less than perfect. The process has several components to it we want to identify and think about, lest these important occurrences in the lives of leaders be missed or misconstrued (see figure 4.1).

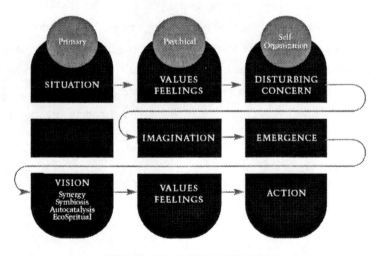

FIGURE 4.1: VISION PROCESS

The vision first arises out of a collision between a leader's values and a world that doesn't measure up. The collision shakes the very ground on which these leaders live their lives, bringing leaders face to face with their "disturbing concerns."[2] Given that a vision emerges out of this troubled ground, we need to consider the role and significance of the leader's *feelings.*

These feelings, churned by the difficult and pressing situation, spur the *imagination.* New images and combinations of ideas are formed, giving rise to the sense that this situation, at the very least, is not a dead end, despite appearances. But for the leader to coalesce these upsurges of psychic energy into a vision requires an appreciation of how something new actually comes into the world. It is not "caused"; rather, it *emerges more or less whole through a process of psychic self-organization.*

We will see from this discussion the variety of visions leaders have. And we will come to appreciate how all of them are necessary in order to bring about larger—or smaller-scale changes in our worlds.[3] Some visions see whole social and organizational arrangements that don't even have a glimmer of existence as yet; another vision points to breakdowns and shortcomings of existing arrangements and links directly with clear solutions; still another vision plays with organizational excellence the way a sculptor shapes raw marble into a striking form, or a musician recasts a melody into new realization; and finally, some visions set out how to raise the bar of performance of an organization by unleashing and then focusing the energies and potentialities of its members.

[2] The term "Disturbing Concern" was developed by Charles Spinosa, Fernando Flores, and Hubert L. Dreyfus in *Disclosing New Worlds: Entrepreneurship, Democratic Action and the Cultivation of Solidarity* (Cambridge, MA, 1997), on whose analysis we loosely base this section.

[3] These types of visions track with the kinds of emergence occasions we identify later in this chapter. Creative leaders use one, several, or all of these forms in order to transform possibilities into real products, service, laws, and/or new societies.

FACE TO FACE WITH ONE'S OWN VALUES: DISTURBING CONCERN

A vision (at least the kind of vision we are discussing) arises when leaders' values are put to the test. Why else would leaders invest so much energy, passion, and enthusiasm into the endeavor if something so basic as their values weren't at stake?

By "values," we don't mean ideals or wishes that the world would be different. We mean something far more basic and intrinsic to a person than that. *Values name the attitudes, beliefs, orientations, and emotions that guide and/or constrain our actual behavior.* If a situation doesn't impel us to act, or at least consciously decide whether or not to act, our values haven't been provoked. If we find ourselves compelled to act in certain ways, even against our "best interests," values are no doubt guiding us.

For example, I may profess that I believe in workplace diversity, but if I don't actively hire nonwhite, nonmale employees (using excuses to myself and others, such as, "I just can't find a qualified candidate."), diversity is not a value; it is just a wish, an ideal, or even worse, some kind of badge my ego needs to display. Or, consider this: Values are the basis of the Self-Trust we exhibit in moments of decision and at times when we venture into generating change in our own lives and in the lives of others. So, as you recall, when, in chapter 2, we talked about Self-Trust, as that state of mind of resolve, we meant that the leader acted in this situation according to undeniable values that, no matter the likely outcome, had to be fulfilled.[4]

[4] Values prescribe (and proscribe) where Self-Trust is able to develop. But Self-Trust goes beyond values by incorporating the concerns, responses, and aspirations of others, both in terms of the acceptance of the need to act on these values, and the sense that something worthy will ensue from the action.

We are more likely to *discover* our actual values than be able to list them in advance. Most of the creative leaders I have worked with didn't always know they had the values they now labor so hard to actualize. There are many things that are important to us, but important things that are also values spur life-shaping actions and exertions and change the lives of the people who hold them. When an impulse or drive to act to be a value, what is experienced feels like a need, an absolute mandate beyond being merely "important." It feels like nothing less than an imperative. A value must be acted on (or consciously decided not to be acted upon) if the person is to feel whole—in integrity, in a connected bond with others—and with a sense of active and worthy engagement.

DISTURBING CONCERN

For the envisioning process to begin, however, these values must be disturbed. Leaders sense that something is missing or is out of whack in the world, and that feeling just won't go away. Since these are leaders, who approach their worlds from standpoints of Self-Trust, they accept that they can make things happen, worthwhile things—they can make their parts of the world better. The vision is drawn out of the resolve, the drive, the passion, to live in the world promised by those values, a world that will come about because it was envisioned and because an organization of many collaborators worked hard to bring it into reality.

This dissatisfaction is not a sudden upsurge of pique. It is experienced as a long-abiding, unsettled feeling. It stays alive and continues to affect the leader because the world is just not quite right. Such leaders cannot get away from the suspicion that with just a little organizing effort the world could be made better. They don't come to this conclusion lightly. They have paid attention to this concern for a long time. It is something of high, if not ultimate, concern.[5] They will have studied the lack, its parameters and boundaries, the attitudes, habits and assumptions, power structures and social institutions that have kept this possibility from coming into being. If these leaders act, placing it within the sphere of their resolve, they do so out of their Self-Trust, out of their recollection of their past experiences, their knowledge of the times and current state of affairs, out of their sense of her own proven capabilities, and the willingness to accept what is possible. To fully understand the leader's vision, however, we have to grasp the *vitality* of its significance, its "feeling" content. This vision—which engenders life-changing actions, stirs resolve, and demands acceptance of a radical proposition—is saturated with many feelings: passion, enthusiasm, excitement, and maybe touches of fear and doubt. It is to the "feeling" dimension of the vision that we now turn.

FEELINGS

The process of coming to a vision begins in the turmoil of experiencing unsettling, disturbing feelings. When something offends a supposed value and doesn't register with a feeling, it probably isn't much of a value. If the genocide in Rwanda passes through my life without inciting sadness, despair, a desire to change something about this world, can I say that compassion is a value of mine? The kinds of values we are talking about—the ones that rouse people from their sleep, tear them away from their "appointment" television shows, make them suddenly uncomfortable with the opinions they have been espousing—are truly held values, ones that stir feelings, and are even raw, alive, "hot" and just waiting to be activated.

[5] To use the term coined by the theologian Paul Tillich.

101

These ideas will make some people very uncomfortable. To even talk about vision, values, or feelings entails that we stir things up and break the routines that allow us to live seamlessly within habit, certainty, and comfort. According to the conventions of everyday life, we go along to get along, and vice versa. Acting on a vision is just not a "normal" way to behave. But for creative leaders, going against the grain, discomforting the comfortable is hardly a preposterous proposition. At some level, at some time in their lives, those who are contented with the *status quo* probably have called creative leaders "a bit crazy."

People can look from the sidelines and feel quite justified in asking, "What's wrong with that person?" and they will not be the creative leaders. "What do they see that we don't?" is a reasonable question for the rest of us to ask of creative leaders. "What's the problem? Why is this such a big deal?" we'd ask. Leaders know what they see and know why it is a big deal. Then the rest of us get to decide whether or not we agree. We get to decide whether we think this person is crazy or is a leader who has a vision, someone we might choose to follow.

FEELINGS IN ACTION[6]

When I pull my hand away from a hot stove burner, a response is triggered. First, there are the sensations: those harbingers and heralds of psychic change. Then come emotions—the driving of a physical response from out of my sensations (thus *e*-meaning "out of"—*motion*). But that surge of self-preserving energy isn't the *feeling*. The feeling, which may or may not occur after the event, is a complex of thoughts,

---

[6] The comments in this section are based on my interpretation of the work of Antonio Damasio, as presented in two of his works: *The Feeling of What Happens: Body and Emotion in the Making of Consciousness* (New York, 1999) and *Looking for Spinoza: Joy, Sorrow and the Feeling Brain* (New York, 2003).

inner changes in body state. The feelings arise later, as I consider how stupid I had been to put my hand near that burner. If I just continue my cooking—probably boiling an egg is the range of activity I'd be likely to be capable of in this instance—there is no feeling involved. If, however, I am, for some reason, really disturbed by that event, a feeling will rise up. The cover is blown on my comfort, and this complex of thoughts, feelings, and images bubbles to the surface.

Let's say the feeling is that of embarrassment or of bewilderment (at my carelessness). The feelings aren't stirred because of the sensation of the heat or because my emotional response was to pull away. That was all natural, instinctive, engendering no further cause for reflection. Feelings are stirred when I see myself as having ignored simple, important, and essential values around the most basic needs of bodily safety. Maybe memories of my fearing mother's voice come up; maybe my father's words encouraging defiance in the face of the world's dangers are triggered. Maybe fears that I am losing some motor skills or my mind is deteriorating with age arise. Stranger things have happened.

So feelings aren't just sensations or emotions, and neither are they solely the thoughts that are triggered as this new and less than satisfactory picture of my self-sufficiency and self-reliance that has been thrust up in my face. *The whole event triggers feeling, and the feeling comprises nothing less than a full-fledged bodily orientation that grabs my attention, alters my train of concentration, and drives a complete complex of realizations about myself and insists on commanding my attention.*

URGENCY

What is the role of feelings in our valuing such that they claim such a crucial component of the creative leader's vision? *Feelings connect our seemingly "solid selves" (these self-satisfied, capable, and self-trusting entities we take ourselves to be) to the outside world, to things that are beyond our control.* In fact, as you think about it, except for our bodily needs, most of what we know as our "self" is actually a bunch of feelings we have cobbled together, from the relationships we have to things outside us. When we are in a comfortable relation with the things we value, when they accept our actions and give back to us what we need from them, we just hum along; and these outside elements hum in the background, moving us blithely along. But when something disrupts that relation, breaks the free interchange of what we value and what that valued entity returns to us, our feelings are stirred. From this perspective, *values are feelings waiting to happen.*

For the creative leader, those stirrings of feeling are occasions that can translate into a vision. So, for the creative leader, a vision is a feeling that this value's time has come. What makes the feeling effective—as something I pay attention to in a way that enables me to reevaluate myself and thus incorporate new information into my self-image—is a feeling that alters my beliefs about the world, and in this case, about myself in the world. By putting huge swaths of my life into play, this feeling can change my orientation to the world, my beliefs, and the level of my resolve and will in the face of certain aspects of that world.

IMAGINATION

Feeling-driven values trigger the imagination. When one's life is stirred in this passionate way, feelings are accompanied, in the words of Martha Nussbaum, "by relevant acts of the imagination."[7]

The imagination, which each and every one of us has, is vastly underappreciated for its power to enrich and vitalize our lives. It is

[7] *Upheavals of Thought* (New York, 2001), p. 65.

downplayed as a factor in decision making or in the determination of the "facts" by which we are supposed to guide our lives. The cultural historian and critic William Irwin Thompson calls the imagination the resource that allows us to bring new vistas of the world into play.[8] "We cannot see what we cannot imagine," he says.

The creative leaders' feelings sustain the energies that spur imaginative activity. They help creative leaders quiet the noise from the environment and direct lively attention, imaginative energy, to the salient events at hand. The feeling's value component frees leaders' time, allows them to put aside other things and concentrate fully on the situation at hand without distraction. And, because the leader does not want to move on, but instead, capitalizes on the mental energy released by the feelings-guided value, the imagination is set free.

The imagination is stirred by the feelings-triggered values which insist that *attention be paid and that something new come out of this moment, that my state of being change.* Thus the life of the creative leader is thrown into flux by this experience of the vision. The play of the imagination is not just a fleeting tickle of energy. It keeps score. The range of thought, knowledge, science, art, history, etc., which imagination encompasses, shapes how a life will be directed into its future. It generates all the material that will be included in the consolidating actions that form the vision, i.e., the actions of "emergence."

EMERGENCE

The leader's psyche is stirred: her feelings tingle, memories are evoked, the imagination is generating ideas, values have been brought to the fore, and old assumptions break down. This "crisis" is the last thing

[8] *Coming Into Being* (New York, 1998), p. 76.

most of us want to go through. But for our leader, there it is, and there is no turning back; there's no point in running away. The leader—under the right circumstances, after a time of rumination and gestation, with the aid of research, conversation, and reflection—comes to a resolution: Something clicks; everything seems to fall into place, and a good hunch about what can be done starts to take shape. A vision comes into view.

Leaders arrive at their visions by a circuitous and largely unconscious route. The process can seem at least mystifying, if not downright mystical, defying the usual procedures of problem solving and establishing causal chains of events. It feels more like a hurricane forming out of chaotically swirling winds and rain than it does scientifically investigating and solving a problem. In these moments when she is absorbed in her disturbing concern and feels her imaginative energies being set loose, the leader's psyche undergoes a self-organizing process that allows for the emergence of a new possibility.

"Emergence" is the name given to a process in which separate and discrete elements intermingle, combine and/or interact such that a new phenomenon takes shape. The new phenomenon may then be "grasped," recognized and reinforced by elements outside the volatile mixture, enabling it to stabilize and become an effective entity on its own. If it is grasped, the phenomenon has a chance of taking hold and integrating into the environment. If it is not grasped, the phenomenon fades away, becoming a mere chimera, a burst of psychic energy that dissipates like a cloud.

EMERGENCE VERSUS CAUSALITY

"Emergence"—what a wonderful concept. Emergence considers the new and unexpected as they rise out of the already present—supposedly known and, to all appearances, stable—world. It is a process that occurs when seemingly simple things that abide in proximity to one another, combine, communicate, and coordinate, and then, spontaneously, produce something completely beyond the capability of any of those original elements. Emergence takes place in nature continuously, at all levels, from the subatomic to the galactic, and in all dimensions, from the inorganic to the living to the purely psychical.

The idea of "emergence" was once anathema to the scientific community. Emergence pertains most directly to systems that evolve and change. Thus the concept would hardly have any place, no less validity, in the mechanistic Newtonian mindset (in which management science has been confined). Of course, Newton preceded Darwin by two hundred years and could not have known about evolution. So the Newtonians who took up the great mathematician's procedures can be forgiven for their mechanistic approaches.[9] But the resistance, even today, to the idea of open systems evolution—the dynamic interpretation of Darwinian evolution—is less forgivable.

In the Newtonian mindset, several tenets are held dear and nearly sacrosanct: only humans have "mind" and "soul"; while nature, out there (as our minds are "in here"), does not generate novelty, it operates, instead, according to strictly deterministic and predictable laws. We, humans (supposedly exalted and divinely created), can, therefore, know all there is to know about nature for all time; and of course, we can dispose of mere nature, lord over it, manipulate it and extract from it, as we please.

This still represents the mainstream thinking presented in most typical management science courses. Even in traditional ethics courses, mechanistic thinking dominates. After all, it does offer a safe and reassuring picture of a universe we can control and an exalted place for

---

[9] Newton himself was not as mechanistic in his outlook as were his followers. The great man was an alchemist and held some very pre-Newtonian, animistic notions about nature. See Gleick's *Isaac Newton* (New York, 2003).

human efficacy over against that universe. And how can we ignore the fact that this mindset has produced such technological wonders as the microprocessor, vaccines that prevent diseases, and a spacecraft that has photographed Jupiter's moons before plunging into the Jovian soup?

While this mindset is capable of isolating a few aspects of nature's bounty that it can manipulate for human purposes, as a complete and life-supporting picture of the universe, it falls short, way short. Look around. Ask yourself: how prevalent is emergence in nature? It is far more prevalent that the specific kinds of causal relations that technologists have to labor so hard to tease out of their combinations of materials and forces. Emergence happens as planets form out of swirling dust; it happens as hurricanes form over the oceans, or when tornadoes form over the plains. It happens as seeds sprout into plants and embryos develop into fetuses, and then into babies. On its own, nature generates new species of living things at a prolific rate (not prolific enough, however, to compensate for the human ability to destroy whole ecologies and habitats).

How likely is it that emergence takes place naturally, in great profusion, in all kinds of different forms? It is so likely that Stuart Kauffman, one of the creators of the science of self-organization, thinks it merits the status of a fourth law of thermodynamics.

This law would state:

As an average trend, biospheres and the universe create novelty and diversity as fast as they can manage to do so without destroying the accumulated propagating organization that is the basis and nexus from which further novelty is discovered and incorporated into the propagating organization.[10]

[10] *Investigations* (New York, 2000), p. 85.

While this is intended to be precisely scientific in its wording, a simpler rendering of this idea for leaders might be: nature's motto is, "Let's go for it, and we'll see what happens."

Why is the mechanistic mindset so destructive to creative leading? Because by being locked in this linear mindset, we miss some of the most important aspects of creative leading, and we miss those aspects of the human condition that are most conducive to sustaining the life of creative leading. By missing the difference between causing something to happen versus allowing something to emerge, by not understanding the difference between coercion and control versus fostering the conditions that allow something to be able to emerge, traditionally oriented leaders have been locked into a command and control model that, on the one hand, cripples creativity and, on the other, causes leader burnout. In fact, I would say that all organizational efforts using a causality model eventually go badly, generate frustration, and in the extreme result in oppression, vengeance, and other needless miseries.[11]

Creative leading, in contrast to traditional models of leading, takes place in the regime of emergence, of nature's seemingly invisible and endlessly mysterious and miraculous generativity and creativity.

---

[11] Still, in fairness, the causal mindset plays an important role. While comprehending the emotions that are driving him to envision and act, it is helpful to get a start and discern clues by seeing "causes" that gave rise to the situation. It is useful for the leader, when starting out, to analyze the situation, in order to enrich his understanding of chains of events and to piece fragments together in a revealing way. But, in the end, causal analysis provides little in the way of understanding, comprehending, or seeing the event in such a way that it can be approached and changed. We are left with the conclusions, "So one event triggered another, and these are the results." What does this tell us about moving forward? Not much." I am sure the reader can see approaching leading strictly and solely from the mindset of linear causality travels on a downhill road.

The idea of "emergence" leaves that kind of thinking behind. It is a forward-looking approach to a living organization that assumes only one thing: nature, and the people in it, can be infinitely creative, under the right conditions. Here we compare the two mindsets when dealing with certain kinds of situations that arise in the context of leading organizations and change. The difficulty, as is readily apparent, is that the emergent mindset takes longer to explain, takes more attention to put into effect, and takes in more information in order to arrive at a decision. This complexity is often shunned in the result-driven business context.

EMERGENCE IN ACTION ONE: CONNECTING

With Stuart Kauffman's fourth law of thermodynamics in mind (and I, for one, have accepted it and added it to my thermodynamic canon), we can see how this universe in which we are so privileged to live is all about *generating novelty*. Creative leaders just grab on to that fact and run with it in the human arena—for the benefit of all.

Apple Computer founders Jobs and Wozniak's mythic story of creating the personal computer perfectly depicts emergence. They took off-the-shelf materials and cobbled them together into a device that anyone could afford and many would be able to use. These parts were all available to anyone who wanted to use them. But while other people played with these parts to satisfy their own "geeky" interests and augment their own specialized curiosities, Jobs and Wozniak approached those same materials with a different orientation. They had a vision: "a bicycle for the mind," Jobs called their invention. He felt that these parts could be put together in such a way as to create an inexpensive appliance that most could afford and this appliance would leverage the creative capabilities possessed by everyone to new levels of accessibility and availability.

So there it is: lots of parts hanging around the environment, lots of energy in the form of many people trying to put them together into useful combinations; and this duo saw something else, tied to the world as it is but capable of changing it. Their values drove them to pay attention to certain things, supplying them a vision that could grasp when the right combination came along and produced a startling new machine, one that took hold and changed everything. All of the components they used were off the shelf. Many people had combined them in various ways to do different things. But all of these uses simply passed away, quietly slipping into the night of disuse.

What the dynamic duo supplied, that others did not, was a vision capable of grasping the low-hanging fruit, or what Kaufmann has called "the adjacent possible." All the material was at hand. They supplied an initial impetus to organize these materials in a certain way. They grasped some quality that these parts could have when put in combination that others did not grasp. This combination clicked, found a niche, was reinforced by repeated use, and was pulled into being replicated (manufactured) many times.

EMERGENCE IN ACTION TWO: TAKING HOLD

That's the "generation" part of "emergence." But our definition includes another phase of the process: the idea has to *take hold.* In the realm of nature, mutation has to be favored, supported, or "selected" by accommodating surroundings. In business, the product has to establish its niche by being purchased. Thus the creative leader realizes that the idea works not only because it was conceived, but also because a lot of really good things happened afterwards (and these events are decidedly not in the leader's control). Success is as much due to the fact that the idea is reinforced by the favorable conditions and responses in the environment as it is to the genius of any one person's inspiration.

The reinforcement happens in many ways. Sometimes the environment provides a rich and fertile medium for the new capability to draw on for its sustenance. Sometimes an outside agent has to nurture the new entity for a while, until it can stand on its own. For creative leaders, conversations with colleagues, followers, and mentors help to give the idea solidity and adaptability. *Thus, in the plentitude of nature and/or the market, things are not so much caused as they occur and are then subsequently taken up as viable and so are reinforced into a viable existence.* Novelty in nature comes about through the agency of the multifaceted, interacting drift of all the elements in play. One thing responds to the other, something occurs, a "thing" "emerges" for a while because it has been reinforced by surroundings. It is responded to, it fits, and so it is able to maintain itself in this niche as a viable entity. Then, the tables turn. The elements in the environment then start to adjust to it, making its emergence an "attractor"[12] for subsequent developments in the environment.

One consequence of this model for generating novelty unsettles the Newtonians: how predictable is it that a specific result will happen from this emergence process? Not very. Could Jobs and Wozniak predict that their computer would take off as it did? Could Henry Ford predict that his methods would revolutionize modern industry? They had their aspirations, but could they predict a specific outcome? Creative leaders can't predict success or the extent of their success. In the mode of Self-Trust, they have to accept that their efforts are worthy, learn from them and stay in the game, go back out into the world, play at it, and enjoy the results. If the capital runs out, so be it.

FOUR KINDS OF EMERGENCE AND LEADER VISIONS

In the realm of the leader's psyche, the vision is the form that emergence takes on in order to generate novelty, increased robustness of our individual lives, societies, and worlds. The vision is akin to biological evolution and the emergence of new species; it is akin to all the processes

---

[12] "Attractor" is an important concept in self-organization. We will consider this concept in detail in the next two chapters.

we see in nature that give rise to awe, surprise, fear, and exhilaration. Thus, what we want to do now is to use nature's emergence processes as guides for better understanding and grasping and therefore appreciating and using leaders' envisioning.

In nature—including the human form of it—there are at least four processes that result in emergent phenomena: Synergy, Symbiosis, Autocatalysis, and Eco-spiritual Emergence. For creative leaders then, emergence takes shape in at least these forms, as well.

Considering these forms helps us appreciate creative leading in several ways. First, it helps us appreciate that by using these terms, leaders are working in the realm of vision and emergence—where there are no guarantees—and not in the safe and sure realm of management "science." Second, considering these forms helps leaders to recognize what their visions comprise, and so better guide and shape their execution. Third, the forms give us a better sense of what this particular vision is going to be able to accomplish. Finally, understanding these forms helps us distinguish these kinds of visionary, emergent actions, from mechanistic ones such as imposing rules, adding mechanisms, force-fitting and ill-matched organizations together in expedient, greed-driven mergers.

EMERGENCE AND LEADERS

For emergence to occur the following conditions are needed:

- ➤ *A supporting, vibrant medium (environment) in which a diversity of elements can be nourished and sustained.*

- ➤ *A continual source of moderate energy (on the edge of chaos but far from equilibrium) that keeps the system's components in motion.*

- ➤ *The right rate and amount ("temperature") of activity and energy flow, such that the environment is in a "Goldilocks" condition: not too hot and not too cold.*

- ➤ *An agent/observer to bring about, focus and/or accelerate the process of creating new combinations that take up position in the environment, instigating its acceptance of the new capability.*

- ➤ *Another agent or capability that grasps, reinforces and then sustains the emergent phenomenon.*

---

1. SYNERGY

Leaders talk about "creating synergy" all the time. Synergy names a process in which existing elements combine in a unique way, resulting in a completely new entity. I think here of atoms combining into elementary molecules, these molecules combing into compounds, etc. In this kind of vision, a leader looks at all the processes and activities of an organization and sees the inefficiencies or the latent potentials. The intent is for all of the energy and expertise of the similarly engaged people and technologies to coalesce into a more robust capability.

Managers perform these functions (that is, they can envision these kinds of opportunities) equally well, or even better than leaders do. They guide the combinations through changes and adaptations so the desired capabilities have a chance to emerge, and the previous deficiencies do not completely diminish that potentiality. Then they guide the new behaviors into repetition and stability.

This ability to foster synergy is often the first indication of the "emergence" mindset being present, in a manager for instance. From this platform, some go on to leading and thus to more subtle and more difficult forms of envisioning and emergence.

2. SYMBIOSIS

Symbiosis is a more difficult kind of emergence to foster. Here, distinctly functioning elements combine parts of their total activities, while withholding some characteristics of their original characteristics in order to maintain a vestige of individuality and independence. For instance, in the stomach, bacteria give up their mobility and migratory abilities in order to have a larger organism to supply them with nutrients. The human body, in exchange, has evolved in such a way as to tolerate these "parasites" within its midst. Accordingly, the body benefits from more complete and efficient digestion of its food, making more nutrients available to it with less effort and energy expenditure.[13]

This is the kind of emergence taken up by Jobs and Wozniak. They took previously independent components and combined certain of their

[13] In their now famous book, *Microcosmos* (Berkeley, 1997), Lynn Margulis and Dorion Sagan show how the process of symbiosis heavily influenced the evolution of living things. While controversial at first, the thesis is now widely accepted in the scientific community. We are adapting this idea to the organizational arena.

characteristics, and not others, to produce the first commercially successful personal computer.

None of these entities could perform the new function without the presence of the other entities. Where nature arrived at its symbiotic combinations by chance, of course, Jobs and Wozniak placed these parts in this new symbiotic relationship through trail, error, and (rational, cause-and-effect-based) experimentation.

Here the leader's role is a delicate one. The old parts have to function, but the individual capabilities of each part have to be linked with other functions. The combination then has to yield an even higher, more encompassing function. The leader has to have an idea of what that function can be, and so select for the capabilities he wants the formerly independent entities to exhibit. Leaders act as agents of symbiotic emergence by being able to identify when, out of a competing or interacting field of components, a new capability is actually happening before their eyes. Often they are actually surprised that what they once vaguely envisioned is now happening. The great leaders are able to recognize that something completely different or even better than they originally envisioned is happening, and they grab on to that as the new capability they want to reinforce.

3. AUTOCATALYSIS

This is a very difficult form of emergence to bring off successfully. Two substances combine to produce a third, and they also reproduce themselves in the process. The result is a growth process that spawns greater numbers of the same kinds of materials, but also spawns the possibility of generating open-ended diversification of forms, substances, materials, and living systems. This is the very basis of all life on the planet, according to Stuart Kauffman. DNA, for instance, guides the production of proteins and also replicates itself in the process. Thus life has the capability of being chemically stable, while incorporating within itself the ability to generate (potentially advantageous, but usually not advantageous) mutations.

Leaders of successful, profitable business organizations unconsciously use the autocatalytic aspect of emergence. The business consists of the products and services being produced, and the marketing, financial, administrative processes that are built around them. The autocatalysis takes place because the products enable the business to survive; the business then promotes and advances the products. The result is more products are produced, and the business is enriched; in turn, the business can subsequently expand production of the product and improve succeeding generations of the product. The whole idea of profit and economic development, in other words, is based on an autocatalytic model.

The essence of seeing this type of emergence is in envisioning how giving something up in one stage of a much larger process (which also needs to be envisioned) results in much greater yields, of what was originally given up, down the road. It is the classic model of generosity coming back to repay in spades the giver. As the saying goes, if you want something, give it away.

4. ECO-SPIRITUAL EMERGENCE

This form of emergence names the process whereby all of the above forms of emergence processes combine into creating whole new environments and life capabilities that had never existed before, and are completely dependent on all the emergences and evolutions that have gone before. I include in this the complex ecosystems of the rainforest, or the plains or the mountains. I also think of the emergence of complex living organisms and mentality[14] as a means of providing for flexible adaptation to changing conditions.

This form of emergence takes on a life of its own in the human realm where language and other symbol-based means of organization create new forms of behavior. I think of realms of activity such as science, economic development, art, religion, and philosophy as constituting distinctive forms of emergence that I would call "spiritual." I do so for several reasons: they are global and highly generative in character; they rely on widely diverse capabilities that are only sustained by large-scale organization; they offer futures that are open ended; they portend further levels of self-organization that surpass even this form of emergence.[15]

The vision at this level occurs at the highest levels of creative leading. These are the visions that reshape societies, sciences, technologies, and the very capabilities of what we are able to imagine. Jesus, the Buddha, Socrates, Newton, Einstein, Lincoln, Gandhi, Mandela, Martin Luther King Jr. are leaders who exemplify the eco-spiritual level of emergence that simmers among us.

[14] In part 3, we will consider this psychical dimension under the rubric of the "neural/ linguistic adaptive system" that produces responsive, conscious, and linguist/symbolic behaviors in higher organisms.

[15] Cyber-emergence seems to be on a horizon of possible transhuman evolution. We'll see.

ACTIONS THAT FOSTER THE VISIONING PROCESS

1. Concentrate your attention and mental energy on the situation. Remain deeply immersed in the problem, hearing and experiencing the pain and fears it engenders. Learn all its lived dimensions.

Then...

2. Clear out conflicting stimuli. Focus on the sights, sounds, symbols, words and images of the situation in a free-flowing, undistracted way. Go off into the desert or the wilderness, or the quiet of a mountain or seaside retreat to ponder the situation. Create a single stream of thinking activity, such as readings, conversations observing similar situations in other contexts, in order to gain a larger, but concentrated perspective.

3. Map the impressions onto a rhythm within calmness. Physically engage in activities that have a rhythmic component to them: walking, working out on equipment doing reps, take a long ride (driving or just riding) through a landscape that can be seen (not an aisle seat on an commercial airliner). Attentive energy is thus simplified; it flows and moves to its own internal clock. Your own, internally initiated values and sense of the "whole" can emerge.

4. Psychically (intellectually, emotionally, imaginatively), listen to the messages. The solution emerges in many forms, some completely unpredicted. Let your Self-Trust have a voice and listen to it. It may come from others. It may be a matter of recovering and renewing former solutions.

5. Capture the intuition. Write down what comes up.

6. Rehearse and explore the intuition through conversations. Articulate both the problem and the vision, to others, from one or several perspectives, in different settings and from different platforms. See how it sounds in those different settings. See how people in different groupings react to it.

7. Organize the vision. Create a new vision, in which all the parts now interact with clarity. Live in the insight, in the intuition, in the values that you have labored to touch.

CHAPTER FIVE

Vision and Organization

WHILE WE HAVE, IT SEEMS,

ADEQUATE CONCEPTS OF MATTER,

ENERGY, ENTROPY AND INFORMATION,

WE LACK A COHERENT CONCEPT

OF ORGANIZATION.

—*STUART KAUFFMAN*[1]

[1] Stuart Kauffman, *Investigations*, op. cit., p. 104.

THE ORGANIZATION CONUNDRUM

In the epigram, Stuart Kauffman, one of the principal architects of the new science of complexity, suggests we don't understand organization very well. What could he mean by that? Down through history, haven't we always used organizations to accomplish our purposes? Of course, we have always used organizations. But just because we use them to accomplish our ends doesn't mean we understand the dynamics of organization. After all, just because we use electricity every day to run our appliances and light our buildings doesn't mean that we understand its physics; or just because we breathe and use oxygen doesn't mean we understand the organic chemistry involved.

He means that we don't have a verifiable, refutable, generally accessible comprehension of how things organize. And, because we don't have this comprehension, we really don't know how to organize ourselves, our collaborative endeavors successfully, at least not by design. We can guess, use our "gut," rely on our intuition or our experiences as a guide, but we really don't know what we are doing. And to anyone who has to live and work in organizations—and that's most of us—such a state of affairs just isn't good enough.

Prior to Mr. Kauffman's and his colleagues' efforts in self-organization study, there was no serious "science" on how discrete, isolated, unrelated entities formed into larger, more complex organizations. Social scientists described the aftereffects of groups' and coalitions' actions on or within an existing organization; they talked about the uses of power within or by an organization, but there was precious little said about the basics of forming and/or sustaining successful and thriving organizations. At another level, we have always known that things grow, propagate, generate offspring and form into larger organizations such as packs, families, colonies, societies, etc. However, up until now, these events have been relegated to the attention of the poets, mystics, artists, and some leaders who seem to have a "feel" for organizations.

Self-organization study changes that. This new discipline brings to the fore dynamics that are completely different from those cited in traditional sciences. Now we find that the advent of organization has characteristics that can be identified, quantified, and reproduced in computer simulations. Kauffman and his colleagues study how relationships form between previously independent entities such that they congeal into more complex structures. The dynamics of organization are still mysterious, but they are not unknowable. They are sufficiently knowable such that we can use them better and take advantage of what they put at the disposal of the creative leader in terms of initiating and sustaining organizations.

We have already cited "emergence" as one seminal dynamic of self-organization. That concept highlights nature's ability to generate novelty. Now we introduce another concept used in self-organization study: the "attractor." This idea highlights how diverse energies, people and/or materials coalesce and gel into sustainable organizations.

The vision, as we have discussed it so far, captures the "emergence" of novelty as the leader's psyche coalesces around the response to a disturbing concern. Diverse and dispersed feelings and bodily states coalesce into a distinctive and seemingly workable response. And then, when the vision is put out in the world, articulated and dramatized by the leader's passion, it adopts that other mysteriously productive form, that of the "attractor" as others sense the potential offered by the vision and organize themselves in accordance with it.

WHY DO WE NEED AN IMAGE OF ORGANIZATION?

Does it matter how we think about organization? Does it make any difference if we think of an organization as an engine, a computer, or a living entity? It does. Consider this real-life client story. It concerns Howard Keats, whom we introduced in chapter 1.

When this story begins, Howard's company has been fantastically successful. Though profitability has been slow in coming, the company's revenues have grown faster than even Howard had envisioned. People enjoyed working in the company. Employees ascribed their enthusiasm and sense of enjoyment in the company to Howard's vision, sense of fun, and energy. All of this was about to change, however.

There was a problem: for all this success, in Howard's own mind, he was a lousy manager. He told himself over and over again how he exemplified the archetypically peripatetic entrepreneur: full of passion, overflowing with ideas, never able to settle down to a routine. The thought that he was an effective leader never occurred to him. Howard lived in a perpetual state of creating new visions: a new sales initiative one day, a whole new nonprofit section of the business the next, a new hire of an exciting new person, and so on. It was absolutely true that although he was very exciting to work for, he also destabilized the ability of the company to attain the sustained and incremental growth he thought characterized mature organizations.

His ennui was understandable. After a decade of building, rebuilding, and, once again, re-rebuilding his company, Howard was tired of the grind. All he knew at this point was that while he loved working on ideas with his people, he hated the day-to-day detail, the numbers, the politics, the constant train of people coming through his office with problems calling for decisions on every sort of issue. Howard decided that it was time to hire a chief operating officer to manage the day-to-day functioning of the company. Not any COO though. In his mind, he needed to hire a predictable, "businesslike" professional to counteract the "day camp" director he felt himself to be.

He found the perfect person to apply the antidote to his own hyperactivity, providing the discipline and order to quiet Harry's inchoate dreams. Hannibal, as we came to call the new officer, was a pure numbers guy. Here was someone who drives the numbers instead of being swayed by opinions, insights, or inspirations, as Howard would be. For a while, Howard was thrilled with what happened. This was just what the company needed, he told himself.

But this was not what Howard's employees felt. People who had worked with Howard for years voted with their feet. Sales did not increase, and because of all the new hiring (due to turnover as well as Hannibal's own visions of glory), operating costs did not go down. Those who stayed on during this purgatorial epoch did so in order to be there when the dust settled, when Howard would need help picking up the pieces. And, eventually, Howard did get the message.

Howard was shell-shocked at what had happened. He was disoriented and felt no small amount of regret for what he had done. And he truly didn't understand why his idea didn't work.

He thought he had made a bad hire and so doubted his "people skills." My presentation to him was this: Originally, he had created an organization based on his Leader Brand. It was a wild place, with lots of ideas, convictions, decisions flying around—some in conflict and contradictory—but one in which many people contributed to the company in many ways. Hannibal took all that away from them and tried to establish a production line in which only he, Hannibal, made the decisions and everyone else implemented his grand scheme.

THE MORAL: WE CAN'T THINK OF
ORGANIZATIONS MECHANISTICALLY

In making that hire, Howard succumbed to the stereotypical account of how an organization is supposed to develop and evolve. This perspective wasn't more consoling to him at first, but it started him thinking about how the situation deteriorated so quickly. Howard was trying to turn the company around on a dime, going from the chaotic swirl of overheated energy to the drill and monotony of a production plant.

Howard did lead the organization, by the "attracting" strength and power of his vision. Maybe his leading wasn't pretty, neat, tidy, and orderly, but he did *lead* that organization, and everyone knew it. The old organization was messy, but it had grown exponentially year after year, and people stayed in it and worked hard for its success. People innovated (maybe too much) around a vision, which he provided, and they all invented around the possibilities that Howard only hinted at. He was always there, validating their excitement, closing the loop of attention and focus. When he withdrew that Leader Brand, he created a vacuum. Everyone felt it intensely; and when someone tried to create a completely different kind of organization, it all came crashing down.

Howard was probably right that processes had to be done better, and I am sure Howard needed to make personnel and functional changes; but not *these* changes. Making a sharp U-turn was too much for the organization to take. By making a sharp distinction between those who created ideas versus those who implemented them, by measuring himself against a very traditional standard of how mature organizations are supposed to act and evolve, he was wrenching the organization's culture from one that was led to one that was *administered*. Whether or not that kind of static organization was even sustainable, not less desirable, in his market (computer network support), was not asked. All of these factors played a role in Howard's costly, nearly fatal mistake.

For a leader to translate a vision into an organization, an appropriate image of how to organize is critical. Starting with the wrong image of that organization will result in inappropriate guidance and failure; the right image, such as we will offer below, has a better chance (no guarantees) of success. So now let's develop a picture of how a dynamic organization comes together, changes and stabilizes, and what the agency of the leader actually contributes.

Self-organization study presents us with an opportunity to clearly view the once inscrutable building blocks of organization. Our attention is shifted away from the nuts and bolts, bricks and mortars, positions and functions of the organization to "conceptual" components. This big shift in our attention frees us from the old models of the organization functioning like a hierarchical army or a controlled machine. Instead, we can use dynamic and naturalistic images of organizations such as networks, brains, and swarms. The organization can be conceived and led as an entity that is alive, connected, adaptive and inherently intelligent and therefore capable of self-organizing.

As a result of this changing image, we can also reshape our conception of the leader's role. Successful creative leaders don't have to be the sole source of inspiration, thinking, and decision making for an organization, but instead can accept the more modest role of offering a context (an arch) within which people can coalesce their energies into collaborative actions. This leader fosters the viability of certain constraints, patterns, and boundaries; the others in the arch, understanding what is at stake, organize themselves. Instead of being the architect, primary driver or master of the organization, the leader acts as an "attractor."

ATTRACTORS

The key idea of organizing a vision into a viable organization is that of the "attractor."

The term "attractor" conjures up images of invisible powers. I think of the magnet under the table, its powers hidden from view as it draws iron filings into symmetrical patterns around the poles. The term also brings to mind how some people "attract" us with their beauty or force of personality, summoning up an image of a benign power drawing us closer together, willingly, energetically, and enthusiastically. And complexity study reinforces this story.

How does the idea of the attractor relate to that of emergence, the self-organizing phenomenon we examined in the last chapter? Attractors were once emergent phenomena, originating in processes like the ones we have described: symbiosis, synergy, and autocatalysis. When these occurrences are reinforced and supported by an amenable, energy-rich environment, they can self-organize into living, dynamic systems. When the coalescing settles into a stabilized process—any one of the four we mentioned—it means that the emergent phenomenon has happened on to a process that can act as an "attractor." The process, relative to the environment around it, is efficient and simple enough to be repeated. The combination repeats, draws energy successfully, sustains itself, and, in the case of life, reproduces itself. The phenomenon has thus progressed from being an emergent possibility into a stable, reproducible entity because it has organized itself around an attractor.

We were hinting at this at the conclusion of the last chapter. Look at the creative process we offered there. When we say that the leader grasps ideas, we refer to the first level of identifying and then stabilizing a process. Then when we said test the concept in conversation and then institutionalize it, we foreshadow the attractor process. By capturing the emergent process's salient elements and articulating them (making the explanations clearer and easier for others to grasp, so they can talk about it themselves), the idea can become an attractor.

PURE ENERGY

The idea of an "attractor" refers to invisible flows of energy. From Einstein's relativity we know that the universe consists entirely of energy (the E of E=MC²), that matter (the M) is really congealed energy, energy slowed and cooled in its coursing through the vastness of the universe.

Organization is another way, besides "matter," that congealed energy forms into something more enduring. Organization results (energy organized into atoms, molecules and all forms of matter included) when energy cools down and some of that energy congeals into patterns, that, while stable, are neither solid nor completely closed off from their surroundings, and instead remain open to the continuing influx of streaming of energies in those surroundings. Organization can be thought of as being a congealed state that falls between pure energy and solid matter.

Some organizations become living organisms – organizations that are actually able to maintain themselves and reproduce other beings like themselves, who are able seek out the specific forms of energy that are most conducive to its continuation as an open, identifiable, continuing system of patterned energy.

THE HURRICANE

The idea of attractor carries with it some other concepts, such as constraint and boundary. For a clear example of how these terms work together to create organization, we'll consider a natural event that we see enacted in all its grandeur and horror every year: the formation of a hurricane.

At first there are only unorganized, passive, undifferentiated elements—air, wind, and warm (energized) moisture—hanging around, inert, indifferent to each other's presence. As a collection of disconnected entities, they generate nothing of note. The breeze blows; the water waves and ripples. Then, amid this smarmy mass, something—the proverbial butterfly—passes through, innocently, with no particular intention with regard to these elements. But its very passing engenders a pattern, an eddy, in the wind. A curl takes shape. The lowered pressure (lower energy relative to the general environment) pulls more wind into its compass, and eventually, these coalesce (self-organize) into a vortex of energy, an "eye."

This vortex has integrity, shape, and cohesion. It attracts more of its kind into itself because, well, it is easier for these elements to combine (the eye lowers pressure and lowers energy within itself) than it is to resist the pressure, remain loose and unconnected and thus avoid the burgeoning system. The environment thus supports the system by feeding it more energy (warm water and wind) and giving it room to maneuver (currents on which to roam). The vortex centers a dynamic system that attracts more energy from wind and rain, pulling them into the storm. This whole system then roams, intact, over thousands of miles, over days and weeks at a time feeding itself on just those elements that conduce to its survival.

Then, when this arrangement among elements establishes itself firmly, it distinguishes itself from the surrounding world and from elements that do not satisfy the needs of the system. This arrangement of elements thus becomes a full-fledged "attractor."

It draws to it, selects for itself, certain materials (and not others) that supply it with energy. The pattern attracts, pulls in energy and materials it can use to sustain its organization. When there is an abundance of this food available in the environment, the system is able to grow. This enduring combination that results in the familiar centrifugal swirl of wind around the eye takes and holds its character as an attractor because all its elements are constrained into a single pattern. If constituents, consistent with their constraining, selecting criteria, are present and/or are abundant (i.e., out over the warm ocean), the system attracts these elements into itself and grows. We have a hurricane.

This *constrained patterning of energy* results in a structure we experience in all its furious glory and to which we give our anthropomorphic names. The circular pattern, the lowered pressures at its center, the uniform directionality of its winds, give the system strength, power, and longevity as it moves over water and, for a time, over land.

The attractor-generated, now highly, robustly patterned system constitutes a *difference* between itself and what is not itself, giving the system a *boundary* vis-à-vis the environment, and more importantly for our discussion, a *"Signature" Behavior, shape, or identity within that environment.* We name hurricanes because they have boundaries and identities; the name doesn't make a weather pattern a hurricane. So for leaders to have an organization, they must establish an identity that marks out a distinctive space, niche, or action in the environment, one that the environment is capable of supporting, but also one that changes that environment, making its distinctive contribution to the new ecology the environment will bear.

ATTRACTOR METAPHORS

The hurricane offers us a dramatic image we can use for understanding how to use attractors in leading, but there are other examples of attractors' roles in organization that are also helpful.

Games and Infinite Combination. For example, there is the game image. Here is an accessible picture in which a few basic rules result in constrained behavior that draws in the energies of attention and motion because it makes sense. Start with a simple rule, jump over the rope as it passes under your feet. Suddenly there is a pattern you can build on. You can then add words, music, and rhymes. You can speed up the rope, or slow it down, or add more loops. Here is a simple pattern that evokes other behaviors and creates a little nexus of activity. Leaders can thus think of simple activities that can be successfully accomplished and then can be added to and enhanced to create more complex and engaging actions.

One of the important insights that self-organization brings to our attention in this regard is that the *only limitation to how emergence can take place—and thus how many attractors can link up, organize, become more complex—is the energy available in the environment to support that combination.*

Catchy Tunes. Another metaphor is that of the "catchy tune." Think of a jingle, a melody that suddenly pops into your mind. Or maybe it's a phrase like "the pattern that connects." You can't get it out of your mind. In every quiet moment, in the car, sitting at your desk, standing in line, the tune pops up. That tune or phrase is acting as an attractor for some excess and idle mental capacity. It is pulling in your attention, activating (or triggered by and then reactivating) other sensations, associations and thoughts, and then coming back to that phrase. A leader gets that phrase or tune or vision going in the minds of followers so that it acts as an attractor for their energies and attentions as well. The lesson in this image is how robust and sturdy an attractor pattern can be. And, through the agency of minds, it can propagate and spread without limitation throughout a population, enabling organization of masses of individuals to form into institutions, groups, swarms, networks, or other kinds of organizations.

Prone to Pattern. Finally, there is brain functioning. In a game that we use in our mentoring group processes, we pass pieces of paper around the group, each person placing one dot on the page. Inevitably, people put the dots in a patterned relationship to the dots placed by others, or they make jokes (exert a specific effort) to break a pattern or defy one. We then ask people to connect the dots, each person connecting three or four dots and then passing the paper on. Again, some can't help but fit their dot into a pattern they can already discern, or some rebel against the patterning they see and make sure that the dot is placed in a position that seems (because it is not) arbitrary. Finally, I ask people to take one of the papers and give a name to the drawing.

The point of the exercise is that *our brains are oriented to notice patterns.* Even more than that, our brains naturally create patterns that center our perceptions. We create fields and grounds, giving some things prominence against other things. Patterns that give order are part of our inheritance from nature's way of organizing. Stereotypes that we create, assumptions, and habits of behavior are all patterns that we use to lower the energy we need to expend in order to survive. We build structures, create products, clothe and adorn these patterns into rituals and centers for ourselves. We are an attractor-creating species, above and beyond all.

NEW WORKING CONCEPTS

The core principles that underlie attractors in self-organizing systems – energy patterns, constraints, boundaries – open up to other key concepts which, taken together, constitute a new framework for leaders to use in creating organizations that actualize the vision.

ENERGY

Thinking in terms of self-organizing systems turns our attention to invisible flows of energy [See the box above]. Using this concept, leaders can visualize connections, flows, patterns that move in a dynamic way throughout the relationships that constitute an organization's internal relationships as well as its relations to the external environment.

HOLISM

"Holism" refers to a system that comprises many parts, all of which function in an interlocking way with one another. The entity cannot be properly understood except on that systematic level. It cannot be broken down in to atomistic parts, In a system considered holistically, change to any part of the system changes the whole system.

Leaders can use this key concept to distinguish self-organizing dynamics from mechanistic ones. The leader asks, does a change in this process – outsourcing a function or process – change the nature and character of the whole organization?

HIERARCHY AND "KINARCHY"

The classical, indeed the only model of organization we have had up until now is hierarchy. The attractor model points to a different kind of relationship of ordering and subordination that I call "Kinarchy."

"Kinarchy," highlights how an organization (my body, a company, a nation, an ecosystem) coalesces, instantly and spontaneously, reflexively and without hesitation, around a focusing event. When a situation commands attention, disparate elements giving way to the need for a system-wide action and/or response, including some subordination and super-ordination. The situation itself organizes the response and deploys the energy as much as does any "commanding element" (such as the brain, or the commander).

CHANGE WITHOUT ENEMIES

Development, growth and change happen without enemies. A growing system may have competitors in the environment, some of those being fierce and death dealing. But any species or living system grows and develops in order to create its own niche, and does not develop its mode of life specifically to enter into conflict with another species.

Thus, the evolutionary dimension of self-organization, points to another critical dimension of organization: *nature's impetus to change is a shared one.* All sectors of the environment feel the effects of changes in an ecology, all species adapt to a greater or lesser extent. Conflicts arise in the process of these changes, especially if the ecology becomes less capable of supporting the diversity of species its once did. Even in these (increasingly frequent) circumstances, the issue is not one of survival of the self as opposed to that of the other, but one of determining whether values that were once important still are, and thus what place the new organization's capabilities (and those that are allied, competitive or associated with it) will have in a new ecological mix.

PROPAGATING DIVERSITY

According to Stuart Kauffman, when nature thrives, it creates not only more members of a species, but it also creates more varieties of species. That is the impeccable logic (not a mystical pronouncement) borne out in human commerce. In his book, *Non-Zero, The Logic of Human Destiny*, Robert Wright notes the increasing proliferation of human creativity in this way:

"During the Upper Paleolithic, the average rate of technological change would be one innovation per 1,400 years, compared to one per 20,000 years during the Middle Paleolithic. Then, after 10,000 B.C., during the Mesolithic, with population growing faster than ever, the rate of technological innovation reached one innovation per 200 years (including such gifts to posterity as combs and ice picks)."[2]

Continuing with that logic, from 0 A.D. until 1500 A.D. there was one invention per every 100 years. After that time, when the roots of contemporary science and technology were sown, and the printing press (developed in 1451) was in general use, the rate of innovation increased to one per year.[3]

Think of all the visions and leaders this means are waiting to take flight.

[2] *Non-Zero,* (New York, 2000), p. 50.

[3] According to the New York Public Library Desktop Encyclopedia.

BECOMING MORE COMPLEX (NOT MORE COMPLICATED)

The occurrence of self-organization at greater levels complexity has meant that organisms combine in various ways so as to become more adaptable and more robust within their environments. They create alliances or foster relationships of dependence and even engender new levels of organized capability.

For leaders this means constantly looking for ways in which collaborations can take shape and can support more capable action in the environment in order to realize the vision. But it is important for leaders' humility to remember that the proclivity toward greater complexity implies neither inevitability nor progress

---

THE LEADER'S VISION AS AN ATTRACTOR

At some level, leaders offer a vision—whether the operational level of making things work better (synergy) or the eco-spiritual level of carving out new ways for us to interact with one another. No one credits the cost-cutting efficiency expert, who merely slashes payrolls and cuts out services, with being a leader. Someone else, who does these things on the way to accomplishing an important vision, on the other hand, might well be a leader. The vision attracts attention, sparks notice, and channels energies in new directions.

Let's think once again about Howard Keats. By hiring a numbers-crunching hit man to take over the operations of the company, Howard underestimated and undermined the attracting power of his vision. He did not acknowledge its indispensable role in inducing self-organization among followers. He fell back on old, outmoded, command—and control-oriented managerial mechanisms.

We can see how much the idea of attractors working within self-organizing systems would have changed his decisions. For him and for leaders in general, this perspective on organizing around attractors starts with this insight: *leaders cannot force people into organization.* The forces that determine the appropriate form of organization are already, always, ubiquitously there, within and outside the organization; or they are not. A healthy organization, in the self-organizing view, flows toward the changes; easily adapting its capabilities and its means of relating to an environment. If the conditions are not present—if sufficient energy is not available, if there are already too many competitors, if the raw materials and catalysts are not already present in the environment—an organization will not develop. The consequences of this realization for leaders are sobering.

The best leaders can do is offer the vision as a resource and response to what is occurring in the environment. If this vision rings true, organization can take place; if these conditions are not met, no organization will be possible.

The change that occurs will always be limited by the environmental conditions into which it is flowing. In the human arena, how often have we seen changes not take hold because the environment was not ready for it? Whatever leaders want to do, the kind of organizations they will be able to establish are limited by the vision itself, by the values it embraces, by quantity and quality of energy they unleash and makes available to others, by the leaders' abilities to sense, measure, and qualify changes around it. The leader's role in the change process is modest. From our survey of what the attractor-based model offers we see that the leader brings four basic contributions to the self-organizing process.

First, there is *grasping the emergence of the vision.* The leader senses what the environment is calling for in terms of change and identifies the emergent possibilities in it. If a business, for instance, is in a condition that requires a turnaround, it is somehow not acting, responding, producing in a way that the environment—e.g., market and customers—accepts. But what, exactly, is the environment calling for? New products, cheaper products, better services? The leader surveys and assesses the environment to arrive at conclusions on this dimension of change.

Second, *the vision provides a focal point for the energies that he or she sets loose and requires.* The leader's vision initiates a pattern of stability and coherence that enables the organization to activate vital energies, compile and coordinate them, and finally direct its energies and capabilities into a flow directed at the changes that need to occur.

Third, *the vision does these things by providing the leader with an understanding of constraints that will embody the organization's potential.* These constraints act as "attractors" around which energy concentrates, coalesces into a new, fresh, vital, transforming energy, and then is redirected into the actions that need to occur for the changes to be accomplished successfully. By embodying that focusing and reflecting "attractor" within the system, the energies of all the constituents of the organization are set free to actually affect the change that is now clearly envisioned, anticipated, and acted upon (as though it were already the fact).

Finally, *the vision assures that the organization remains connected to all salient aspects of its own internal processes as well as those of the environment in which it is situated.* The organization dies when the environment cannot support its processes, or when its process spins out of range of what other components of its system can support. Cancer is an example of the former; human overuse and damage to the environment is an example of the latter. Both are conditions that lack salient attractors capable of organizing the system appropriately.

As we conclude this chapter, let's revisit Howard's situation and consider *what he might have done differently if appreciated his vision in the ways self-organization suggests.* First, since he would know that he provided his people with the prime attractor around which their energies were clustered and focused, he would not have thought that to extricate himself from the day-to-day affairs of the company was a viable idea. Did his role need to change? Yes, it most certainly did, for his sake and health, as well as for the sake of the organization, but not so drastically that he, embodying the vision, would disappear from sight.

Second, he would have taken stock of his company and tried better to understand its dynamics, its emotional needs and frustrations. He would have searched for what his company's capabilities for "emergent," "visionary," and stable growth were. He would not have tried to jerk it, kicking and screaming, into a new regime. Instead, he would have charted a path for change: a many-stepped, incrementally developmental approach to solidifying its capabilities and potentialities for stability. Through all of this, many individual's roles would be changed, not just his own. And new leaders would have been seeded throughout the organization. If none could be found, he would make many small changes and/or hires to plant these seeds for stability and continued growth. Still, through it all, he would be in view, available, exchanging ideas, energy, and passion about the company's future.

So while the idea of a COO position may have been a good one, he would have searched high and low for anyone but the person he did hire. He could have found someone who could fully grasp his message and "attractor" qualities and amplify them throughout the organization. Or he could have quietly mentored someone in the company, while other changes were going on (maybe through the use of a professional mentor), so that eventually this person could take on greater responsibilities.

Finally and most importantly, he would have undertaken a concerted project to elevate his own vision of leading. Of course, this is exactly what he did after the debacle of Hannibal played itself out. My firm was part of that process, I am glad to say. We found him to be so open to learning—and not the skill-based, expertise-level claptrap that passes for what a leader needs to learn. Instead, he was able and willing to dig deep, examine who he was as a leader, including appreciating what his leading meant to those around him. He found that by relaxing and accepting in Self-Trust, he actually was effective in leading if not in day-to-day managing.

And lead he did. He personally focused the mission of the company, drove sales, culled marginal activities, and reenergized his organization. As of this writing, one of his internal people, without the title, has taken on many COO type of duties and loves the role.

CHAPTER SIX

Embodying the Vision

WHAT WE UNDERSTAND THE WORLD TO BE LIKE

IS DETERMINED BY MANY THINGS:

OUR SENSORY ORGANS, OUR ABILITY TO MOVE

AND TO MANIPULATE OBJECTS, THE DETAINED

STRUCTURE OF OUR BRAIN, OUR CULTURE

AND OUR INTERACTIONS IN OUR ENVIRONMENT,

AT THE VERY LEAST. WHAT WE TAKE TO BE TRUE

IN A SITUATION DEPENDS ON OUR EMBODIED

UNDERSTANDING OF THE SITUATION,

WHICH IS IN TURN SHAPED BY ALL THESE FACTORS.

TRUTH FOR US, ANY TRUTH THAT WE CAN

HAVE ACCESS TO, DEPENDS ON SUCH EMBODIED

UNDERSTANDING.[1]

—LAKOFF AND JOHNSON

[1] Lakoff and Johnson, *Philosophy in the Flesh* (New York, 1999), p. 102.

ORGANIZATION ATTRACTORS

Creative leading is neither control based, hierarchical, nor power driven. What's left? Without those levers to pull, how does a person lead? you might ask. *Creative leaders guide and strengthen the formation of the organization's attractors, and the way that is done is by embodying those attractors.*

To highlight how this is done entails traveling on, moving along the path and entering the second destination, the marker we call the Arch of Vision and Organization. *The leader enters this arch when she decides to act on her vision.* The arch encompasses the organization that results from the vision. Thus, the components of the arch now represent an organization's Identity, Behavior, and Structure—the three different kinds of attractors that comprise the heart and soul of the organization. The arch still does represent the "psyche" of the leader, however. Organization and leader merge in this arch, as the leader's life becomes devoted to forming an organization around her vision. The attractors of the organization have their most potent effect when they are "embodied" by the leader.

The Arch of Vision and Organization emphasizes concepts: ideas, words—things of gossamer and air. For instance, an organization's "mission" is one of its spires. A mission statement, no matter how well written and descriptive, will have effect, will come to life, only if the organization embodies and lives it day in, day out, or dies trying. How many times have you attended a conference at which your executives sat around tables at luxurious retreats creating a mission statement? Then, when it is brought back to the company, it gets printed up, hung on a wall, and conscientiously ignored by one and all! In this chapter we get the mission statement off of the wall and into the actions of the organization's members.

A complex organization depends on the interplay of many attractors. An organization comprises three different kinds of attractors:

143

(1) Identity attractors (spires), (2) the Behavior attractor (keystone), and (3) Structure (process) attractors (arch's interior).

Identity attractors comprise those concepts that define the organization as a singular entity within a larger environment. Identity attractors include the values, mission, strategy, and culture that give an organization coherence and that help people settle back down on the basics, the most common denominator, and the clearest and simplest purpose.

The Behavior attractor, the keystone of the arch, encompasses all the actions, ideas, conversations, and experiences that directly mark the organization's presence in its surroundings.

We call the organization's Behavior attractor its "Signature Behavior." All the spire's energies, once again, flow into this keystone, making the Signature Behavior a completely unique occurrence in its environment.

The Signature Behavior is not the endeavor's products or services. The attractor includes all the ways, means, tactics, communications, resources, and thoughts that are used to make those products and services a viable part of the market or community.

Structure attractors comprise the ongoing activities and processes of communication, monitoring and measuring that continually link the myriad activities that go on in the organization to accomplish what its identity calls for.

THE ARCH AS EMBODIED ORGANIZATIONAL ATTRACTORS [2]

Some of the names of these organizational components are quite familiar to you, but as you read on, don't expect to see the same old definitions. When viewed as attractors, and not as mechanical projections of mere

[2] See the appendix for a complete, comparative depiction of the terms of arches.

functions, these once empty concepts open up to avenues of creative organization making, innovation and imaginative play. As we have said, attractors are components of dynamic systems, some of which are living systems. And we consider an organization to be, at least potentially, a living, dynamic system. Seen in this way, when *the organization is understood as a living entity, creating collaboration comes easily to the creative leader.*

KEYSTONE: SIGNATURE BEHAVIOR
INTERIOR SPACE: PROCESS AND STRUCTURE

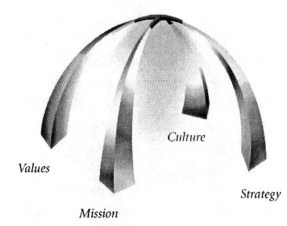

FIGURE 6.1: THE ARCH OF ORGANIZATION

THE SPIRES: IDENTITY ATTRACTORS

The organization's four Identity attractors—Values, Mission, Culture, and Strategy—answer the question, "Who are we?" They envision which actions the organization supports and which it prohibits. When people in the organization have a clear idea of which actions a leader promotes and which are prohibited, they can perform with clarity, and they can act with confident forcefulness. The Identity attractors comprise the most basic and conceptual domain of a leader's direct action and attention. These are the attractors leaders talk about when they "walk the talk."

VALUES

The organization's "Values" comprise how the organization acts to enhance certain features of its global environment (and opposes and/or does not support other aspects). In the context of the (first) Effectiveness Arch, this spire designated Self-Awareness. Self-Awareness implicitly included values in the sweeping recollection of the stories and experiences that brought a person to the endeavor of leading. In this second arch, the spire summarizes conclusions about how certain actions are likely to produce certain results in the world. It spells out judgments about what actions are beneficial to that world and which are not. These judgments involve sweeping assessments about the state of the organization's world and make clear why this organization acts in certain ways and why it refuses to act in other ways.

Leaders embody values by taking primary responsibility for having their actions match their words. Leaders' actions act as benchmarks against which members of an organization assess their own values. Those whose values align with and are in accord with the leaders' values will stay; those whose values clash with those of the leaders will leave.

MISSION

The organization's "Mission" amplifies the leader's Practical Insight into a focused, laserlike beam of attention on the *organization's intended effects on the experiences it generates for others.* It enumerates how the organization offers others an opportunity to form new patterns of perception, understanding, attitudes, and/or behavior that will be beneficial for themselves, their communities, and their surrounding ecologies. Furthermore, the mission describes *how only this organization is capable of delivering this effect on other's experience.*[3]

A leader models the actions that he or she thinks will induce new experiences for the organization's constituents. The leader is the primary measuring and monitoring tool to assess customers' responses to the actions that are directed at fulfilling the mission.

CULTURE

The organization's "Culture" directly extends the leader's People Skills to include the whole organization. *"Culture" summarizes the attitudes and expectations people create as they actually interact within the organization to get things done.*[4] People expect their colleagues torespond in certain ways to their requests and actions, forming an internal map and model of what one's behaviors will mean to others inside the organization.

[3] A Mission, then, is not a list of the products a company makes or services it offers. An organization succeeds by fitting within and making a worthwhile contribution to its environment. The mission states of how all the organization's members collaborate in order to instill some pattern of behavior that others will welcome, adopt, and, in the case of a business's offerings, for which it will pay a premium (profit to the business). Neither is a Mission a statement of revenue or market share goals. Those can be specified elsewhere (in the strategy, perhaps, or in the goals and purposes that focus on process and structure).

[4] Culture is tied to the organization's values, of course. In our terminology, however, values refer to how the organization envisions its world and clarifies itself in that world, while culture refers to actual expectations and actions within the organization that transpire in the fulfilling of those values. When we speak about the underlying expectations that form into a culture, we use the term "drivers," rather than "values." Drivers name concrete expectations that people have about their daily interactions with others within the organization. Either these drivers have "teeth," and violating them will engender consequences, or they will be dead ends, stimulating frustration. If one of my organization's drivers is teamwork, as the organization's leader, I will either fully expect that others will offer teamwork, or I anticipate that they will not stay in the organization.

When I act to create a customer experience that is consistent with what the organization wants to create, and in a way that emulates what the leader embodies, I expect to get positive feedback from my colleagues. When I act contrary to those things, I expect castigation. If I know I am constitutionally unable to act in those sanctioned ways, I'd better find another job, in a hurry.

Again, *matching words to deeds is the critical step for leaders with regard to culture.* If the espoused drivers are out of sync with the behaviors that actually occur, the organization will suffer from cynicism and bad politics. If the drivers do accord with the values, people will be able to act forthrightly, with directness and no energy wasted in second-guessing or trying to swim against the tide. Leaders exemplify the drivers clearly and demonstrably, and they articulate the expectations that these drivers will be followed throughout the organization over and over again.

STRATEGY

The organization's "Strategy" develops the leader's Drive into *the organization's actions that will change the situation into what the vision declares as a better world.* The strategy describes the change that is being created by the organization, it envisions its effects on the world, including how it will affect its immediate or tangential environments, and it also envisions a larger intent on how its actions will add to the general climate of the environment, consistent with its values.

A Strategy describes how the organization as a whole is taking itself into a future, into an environment that has not yet experienced its efficacy. It is envisioning how it will become a factor in that environment, creating a new pattern for potential connection in the environment. It is a statement of its own intentions to act, not an envisioning of specific results from concrete actions.[5]

A Strategy is really a hypothesis. It states that its actions are testing certain features of the world in order to get a certain result. If the test shows that these actions aren't effective, then either the actions or the hypothesis will be changed. *The leader is the first and foremost testing device and measuring tool of the Strategy.* Just as the leader assesses whether the Mission is offering an appropriate attractor, she must assess if the Strategy, its business model and means of delivery of the Mission's intention, is appropriate. All the organization's leaders have to fully grasp, in the heat of action, whether success is in progress or adjustments need to be made. The Strategy is never written in stone.

THE KEYSTONE:
THE ORGANIZATION'S SIGNATURE BEHAVIOR

In the Effectiveness Arch, the keystone represented the leader's Self-Trust. The leader's energy released into the interior of the arch, projecting through speech and actions, what her Leader Brand specified. Here, in the Arch of Vision and Organization, the leader's Self-Trust, resolve and acceptance are magnified by the whole organization's energy. They radiate in two directions: into the interior of the arch and outward into the world.

Radiating outward from the keystone, into the world, the energy forms the organization's "Signature Behavior." The Signature Behavior mirrors the Leader's Brand. It comprises those constant, clearly identifiable and

---

[5] The Strategy in a business context thus incorporates its "transaction or business model." This aspect of the strategy answers the question: What are the exchanges that the organization sets up so as to offer benefits to others and be able to derive energy (profits) for itself? It also envisions the scale and scope of its actions, and accordingly, the rate of return on its actions and investments that will be required to sustain it at its scope of action.

intentional actions for which the organization is known in the world. Just as the Leader's Brand resulted in a coherent response from those within the arch, the Signature Behavior projects set of actions that trigger certain, definite responses in the world outside the arch.

It is a "Signature" Behavior because, as a fulfillment of the leader's singular vision, it uniquely occupies a niche in the environment that is all its own. Offering itself as an attractor within its environment, the organization takes action, indelibly making its mark on the world. This is what the outside world sees of the organization. In other words, the organization offers its behavior to the environment for it to subsequently become an attractor for the behaviors of other systems.

Leaders cannot, in any way, tolerate behavior that violates the intentions of the Signature Behavior. The latter may have to be adjusted to fit the environment more appropriately, but the organization must remain true to its identity and must fully honor the niche that it wants to carve out in that environment. Of course, everyone in the organization must fully and accurately judge whether or not that is taking place. In reality, however, the leaders have to make the final call, formulate the decisions and make the adjustments necessary for keeping the Signature Behavior clear, compelling, and feasible.

INTERIOR SPACE: STRUCTURE THROUGH PROCESS

The interior of the Organization Arch represents "Structure through Process." The interior structure is not a rigid architectural feature. Instead, *the interior is saturated with the leader's energy. It is focused and informed by the energy generated through the arch's spires, the organization's Values, Mission, Culture, and Strategy; and then it brims with the repeated, patterned actions of volunteers, or customer service people, sales people, marketing and finance people, floor workers, service specialists, and others.* They all perform activities that are different from one another, and in the spirit of collaboration, fulfill the vision by enacting the Signature Behavior.

Because these activities entail division of labor—each member performing only part of the totality of actions necessary to carry out the intended Signature Behavior—communications, monitoring and measuring activities are also necessary. Managers, dispersed throughout the organization, perform these functions, keeping the organization working as a whole. They enable the Structure to optimize its use of energy (money, material, equipment) in striving for the organization's success. And as a result, because these actions are performed in certain ways, cyclically returning to methods, standards, and measures as indications of their success, the organization's patterned behaviors provide Structure.

NEW PERSPECTIVES ON
ORGANIZATIONAL ROLES

Self-organization also changes how we view the roles that people adopt when undertaking these activities; and the self-organization model also changes the way we view their interactions. This change is critical for leaders.

Instead of viewing followers as having "jobs," within which people execute certain actions and have specific, limited, highly defined results, leaders view each person as enacting and embodying certain aspects of the organization's Signature Behavior and identity attractors. Thus, in this way, each follower actively determines the organization's ongoing structure and vitality.

We thus introduce new terminology around the self-organizing life that goes on within the arch.

An *Area of Responsibility* describes how a member is responsible for certain aspects of relationships to the people who are affected by the organization's Signature Behavior. If, in a business setting for instance, a patterned activity (the content of a person's "job") is going to be valued by a customer, the employee must assure that the action takes place in the way it is intended as defined in the mission, values, culture and strategy. That is a "responsibility," not a job, because it entails continual self-monitoring by the person who is performing the action.

A *Core Action* is an action that must be performed, day in, day out, over and over again, if the Signature Behavior is to be enacted.

A *Critical Success Factor* defines how those performing certain activities know whether or not they have succeeded. Success is determined by identifying the responses from those affected by the Signature Behavior and results that are anticipated when the organization's niche is established. They are worded to be as specific as possible, so the results being assessed can be identified as being present or not, as quickly and as independently as possible, by the person performing the action. No supervisor, manager or overseer is needed. Each person publicly commits to attaining these results. They are coordinated with others in a flow toward accomplishing the Signature Behavior; and if the results are not being obtained, each person assesses what in the mix needs to be reassessed: the action itself, the measurement or the expectation.[6]

[6] For a detailed explanation of this view and how it is incorporated into ongoing organizational assessment, evaluation and human resource processes, see Michael Shenkman's *The Strategic Heart: Using the New Science to Guide Successful Organizations* (Westport, CT, 1996).

The role of leaders in regard to Structure/Process consists of projecting their Leader Brand and embodying the organization's Identity and Behavior attractors. Other than that, their role is to assure that managers and other leaders in the organization are performing their roles of communicating, monitoring, evaluating, and adjusting to changing conditions and/or mistakes. The leader assures that the Core Actions and Areas of Responsibility are constantly updated and attuned to environmental demands. Sometimes the leader needs to insist that the time has come to make major adjustments in the Structure to assure that they remain effective, but even so, it is up to the people on the ground to determine what, finally, must be done to keep the organization's structure viable. The leader also maintains balanced collaboration. If people engaged in one process start to display behaviors that aren't appropriate (don't align with the organization's Identity attractors and Signature Behavior), the leader has to step in to get those people back in line, or urge them to move on.

LEADERS AS ATTRACTORS

There is one more attractor we need to consider. To act as a living community of talents and energies, an organization must establish its Identity, Structure, and Behavior attractors. Still, at best, these attractors are just words, merely propositions, promises, plans, or assumptions. *By giving these concepts a living form, with eyes, ears, heart, and determination, by bringing everyone under the consolidating and coalescing light of her attention and care, by walking around the organization and having people see and touch and talk to her, the leader brings the other attractors to life.* Without the leader's living presence, no organization has a chance of fulfilling any vision, no less ones that bring about significant transformations for large groups of people.

153

We have already talked about how the leader does certain things to make these attractors viable organizing tools. But we must remember, the arch symbolizes leaders' psyches as they bring their vision into an organized endeavor. That means all these attractors we have described are parts of, components of the leader, whose vision and presence, we have already explained, generate the need and viability of the organization's existence, no less its effectiveness.

So, in addition to these "component" attractors, we need to pay attention *to leaders themselves, who are attractors*. To do this, we will offer a few focusing (attractor-like) "mantras" that leaders can play in their heads, again and again, as they sort through the claims on their time and energy. Using these phrases as their guide, all the dimensions of the originating vision will be continually recalled and reactivated. Our mantras are (1) define the "whole"; (2) make sense; (3) make it come alive; (4) create aspiring roles. Let's look at each of them.

DEFINE THE "WHOLE"

Too often it is just assumed that everyone knows what the "whole" is. But this assumption couldn't be more mistaken. Ask a number of people in a developing organization, "What's the whole that we care about?" and you'll get any number of answers, all of them stated with complete confidence: "Why, of course, it's the company," one might say. Others might say that it's the organization, or the department. "What else could it be?" they'd be thinking. Well, for instance, think about this: in the business world, a company doesn't exist without customers, markets, a financial system, other supporting products, communities that are culturally and financially able to buy the product, a government that protects and advances the interests of the whole community, a natural environment that is either benefited or harmed by the company's actions. Aren't these parts of the "whole" that the organization needs to consider in its attractors? Of course, there are limits to the whole that the organization addresses, and these limits also need to be incorporated into that definition.

So then, what is the whole? *The whole envisions all the populations, groups, and/or conditions that greatly affect, and/or are greatly affected by, what the vision and its organized realization encompass.* The whole is the world as seen by the organization, which the organization influences in ever-decreasing intensity as that world extends out from the reach of its actions. Again, it is as crucial to identify what the organization *does not affect* as it is to identify what changes the organization is capable of making. Humility and perspective must enter into the picture. The whole, properly defined, mitigates against grandiosity. How far the vision extends out into a wider world, beyond even what the organization affects, depends on the initiating values that engendered the vision and necessitated the organized response from the leader and her followers.

We all want to be "whole," to live with a sense of completeness, as opposed to fragmentation or emptiness. The wholes by which we define ourselves are the primary experiences in our lives. We divide and compartmentalize our worlds in order to accommodate (or adjust our energies to) the least of what experience brings to us. Ultimately however, at some time, in some place, the energies of the wider world destroy those convenient, expedient, self-justifying boundaries. As we said in our exposition about attractors: this is a mode of thinking that entails porous boundaries. Our wholes are constantly in flux. We live in a world that constantly redefines our "wholes."

No one feels the shifting of the boundaries of what we define as wholes more than creative leaders. Creative leaders define wholes that are more encompassing and inclusive than what had gone before. I just can't think of a creative leader who stirs emotion by dividing a functioning whole into smaller sects. Creative leading takes on the burden of inducing emotions that give people a sense of belonging to a larger world, and of collaborating with wider networks of people. What is "creative" about appealing to fear, acting out of fear, and responding to others with blunt acts of dismissal, disdain, or even violence? But how do creative leaders depict a way of living that enables boundaries to melt away, that uncovers new grounds held in common, or that cuts new avenues for understanding, sharing, and collaboration? That is the hard work that creative leaders do first.

The difference between leaders and even their closest and most capable of followers is that leaders act to evoke, depict and preserve the whole, not just get things done. Creative leaders know that change always exacts a price and they make calculations as to what prices will produce the best returns for all concerned. Creative leaders are preservers and protectors, first and foremost, rather than revolutionaries and predators.

MAKE SENSE OF NEW WORLDS

The creative leader's vision is triggered by an experience in which something isn't right. *Then the creative leader's vision elaborates on a picture of how a different, larger, more encompassing, but not yet existing world makes even more sense than does this older, more confined and restricted and actual one.* This is a difficult task. How difficult? Think about how we normally respond when we confront completely new situations. Most of us take the attitude, "There is no need to change things; what happens happens; you can't force us to change. This is the way we've done things in the past. This is the way it's always been. And it's good enough."

How do creative leaders respond to this complacency and/or fear of the new? They make sense of this new, enlarged world by means of language, first of all. They generate "an inexorable flow of explanatory power from one realm to another," as one writer put it.[7] Using strong verbs of action and determination and weaving them in with compelling metaphors that stick in our minds, maybe forever, e.g., Martin Luther King said, "I have been to the mountaintop"; Lincoln's "a government of the people, for the people, by the people." The leader paints pictures (and evokes metaphors, as we will see in the next section) in which all can envision that this new world is among us, if we only grasp it and start acting in it. In this world, people envision themselves living in different ways, engaging each other in different, more preferred actions that create a large whole and enlarge our own selves and lives as well. Then the leader makes sense by laying out the sequence of events that need to transpire to bring the new world about. People can envision those events that occur along the way and take up the actions that will bring those events about.

The collaboration was initiated because the creative leader and then followers believed there was a better world out there that could be brought about. Thus, as a client of mine put it, "My job isn't to get things done. That would be a waste of my time. My job is not even to drive other people to get things done. That would be condescending to my followers. No, my real job is to help others to make bridges for

---

[7] Jack Hitt, *A Gospel According to the Earth* (Harpers, July 2003), p. 43.

themselves, so they can get over the rough spots, the fears and disappointments that go with change. I help them get into the next creative, productive action—no matter how anxiety producing it is at the outset—so we can accomplish what we set out to do." Creative leaders engender collaboration in order to help followers push themselves through the fear, stress, exhaustion, and disbelief so they can move on to tackle the tasks at hand that, collectively executed, will amount to real accomplishment.

BRING IT TO LIFE

"Making sense" is no intellectual proposition. People are being asked to act, to take risks. But to get people to collaborate around a vision (a mere notion that has yet to take up its place in the sun), that vision has to inspire, offer a breath of prospect and excitement. The leader's vision needs to become emotionally compelling, and most of all, *alive.*

No project or process in and of itself has life in it. We all know about these deadening processes to which we are subjected. There are tasks to be executed, there are numbers, up or down, positive or negative, to be generated. The leader knows one thing for sure: people do not collaborate because they yearn to be employed in a repetitive, functional, clean, and efficient process. They will collaborate under certain conditions: when they feel engaged; when they feel more alive working with others on a compelling mission than they do as single contributors; when they feel their actions and lives embody important values; when they see something new and worthwhile take shape; and when they know that they can put their name on it. They are following a leader in order to accomplish something that matters. Defining a larger whole and creating a picture that gives sense and tangibility (even if it is only a dream) to this new whole is what energizes the leader's endeavor.

Making it come alive entails drilling down into the concrete, day-to-day, person-to-person aspects of the effort and making them a part of the new whole—a vital part, without which the whole could not endure. Creative leaders offer a "presence" (Leader Brand) that guides others' experiences even when they are not present. Creative leaders are often people who are personally memorable and vivid. Their mannerisms, their speech and words, all have to be easy to recall. Their energies cut through the fog and clutter of the swirling happenings of change.

When leaders "create the experience of change," their presence fills the pores and ignites the synapses of people's lives within the organization. As human beings, we respond to others' voices, to the intonations and connotations of their words. "It is the 'inner sonority of speech,'" one CEO said, "that people respond to." The experience of change is created in all the unspoken sonorities, all the expressions and means of embodiment that a leader puts forward. Those who engage in creative leading know this in their bones.

ASPIRING ROLES

Leaders treasure their successful managers. Like the body's nervous system, managers keep the organism coherently together as it strikes out into the chaotic territories that get the heart pumping faster and the mind whirring more forcefully. Leaders put people in those roles who love order, who thrive on constraint and pattern. But there are others, leader colleagues, who, even as they get the specific things done that enable that new world to come about, aren't doing things merely

159

to sustain the usual. They are adding a brick, driving a nail in the edifice of the new. They know process but don't dwell on it. They see the familiar, the patterned and customary as a template, but don't feel any obligation or inclination to replicate it. They are the people for whom the vision has the best chance of coming alive, and they are the people who will most likely populate that group of followers so treasured by the creative leader. They are also the people to whom the creative leader must first appeal in order to establish the ways that collaboration will bring the vision to life.

People can incite others to act by appealing to many emotions—fear and revenge are the most common. *But creative leaders appeal to people's sense of aspirations that encompass a larger whole and embrace a wider spectrum of life, rather than prey on fearful emotions that exclude, replace, or deny.* As one colleague of mine said in a recent conversation, "Leaders influence through aspiration." Aspiring to the vision, after all, drives the leader, why wouldn't aspiration drive followers as well? While the athlete or the monk might seek to enter into his or her efforts in order to fulfill their aspirations for themselves, the leader enters into the endeavor in order to have others—followers and even those who have not yet chosen to follow—achieve their aspirations.

PART THREE

What Makes a Leader Great?

INTRODUCTION

Beth struggled for two years in Zee-Tech.

The company was stressed and its atmosphere was tense from the start. The investors only put up half of the amount the founders thought they would need to get to a commercially viable product. Then, it was much harder to get technology into mass production than the founders had thought it would be. It is not unusual in these situations for the engineers to get quarrelsome, and many fingers were being pointed at various people. As in any technical company, the engineers typically blame marketing, and vice versa. Beth, in her marketing position, was a convenient target—being the only woman on the executive team didn't help either.

Matt tried to help her keep in mind what she was trying to accomplish for herself: to have her values count, to have the organization be known for its clear and compelling signature behavior, and not just its technology. But when the fur started to fly—and fly it did—Beth reverted to old behaviors and traditional business organization models.

As time went on, Matt had to tell Beth how others in the company found her to be rigid, for instance. She had her way of doing things—and Beth was sure they were the right way—and would brook no interference in her group's operations. She stood up for her values, all right, but did so by drawing the wagons around her department. Eventually, people just stopped coming to her. There were days when she wondered why bother coming to work.

She also heard it said that her group's research was "useless" to Zee-Tech. Sure, the complaint went, the kind of statistical market assessing she did may be great in a big company with lots of established customers, but it wasn't helpful in getting this start-up's products into the market. The engineers felt that all Beth had to do was ask them about what was needed. But Beth hadn't asked anyone within the company to offer their opinion. Either, the engineers said, the product had more to offer, and so could command a better price, or it wouldn't be worth it. The market was looking for quantum leaps, not incremental improvements, they told her. Of course, Beth's retort was either they had to get the performance promised out of the device or there was no value proposition to offer.

While Beth had no control over the actual performance of the device, it stung her that her marketing expertise was being called into question. Her veracity and competence had never been questioned like that before. The engineers got downright nasty. They called her "Presentation Queen," meaning all show and no substance. She found that after the first year or so she was not invited to go along on some customer calls. "We're just doing engineering," she'd be told. The investors were getting restless as well. They were wondering if the company could offer them the multipliers of ten or even five they had wanted.

From Matt's perspective, the situation was becoming toxic, and he could tell Beth was shutting down. The more accusatory the engineers, the more rigid and formal Beth became. The mentoring sessions also became drab and uneventful. Beth sometimes seemed oblivious or even in denial as negativity swirled around her. She clung to the fact that presentations to potential customers went well and that the investors were satisfied with the business plan. She talked about how the people in her group were doing such good work, but weren't appreciated. All well and good, but Matt knew she was stonewalling, as she broke one appointment after another.

And then the post-dot-com downturn hit the high-tech market. No one was buying anything in the markets Zee-Tech had courted. Companies like Zee-Tech disappeared one after the other. Every day, the drip, drip, drip of new bankruptcies in Zee-Tech's world was reported in the trade journals. And, to make matters worse, during this industry-wide downturn, Beth and the other executives were leading the company's efforts at getting a second round of *capital funding. Some funding firms didn't bother returning phone calls. Others offered meetings with their research staffs, but not with partners who actually made the investment decisions. The well was dry, and the temperature in the company was hot.*

As the firm's money was drawn down to the final months' supply, the first investors decided to put up another round, with onerous terms, however. The funds offered were half of what the executives were looking for, and the investors' share of equity was nearly exclusionary. The company would survive long enough to get through the market downturn, but not with its current burn rate. Drastic cuts would have to be made.

The situation was clear to Beth. Zee-Tech would not be selling any product for at least eighteen months. Who knew what the markets would look like then, or if Zee-Tech would even be selling into the markets she had researched and explored? She was no one's favorite in the company. She had to go. So did Matt.

Matt assured Beth that he would continue to be available to Beth as her mentor, despite the change in circumstances. Matt and Beth met in a local café a few weeks after the layoff. Beth's pain at this juncture was palpable. As they sat across from each other at the outdoor patio table, in the bright sunshine of this spring day, Beth mostly looked down at the table and would only occasionally look up at Matt. Often she would sigh, and the conversation moved slowly, with many long pauses that Matt made no attempt to cover or shorten. Let the feelings flow, he thought.

"You know, you do everything right, and it's still not enough," Beth pushed out. Sadness and no small amount of anger mixed in her voice, as she wrapped on the table with her fingers.

"What do you mean by that?" Matt asked.

"You go to business school, to learn all the right skills, learn how to run scenarios, plan optimal and worst case budgets, and you find out that none of that matters."

"*You mean these skills aren't useful once you reach a certain level?*" Matt pressed.

"*No, these skills are always useful. It's just that people want more, or something else. I wanted to be a leader in that company, and I failed. That's what I've been thinking, in the last few days. Maybe I really learned something, that leading isn't about those skills. Leading is about being yourself, being open with and to other people. So you need to know who you are, and you need to be able to express that to others. You really need to know what is important to you. They don't teach you that in business schools, and your bosses along the way never really help you with that either. Maybe it's not in their interest to help you with that, I don't know.*

"*This is something you end up discovering on your own,*" she continued. "*Or maybe, if you are lucky, you get to a mentor to help you discover it. But really, since I have been working with you, for instance, it has felt almost as though I was starting over.*"

"*Was that a bad thing?*"

"*No, but I was surprised. I thought I had everything I needed to succeed, and that wasn't true. I felt let down, in a big way. I never failed before.*

"*You know what gets me? When they say, 'Beth, it's nothing personal; it's just a business decision.' Well, bull; it's damned personal to me. I failed; I was rigid; my marketing decisions were criticized.*"

"*But, Beth, the market . . .*"

"*Come on, Matt. You and I know better. I really blew it here.*"

"*And now?*"

"*I don't know. I did get a great severance package. My last job paid me bonuses—paid me bonuses for the job I did—so I have some money. Maybe I should take some time off and get a life.*"

Matt was glad to hear her say that. Beth's self-image was bruised, but her spirit was still alive and kicking. "*Actually, Beth, that's what I wanted to talk* to you about. I really think it's time for a break. I think you should take a serious break, maybe many months or even a year. I think you need to reset on some things, at least in terms of getting your life together in a way that supports leading."

"Like what?"

"Well," Matt paused while Beth settled into listening to what was coming next, "like you said, you need to get a life. You are in your midthirties; you have no interests besides business; you have no significant other; you haven't seen your mother in a year. Beth, leading isn't about being a workaholic. You said it yourself, all those skills maniacally focused on business processes aren't enough."

"So what do I need that I don't have?"

"Well, that's what you've got to find out for yourself. Again, you said it yourself: you don't even know what you need in your life. When are you going to find out? On your deathbed?"

"I don't know. Maybe I won't look for a job for a while. But I tell you, Matt, I'm not so sure anymore that I want to be a leader. What do you think of that?"

Finally, they laughed.

"No, Matt," she inserted, "I am serious. I don't know anymore."

"I know you're serious, Beth. But before you decide anything, you're going to have to have some fun. I'm serious about that too."

The conversation wound down and each departed.

Matt didn't know if he'd ever hear from Beth again. But Beth had to make a decision. It turned out she met with him at least every couple of months for the first year. Then the journey took a surprising turn: Beth didn't go back into the workforce for several years. She met someone, got married, started a family, and began a new life. There was no telling what would happen next.

GREATNESS IN CREATIVE LEADING

Beth blew it. Or so it would seem. While succeeding on her terms would have been difficult under the circumstances at Zee-Tech, she blew it because she reverted to her managerial training rather than step into leading. While it may be true that she would have ended up resigning anyway—given the downturn in the markets—she didn't take the difficult opportunity to listen, learn, open herself to the sufferings that the engineers and others in the company were undergoing. Instead, she defended her old ways of doing things. She completely forgot about the lessons from her father and the vision she wanted to establish for this tabula rasa, Zee-Tech.

Beth's story, to this point, illustrates how managerial prowess does not necessarily point the way to leading greatness. By "greatness" I mean the recognition offered by others that a leader has had a lasting and profound influence on all the lives of those affected by the endeavor. Great leaders may or may not accomplish the objectives or institute something new, but whatever the outcome of the endeavor—most often beyond the control of any leader—they do affect the way people see themselves, each other and their shared communal and environmental worlds. Great leaders may not transform the world, but they do make a difference in the lives of those they touch. It is the opportunity to affect people's lives that Beth forfeited in her reversion to managerial prowess. Let's be clear: media-based fame or even high positions of established institutional power or title have nothing to do with our standard of a creative leader's "greatness." When our clients describe the leaders they most remember, they recall leaders who sparked a desire to learn and grow, to undertake their own paths to living with risk, and learning its potential for sadness, or joy, or both.

Greatness can be experienced in leading the PTA, in leading a local community action group, or in leading an effective task force in a business. The people who do so may never garner fame for their efforts, and most great creative leaders do go unrecognized (or they, like Beth, fail). But if they exhibit certain dimensions of character, there will be people who will say of them, "She really had an impact on my life." *For us, greatness means being recognized in a singular and personal way as making a difference in the ability of people to live more meaningful, encompassing, and energetic lives.*

THE ARCH OF THE LEADER'S ETHIC

Again, as we approach a new arch, the Arch of the Leader's Ethic—the third and final arch—we consider the leader's character on a whole new level of self-comprehension and integration.

The Self-Development spire, where we encountered Self-Awareness (later, Values), is enriched by Moral Learning.

We see how one becomes a great leader not only by being aware of one's own life, but how one's life plays within a larger context of family, society, world, and environment. Great leaders study and reflect on them all. They internalize this learning as being significant for themselves and for all those who are affected by the endeavors they lead.

The Action spire that symbolizes Practical Insight (later, Mission), now enjoys the expansive play of Moral Imagination. Again, the great leader not only has a great idea about how to address a situation but also appreciates and weighs its implications in changing others' lives. The impetus here is "imaginative" because of its expansive and emphasis on greater encompassing of possibilities, helping all people to live well. Great creative leaders have no illusions about being able to impose "imperatives" or "dictates," or to declare what is to be considered the "final or divine word." The great leaders imagine the possibilities ("I have a dream today," said Martin Luther King Jr.) and invite the willing to take up the challenge of realizing them.

The Interactive spire, where we considered People Skills (later, Culture), becomes Decision as dialogue and narrative. Here the leader works with people in such a way that they collaboratively weave stories of the future of the endeavor and cast themselves as characters in the drama. True to the intent of the arch, the leader's decision is thus cast as the way all those within the arch concentrate and interweave their energies so as to create a completely unique experience for all involved.

We take up the fourth spire, the spire of Vitality, in part 4, under the heading "Flow."

CHAPTER SEVEN

Moral Learning

HUMAN BEINGS ARE IMAGINATIVE SYNTHESIZING

ANIMALS. EVERY ONE OF US IS CONTINUALLY ABOUT

THE VITAL BUSINESS OF WEAVING TOGETHER THE

THREADS OF OUR LIVES. IN ORDER FOR US TO HAVE

COHERENT EXPERIENCES, TO MAKE ANY SENSE AT ALL

OF WHAT HAPPENS TO US, TO SURVIVE IN OUR ENVIRONMENT,

AND TO ENHANCE THE QUALITY OF OUR LIVES,

WE MUST ORGANIZE AND REORGANIZE OUR EXPERIENCE

FROM MOMENT TO MOMENT. [OUR] IMAGINATIVE MECHANISMS

MAKE UP A LARGE PART OF OUR UNDERSTANDING,

BY WHICH I MEAN, NOT JUST OUR BELIEFS, BUT RATHER

OUR BODILY, IMAGINATIVE, SOCIALLY CONSTRUCTED

WAY OF BEING IN AND INHABITING A WORLD.[1]

—MARK JOHNSON

[1] *Moral Imagination* (Chicago, 1983), p. 152.

FEELING ALIVE

Our greatest need is not that our lives have meaning, but that we feel *alive*. So says Joseph Campbell, the late proponent of the power of myth. At least as concerns creative leaders, I couldn't agree more. For these people, leading is the endeavor in which they feel most alive.

Harry Kaufman literally suffered when his organization-making prerogatives were compromised. Harry left three major executive roles for that reason. In one situation, corporate officers offered him an opportunity to be one of them, working at their august headquarters. Harry saw this as being offered the chance to drown in endless politics and bureaucracy. He left that company after more than ten years. In the next situation, the corporation completely centralized strategic decision making and personnel policy making, undermining Harry's role in creating the kind of company he envisioned. Then, the entrepreneurial chairman at his next job was incapable of letting Harry, the nominal CEO, run the company. Harry resigned, in this case leaving significant money on the table in the form of options that hadn't matured.

We are interested in creative leaders precisely because they do feel so alive when they can grasp emergent possibilities lying hidden and/or latent and turn them into organizations that make real-life products, services, and new social formations. New possibilities rise to attention in such a way that these possibilities are experienced as being already real—there, present, palpable, viable, and worthy of attention and action. While most insist that they don't create organizational actions just for the sake of novelty, or even just to keep themselves moving, they do feel compelled to make what they envision as possible into real things that engage and challenge other people.

Since leaders enter on this path in order to feel alive, it should not come as a surprise that the paths they chart are not often straight lines. What is more boring than plodding the straight and narrow, step by step, as has been done many times before, to reach a predictable end? Frankly, creative leaders typify those people who don't read the manuals and clog customer service queues with questions like, "And where is the switch?" If, as kids they built models, they probably didn't follow the instructions. In all of these twists and turns, the leader feels alive; in pursuing what the vision portends, the leader and his followers supply the particular life energies, making this possibility into something real.

THE THIRD ARCH:
THE ARCH OF THE LEADER'S ETHIC

KEYSTONE: ATTENTIVE RESPONSIBILITY

INTERIOR SPACE: PRACTICE

Dialogue
and Narrative

Moral Learning

Flow

Moral Imagination

To understand how people can summon the energy to live this way, we enter our third and final arch. When we stopped and surveyed the components of the first arch, we looked at leaders' psyches in terms of the Skills of Character they needed in order to be effective in creating followers. In the second arch, we saw how a leader's vision translates into organizing people into an effective, collaborative endeavor.

Here, in the third arch, we look at the way leaders (who are already effective in creating organizations that turn a vision into actual products, services, and/or relationships) keep their energies and capabilities vital and fresh. In this arch, we consider questions such as these: How do great leader stay open and fresh to a pressing situation in ways that others don't? How are leaders more able to wrest an attitude resolve out of the ambiguities that discourage or frighten away others? How do these creative leaders dig deeper into both themselves and into the situation at hand than do other people and thus see new opportunities?

These are the most complex questions we have approached so far. This arch poses the deepest challenge and most lasting, life-shaping experiences for the leader. We will take our time in the exposition of the components of this arch for that reason.[2] That being said, once the leader leaves the demarcated space of this arch, he or she walks on unencumbered by the need for the structures and shelters these arches once offered.

In this chapter, we begin our examination of the third and final arch, the Arch of the Leader's Ethic, by looking at the spire we call "Moral Learning."

---

[2] We will only consider three of the spires in this section. The fourth spire and the keystone will be considered in part 4.

MORAL LEARNING

Moral Learning builds on the energies set loose in the Self-Development spire. It deepens Self-Awareness, then sets the leader's Values free from any entrenchment or dogmatic conviction. In the Arch of the Leader's Ethic, a leader's recollections and values are no longer taken to be the final word, to be accepted "as is." They are taken as the raw material for a new challenge, as the basis from which whole new perspectives on how they can be effective leaders in the world begin to be formed.

MORAL

The term "moral" typically (unfortunately) refers to prescribed rules and manners of conduct. We don't use the term in that way. Here, the word evokes *deep understandings of how we are to live well with others (other beings of all kinds) in our worlds:* how we make decisions about what is good for ourselves and others; how we determine if our own lives are to have worth, integrity, and dignity; how we comprehend our lives, attitudes, actions, and decisions within the larger communities, environments—wholes—in which we are immersed. Creative leaders live much of their conscious lives thinking about such things, testing their sense of worth, integrity, and dignity against what they had once professed as being good for others, their community, society, environment, and beyond. They insist that their lives constantly drive toward a higher or deeper, more encompassing, welcoming and inclusive good for themselves and others.

On the world stage, we all know the stories of how Lincoln, Gandhi, and Mandela lived by challenging themselves to measure up to the circumstances they, in large part, generated. But creative leaders, in all walks of life, live that way. More locally, we have seen how Howard, Brian, and Harry thrive by testing their beliefs on ever-larger scales. Harry has always moved to either larger organizations or more difficult challenges. Brian is always seeking ways to work at a larger scale, putting into place completely new organizations that can realize possibilities once thought to be impossible. These people want before them, all around them, touching and enveloping their psyches and attention, the largest "wholes" they can accommodate.

LEARNING

When we are learning (as opposed to merely being trained), we find out how we can change ourselves in order to live in ways that better our worlds; we open ourselves so as to be able to more fully invest in making that world a good place. We suddenly have a new light thrown on to our psychical predispositions, assumptions and prejudices. We come to appreciate all the ways in which our lives are bound up with how ideas, people, institutions, material things—natural, cultural, and technological— connect to us. (We can also learn to shut down. But patterns such as anger, fear, cynicism, and despair do not concern us here.) New facts or even new rules may come to the fore, but when we learn, we come to new realizations about how these facts and rules contribute or detract from our lives; we have learned something when the information involved is used by us in the course of making our decisions and guiding our actions. The world can appear in a new light because we are learning, i.e., a new light ignites in us.

We are engaged in Moral Learning when we are discovering the possibilities life holds: how our living works, how our lives have place and purpose by being immersed in larger worlds. "Moral," as we mean it, carries with it the sense with which we speak of the "soul," that part of our being that connects, with passion and inexorability, to completeness and greatness. Acting morally, our puny individuality dissolves, and in so doing, we feel the larger energies of friends, societies, humanity, nature, and even beyond that. *In our moral learning, these larger connections teach us that we need not make our individuality primary; we only need to make our singular life count for something.*

There are always new deeds to be done, more connections to be made, new discipline to be applied while bringing larger conceptions of what is occurring into clearer focus. Many, most of us, choose not to engage in these kinds of activities. Most of us live our lives like a young branch on a tree: once bent by the wind in one direction or another, it never grows in another direction. We learn only once, and from then on, we live within our habits, following the codes, the rules, the moral lessons we were once taught. Creative leaders don't live that way.

THE EVIDENCE

Is there really such a thing as Moral Learning? Yes. The evidence for its reality and efficacy is irrefutable. For instance, in the United States, during the last forty years, we have witnessed the acceptance of completely new moral perspectives and convictions that are not only espoused, but that shape our everyday conversations and decisions about how we act with each other in any situation we are in.

Think about it for a moment. As guided by the thoughts of Paul Ray and Sherry Ruth Anderson, in their striking book, *The Cultural Creatives*, ask yourself how many of these things, once accepted as the truth, as the correct moral stance, would you accept today:

➤ *White supremacy: using systematic violence and discrimination against people whom we designate as in need of our assuming our "White Man's Burden," including Native Americans, Asians, Arabs, Hispanics, and African Americans.*

➤ *Discriminating against women in the legal system and the workplace, and abuse common at home.*

➤ *Corporate actions that cause large-scale environmental destruction and harm people's health.*

➤ *Ignoring massive global extinctions of plant and animal species.*

➤ *Creating a hair-trigger risk of nuclear war, in which "mutually assured destruction" is the main strategy.*

➤ *Millions of deaths from heart disease and cancer, caused by poor diet, uncontrolled pesticide use, or smoking.*

➤ *I would add the license to abuse the environment, extracting materials from it and depositing waste into it at will.*

And the list goes on, touching all aspects of our lives. These changes in our demands, expectations, and criteria of acceptance are indications of Moral Learning. How did these changes take place? They took place in the cauldron of actions by men and women who individually and collectively realized something was wrong in society, and therefore the beliefs they supported had to change. People felt that the prevalent cultural ideologies forestalled important conversations we needed in order to feel alive. The changes came from exercises in Moral Learning. Many of the changes listed by Ray and Anderson came about through movements, large and small, that had leaders who articulated a new vision. And these leaders, many of whom are cited frequently in this volume, struck their chord of legitimacy and passion because of the Moral Learning they displayed during the course of their lives.

This "impetus" for transforming our worlds in ways that are more encompassing and engendering of opportunity undeniably exists. It has been noticed in many different ways. The philosopher Hegel called this impetus "the cunning of reason," giving us science and the Western way of life. Lincoln saw divine providence in the coming of the Civil War to purge our society of the unadulterated evil of slavery. Darwin gave us the idea of evolution, in which we now see how life moves toward greater diversity, complexity, and capability. They all point to a level of living that drives toward more encompassing ways of embracing our capabilities such that life itself is more robust. Creative leading, in this light, is one of the ways our species has developed to do this: we are born with an innate ability to gather in a social organization so as to maximize our choices, and to even generate new choices. We choose a leader because she or he is able to help us recognize a new alternative and point a way to guide our actions toward that better end.

MORAL LEARNING'S NATURAL BASE

This all sounds very heroic and dramatic. Change? Convert? Transform? Learn and grow? These seem like mystical concepts. But, from the standpoint of the new paradigm of self-organizing systems, this kind of creative, novelty-engendering activity happens all the time, throughout nature and even in the rather overly rule-bound human arena. The self-organizing paradigm puts Moral Learning squarely in the context of ecology, biology, and studies of cognitive process and behavior among living systems and so makes it a structural constituent of our most basic organisms. Our brains, our psyches, along with the rest of our physical organism, the self-organization model demonstrates, are immersed in the actions, responses, and adaptations of our natural, social, and global environments that continually go on all around us.

We are part of an ecology that includes the dynamics of nature and the needs of humanity. Any and every living organism must fit and meld with those that comprise the larger environment. Accordingly, our embodied selves, in completely natural and unconscious ways (albeit through definitive sensing capabilities), respond to the world around us. *Moral Learning is a means by which we adjust our individual lives to the larger wholes in which we live and from which we draw our sustenance (mental, spiritual and physical).* This is not something especially reserved for leading. All organisms modify their behavior to support the whole, as they meander through successive adaptations in response to what is occurring in their environments.

In effect, the self-organizing model presents us with a startling jolt to our prescriptions about living: it is Moral Learning, not our habituated, consumerist-fed existence, that is the norm.

I find this model liberating. Moral Learning is not a mystical process of which only the specially "touched" or "blessed" can partake. Yes, only a few choose to partake of the experience (you can bring a horse to water, but you can't make him drink); but that is not because this process is biologically out of reach. To the contrary, all living systems participate in this process. When they do not, they become ill. Animals exhibit listless or compulsive behaviors; and humans exhibit the same, but add illnesses such as depression, neurosis, and psychosis. Moral Learning is completely accessible within the structures of our experience, if, that is, we choose to "tune in" and listen to the music. The process is "natural" and universal if not customary and comfortable.

ADAPTATION

As living things, we make decisions that guide behavior toward supporting the larger systems, the wholes, in which we live. Evolution can be seen, not as a Lamarckian march to perfection, but as an unguided, random walk, as an ever-diversifying process of behavioral and/or genetic wandering. Amid this profusion of meandering life, some organisms have developed a nervous system, and then other modalities (of locomotion, perception, conception) that expand their range of choices and their ability to make choices about how to adapt to what occurs in their worlds. *Adaptation* is a term used to signify evolution's way of assuring that individuals within a species, and a species within the local ecology of many species, make decisions and guide organisms into new and/or appropriate behaviors in order to support both their continued existence or thriving and the well-being of the larger wholes in which they live.

Moral Learning, in an evolutionary, self-organizing context, is a specific form of adaptation that is available to species with highly developed mental capabilities (consciousness), which enables an individual organism to change its behavior, rather than wait for genetic adaptation in order to respond to environmental conditions. Using their higher mental abilities for Moral Learning, an individual organism assembles vast amounts of data from its sensing of its environment and then uses that information to make decisions specifically oriented toward the betterment of the whole (meaning the whole individual, the organism, or the family or species, depending on what is at stake in a given situation).

CONNECTION

Moral Learning is one of the more interesting outcomes of evolution's meandering adaptations to changing circumstances. As living organisms have become more complex, evolving from single-celled bacteria to plants, animals, the range of adaptive options available to creatures expanded. Consciousness, that key "neural linguistic adaptive" feature by which "higher" organisms are distinguished, enables these select creatures to increase the range of adaptive choices available to them. Rather than wait for an evolutionary mutation to change an entire population of a species over successive generations, Moral Learning in conscious creatures enables them to change *behaviors*, on the spot, individually, in order to benefit the larger groups of which they are a part.

My dog Tasha, for example, is a very wise creature. I can actually see her "wheels turn" as she decides whether to chase after that rabbit or obey my command to stay. As she decides, she turns her head back and forth, looking at the rabbit to one side of her and me on the other. When she was a pup, she would automatically leap off in pursuit of a rabbit that crossed her path. Then she went through a stage of pausing to look back at me before she launched into the chase. Now she stands still and actually deliberates, looking back and forth between options, often letting the rabbit go. Since we do not "punish" her for going her own way, her decision seems to me to be based on the weighing of the relative values of pursuing her own compulsion or deferring that for the more general satisfaction of having her behavior contribute positively to the pack (the larger whole). We, members of the pack, signify our appreciation of her decision by the lavishing of praise when she decides in our favor. That progression of maturation displays, in my opinion, her capacity for Moral Learning, for expanding or changing the options she considers best suited to place in the world and her own sense of thriving. If my dog can exhibit Moral Learning, then, of course humans can, if they so choose, engage in the practice as well. Accordingly, *"Moral Learning" is thus a variant of the ability of living organisms to adapt to changes in their environments in ways that benefit larger groupings—* packs, families, or species, for instance. Moral Learning enables high level, mentally complex creatures to continuously modify their individual behaviors (as opposed to mutations in its physical characteristics) in order to respond to the environment for the benefit of the larger evolving system or ecosystem of which it is a constituent part.

COGNITIVE RESTRUCTURING: HOW MORAL LEARNING HAPPENS

The means by which we interact in the world are hardly static, monolithic, purely mental structures. The cognitive structures of Moral Learning are based on the vitality (the self-organizing adaptive capabilities) of our entire organisms and are not just machinations of our cranially enclosed brains. This new model of how our complete cognitive awareness arises gives us insights into how to foster certain kinds of life practices that keep us excited, attentive, alert, and involved in this great drama of life. It gives us reasons for why it is worthwhile to take the time to engage in these practices and gives us a basis for discerning the contributions those practices make to our creative leading and thus to the experiences of those who choose to follow us.

The work of the pioneers in psychology and philosophy of ecologically immersed mind—such as Antonio Damasio, Gerald Edelman, Terrence Deacon, and Federico Varela, for instance—have

183

created a new picture of how we engage in our worlds. In this new model, an alien, external world is not "represented in" the brain, to a sort of "internal" self that, while commanding our conduct, is itself remote and distinct from our actual daily living. The new model perforates that (false, illusory) boundary between the self and the external world, rendering our boundaries as semipermeable, in the way we described the boundaries of a self-organizing system in chapter 5.

RESPONDING TO MORAL LEARNING'S CALL

Most people just want to get through, and get out of, this moment and get back to "real life"—meaning, the comfortable habits and conventions of customary daily interactions. *Moral Learning engenders extreme discomfort by upsetting the habitual patterns we mindlessly engage in.* It sets the mind to spinning, stirring fears and great feelings of loss, as old verities are revealed as being less than certain. The world seems to hover in the mind in a way that is oddly cut loose from its moorings. But the psyche is still pulsing.

So, in opposition to this feeling of being cut loose from conventional patterns of life, we vividly experience that surge of living energy, the impulse to be alive and to take a part in the great human and cosmic drama. In this divided crucible of the psyche, many of the conventions and habits of our interactions are subjected to scrutiny against a standard of this large, oceanic, undefined but undeniable sense of life that is irrepressibly making itself felt. Maybe some aspects of the old world are confirmed in these moments, and often they are. But they are being tested, extracted out of the flow of the obvious; and so these old worlds, once comfortably assumed, now have to withstand a test.

Brian Thomas, for instance, agonized for a long time about whether or not to undertake a new start-up. He had just completed one, with some success, and had taken a few months off when he was approached by a group from a university who were on the verge of signing a term sheet for seed capital if and only if they were able to bring on a competent, experienced CEO. Brian was the mutual choice of the VCs and the professors. He did his due diligence on the people involved and was lured to the company by the prospect of working with them.

But then he had to do due diligence on himself: was he up for leading a new venture? He decided to do it, not for the money, not for the technical challenge, but because he wanted to take what he had learned and see if he could go even further, maybe take the company public (his last venture was bought by a corporation) and establish an independent company that would produce value on its own merits. He also had a desire to mentor the founders. He didn't have that advantage when he broke into the business world from out of the cocoon of a government lab.

In other words, he wanted to engage in a different level of learning and exercise aspects of his life that he felt were not accomplished.

What others don't see, as Brian cycles through these doubts, is that he is also generating parallel questions on another level of his life. He is not only asking whether the market will be ready for this technology his company is producing, or this is a technology that will actually help people and be humane in its application. He is also asking how ready for and worthy and capable of taking responsibility for putting this technology into commercial use are he and his collaborators. He is questioning whether the life he has so far led is really up to the challenges now being placed before him. He is wondering if this endeavor is equal to the values against which he wants to test himself.

The learning we envision here has a quality of being "uprooted," even of suffering. The comfort or complacency in which we live most of our lives is disquieted as the demands of fresh experiences make themselves felt. This happens in the form of experiences that don't map on to our habituated behaviors, or our habits cause us actual harm, delivering a big message about changes we have to make in our lives. Most of us try our best to get to the other side of these unsettling times as fast as we can and get back to our normal lives.

People defuse those electric moments when Moral Learning beckons in different ways. Some become cynical. They sit back and discredit what creative leaders, artists, and reformers are trying to accomplish in order to take some of the suffering, prejudice, and ignorance out of the world, but offer nothing of their own.

Others ignore the feelings, putting them down and out of the way. Their psychic effort is directed at restoring that happy face. "Tomorrow's another day," as Scarlet O'Hara (the Southern belle character in the Civil War drama *Gone with the Wind*) said, might still be their motto. Let's get on with our lives, they say, meaning resuming the same customs and attitudes and routines.

Another strategy channels the feelings into rage and revenge— striking out at the terror of the new and attempting to obliterate the new situation at its root. Alternatively, a person might turn to an encrusted, over-simplified religious dogma or a patriotic symbol and invest these with the feelings that arise. This response serves to both elevate the feeling to a lofty level and disperse it in a fog of abstraction or sentiment.

Creative leaders, however, at some level of their beings, actually relish these stressful times and find ways to thrive on the tensions created by ambiguity. They are enlivened by all the feelings that test and probe the constraints by which we have previously defined our selves. Creative leaders don't see their roles as being that of intellectuals or philosophers who have to justify how they make sense of things in a logically consistent way. Rather they see it as their roles to envision, at some level of wholeness, a concrete, behavioral, organized response or adaptation to the situation that encourages a better life, a more complete sense of goodness, which supplants the old patterns.

MORAL LEARNING AND FEELING ALIVE

Creative leaders choose to stay in the fog and actually renew the dynamic engagement, ambiguity, and uncertainty that mark the calling card of Moral Learning. They exert no energy at all toward "getting back to normal." They keep the possibilities of seeing things in new ways going on and on. They resist settling down into what is finished. They let the inchoate live and have its way. All of this makes a leader like Brian, for instance, hard to take.

And what is even more contrary to the norm, they feel that they need to keep this struggle going. They seek out opportunities to unsettle their worlds and engage in Moral Learning. After all, the new insights are hardly as crystallized or certain as are the old ways of doing things; the new insights have to be proven by being enacted in the real world. These new insights meet with real opposition.

They aren't interested in "trying something." They completely skip over "trying" and get right into "doing." They live that future now and then see the consequences, whatever they are, unfold. The more that the present situation doesn't match up with that possibility, the more galling the present situation is, the more pressing the vision becomes, and the more the leader insists that actions engage the world's *status quo* now and change it. It is a vision, and not a solution, because the situation is a test, the situation itself is being created so that solutions within that vision can be tried out and measured against that vision.

The situations leaders call into question are populated with people who believe in and have a vested interest in the status quo. The leader has to keep the newly generated suspicions about the nascent possibilities (coiled within what seems so solid and sure) alive and vibrant if they are to have a chance to even be tested. And this is no intellectual exercise. Philosophical niceties such as deliberation of validity, justification, or even truth are not foremost on the leader's mind. The leader's whole being engages in this process. The leader's response to Moral Learning is to strike out and replicate, in the larger world, what her whole psyche experiences in these moments.

Brian Thomas, who puts people together around a promising technology and lets them discover the power of the dream it portends, is a prime example of the creative leader's expectations about what follows from the decision. They cannot guarantee an outcome, but they do promise undying dedication to the effort and to those who take up the cause. Actually, the fact that the ultimate details of the dream won't be realized exactly as originally envisioned may be a boon. As Bob Dylan said, "There's no success like failure; and failure's no success at all." With failures, there are lessons to be learned (what could be better); and because it is failure, there is more to do (that's what's better).

The project is vital, alive, and brimming with a sense of possibility, and it will stay that way for quite a while. People get to stay together in that world of energized anticipation; they become better friends and help each other grow and develop. The imagination continues to be called into play as adaptation needs to take place; the moral learning is extended and enriched through the sequence of unexpected delays and obstacles. They have to regroup and create new ideas and alternatives that make more sense, all the while keeping the dream alive. What could be better?

This makes creative leaders seem odd to many of us, and maybe a little intimidating or scary. They certainly are not people we would think of first when wanting to have a quiet, relaxing, conformity-confirming evening of relaxation. Some may seem self-absorbed, remote, and inconsistent. They stir things up, raise troubling issues and may even seem oblivious to the fact that others may not want to talk about these things. Brian Thomas's employees often feel that way about him. But to think that leaders are rocks of consistency and leaden certainty is to miss the point: creative leaders aren't settled and sure; they are testing and exploring just what it is that is true, meaningful, and just plain "good" for them and others. It is a struggle, and that means these leaders don't come across as stereotypically "heroic" John Wayne types who, with guns blazing and egos blustering, find affirmation of their own certainties.[3]

---

[3] Of course creative leaders aren't the only ones who respond to Moral Learning in this "inverted" way. People who adopt the other transformist roles also consciously dwell in this realm of moral learning. Mystics such as Meister Eckhart or the Zen Master Dogen, or Thomas Merton engage in Moral Learning by linking the experience of disruption with high order symbols that grasp the transcendent dimensions of both the eternal and the change in the engagement with our world. Poets such as Emily Dickinson, T. S. Eliot, or Sylvia Plath, choose this arduous path as well. They and other artists—from Picasso to Copeland to Rodin to Gehry—integrate these feelings with other mental or motor skills to produce poetry, paintings, sculpture, music, literature, drama, architecture, that accompany us in the otherwise lonely experience of moral learning. Prophets and teachers such as Michael Moore, Martha Nussbaum, Joseph Campbell, or Einstein speak out in order to make the new integration of our world an undeniable imperative that we ignore at our own peril, so that we have to face it with honesty and integrity, or turn away from it in some mode of shame or self-justified prejudice.

THE INVERTED PSYCHIC PROCESSES
OF CREATIVE LEADERS

That quality of greatness with which we began our discussion depends on the extent to which the leader engages in Moral Learning. I find it interesting that some people that are creative leaders within a corporate setting are rigidly conservative of the status quo on the level of politics and society. Many former military officers that make a transition into business act this way. I understand it as a response to the fright and disruption of Moral Learning. In order to be open, generous, and flexible in terms of the internal organization, this person draws a hard perimeter around it, insisting on certainty and rectitude outside that messy perimeter. Others, however, are able to accommodate much wider ranges of flux and change and are often anxious to participate in the changes that are taking place in these wider arenas as well. Then there are the Lincolns, Mandelas, and Martin Luther Kings of the world, who can embrace the challenges of whole societies. Finally, there is Jesus of Nazareth and the Buddha, and Gandhi, who placed no bounds on the Moral Learning they took on.

Creative leaders take on the widest possible challenges to the fullest extent that they can endure (emotionally, experientially, financially), in whatever domain they have chosen as their life path. No matter what their sphere of activity, whether it be a corporation, a start-up, a small nonprofit service organization, they integrate their energy for change with the state of the world, with the social, institutional historical and ecological relationships in which we have lived and use their feelings as an impetus to change them. And, despite the obstacles, discouragements, and failures along the way, they keep the feeling alive, in front of them as a vital possibility that is worth a life's devotion.

It is the ability to translate the experience of Moral Learning into an effective organizational response, which gives us the leaders we call great. We feel them opening up their lives and thought patterns to new possibility, even as they give shape, direction, and focus to their organizations. And so, as their followers, we feel that we have a way to contribute to realizing that vision. We participate not only in the processes that give structure to the actions of great organizations, but we help shape the learning experiences that everyone, the leader included, gain from the endeavor's work.

To the follower entering the arch of the creative leader, the ambiguities of the endeavor, even the vacillations of the leader, are not an impediment to participation. These soft edges and hazy horizons engendered by Moral Learning offer an invitation to nothing less than feeling alive. The hours may be long, the conversations infuriating, the results disappointing, but both leaders and followers might say, "This thing is ours to make happen or not, make great or not. Let's turn it into gold. Let's do alchemy."

CHAPTER EIGHT

Moral Imagination

WHAT IS HAPPENING WITH METAPHOR?

WELL, EVERYTHING: THERE IS NOTHING

THAT DOES NOT HAPPEN WITH METAPHOR

AND BY METAPHOR. ANY STATEMENT CONCERNING

ANYTHING THAT HAPPENS, METAPHOR INCLUDED,

WILL BE PRODUCED NOT WITHOUT METAPHOR . . .

AND WHAT GETS ALONG WITHOUT METAPHOR?

NOTHING, THEREFORE . . .

—*JACQUES DERRIDA*[1]

[1] Wolfreys, "The Retrait of Metaphor," *The Derrida Reader,* Writing Performances (Lincoln, NE, 1998), p. 103.

While Moral Learning is often an uprooting and disquieting experience, it need not be one of despair. We put ourselves on the road to despair in many ways: when we assume a defensive posture; when we feel guilty that our values have fallen short; when we discover we don't have the strength or the courage to accomplish something; or when we realize we have abandoned something or someone and tell ourselves it was their fault. All of these realizations bring us down, raise our anger, then laden us with feelings of sadness and loss. But these feelings, in creative leaders, spark a different resource and bring a different kind of experience to the fore. And that resource, that experience, we call, *Moral Imagination*.

THIRD ARCH, SECOND SPIRE

Moral Imagination develops the spire of the Active Self. It goes to the source of Practical Insight described as the first arch and deepens our understanding for how the Mission in the second arch could be conceived at all. In this, the Arch of the Leader's Ethic, the creative leader sees far beyond the immediate situation to appreciate subtle but powerful connections to larger worlds. The leader *imagines* how these larger worlds can be affected by the endeavor's efforts.

DEFINING MORAL IMAGINATION

Moral Imagination is that dimension of our lives in which we gain insight into our values and our world in such a way as to stimulate change in both. I engage my Moral Imagination in order to see how I can expand my sense of participation in and contribution to the world; and I engage Moral Imagination to see the world as a place that is amenable to relations, practices, and institutions that make life better on this planet, to picture what my role in that effort will be. Moral Imagination is the means by which we turn the lessons of Moral Learning into concrete realizations we can then act on.

This may sound like an imposing experience, piling on too much of a load for the ordinary mortal leader—even a creative leader—to bear. For most of us, this experience is indeed way too much to take. We want things to fit neatly within the worlds we know, the worlds within which our expertise has status and merit, and in which we have carved out our comfortable niches. But I have worked with scores of people who, in parts of their lives at least, do take this path to Moral Learning and Moral Imagination. Howard, Harry, Brian, and the others I mention in this account have done so at least in their professional or recreational or volunteer roles, in activities in which they have taken on creative leading. Our task is to see how, while imposing, engaging in Moral Learning and Moral Imagination is neither impossible nor untenable as a life choice. Just as we saw that Moral Learning was a natural process of which living things, even humans, are capable of, so too can we demystify Moral Imagination and make it a more accessible tool for those who are on the way to or are already engaged in creative leading.

The work being done in self-organization, once again, points the way. In this case, the term "Moral Imagination," and much of its description and analysis, was used by Mark Johnson (who wrote a book with that title) and his colleague, George Lakoff. Adapting their work, we can see creative leaders as being people who revel in the opportunities to excite Moral Imagination. When this psychical resource is called into play, a situation takes on dimensions of play, excitement, possibility, and offers the creative leader chances to express choice, exercise decision, and engage in collaborative actions that bring about new opportunities. Using their Moral Imaginations, creative leaders (as well as mystics, artists, and prophets) defy the habits of despair and take the road less traveled.

The keys that unlock this kingdom are the ones that lie right before our eyes, are inexhaustible in their productivity and are unrestricted by any limitation to access except for the limitations we impose on ourselves. The keys that ignite Moral Imagination are *metaphors*.

SPONTANEOUS CREATIVITY: METAPHORS

"Metaphors?" you say. "We are talking about something as important as leading people in difficult situations or changing worlds, and you want to talk about mere words?"

Yes, I do.

Remember learning about grammar back in grade school? There were nouns and verbs and adjectives, etc. But then there were these elements we were instructed to use in order to color a scene in an essay, or to make a joke, or to evoke emotion. They made writing or speaking come alive. These elements, of course, were metaphors. They were effective in making our essays on "What We Did Last Summer" at least a bit more interesting because they evoked definite feelings, vivid images, or whole complexes of thoughts and stories, by pointing to common experiences we easily recognized. They offered a word, phrase, image, or symbol that situated a general idea or new idea within concrete and familiar terrain that we comprehended and felt.

The connotation of the word "metaphor" itself infers this connection between feeling and moving to new terrain. According to *Webster's New World Dictionary*, "meta" means between, and "phor" comes from the Greek, meaning "to bear." Thus, a metaphor "bears" something from one place to another. In the idea of "bearing," we envision whatever is being carried as having weight.

It, at least, has enough substance so that its mass imposes a burden. So the metaphor, as a "bearing between," is something that commands notice; it demands a behavioral response from us. It is a use of speech and writing that intends to be itself an experience of note. The metaphor, in other words, is not psychically trivial, merely flitting between utterances. It signifies a kind of experience in which we are bearing something of value to somewhere else, applying its weight and significance to another new destination.

THE METAPHORICAL MIND

Metaphors originate in our physical actions and gestures. When we climb a mountain or swim a mile, we create metaphors: we engage in direct kinesthetic interactions with the world that we can later use to make our more abstract and mental ideas take on qualities we can actually feel—as though this mentally stressful event were a simpler, more direct physical exertion. When we hear a melody, feelings are being elaborated and extended into pure sounds and rhythms. All of these experiences at some time or other serve us as metaphors for other experiences. By means of metaphors, we bear ourselves into a future in such a way that we can test that future against the patterned comprehensions of our known, familiar, more sensual experiences.

Metaphors perform heavy psychic lifting. In metaphors we compress large, difficult experiences into bite-sized images. We create smaller, bite-sized experiences that mirror back to us the state of mind we are in at the time as we undergo the challenges of the larger experience. We use physical metaphors, like climbing mountains or swimming in oceans, or playing golf, for instance, to act as analogues for long-duration, stressful, and uncertain ventures we undertake in the transforming endeavors scoped out by creative leaders.

These metaphors turn our ambiguous, open-ended experiences into things that we immediately relate to, that we have feelings about and take action on (or they express the experience of not being able to do these things). Metaphors permeate all aspects and dimensions of our lives. They are automatic and reflexive. They are done without any mental processing or thinking at all. We can then use these compressed, single-screen images to arrive at necessary assessments about the complex situations in which we find ourselves from moment to moment. The most primary, most readily available metaphors are us: ourselves—what we do; what we look like to each other; what we, in our actions, convey of our grasp of our lives—thus the allure of plays, movies, sporting events (how often do we use sports metaphors and analogies to explain ourselves). Every moment of the day we generate metaphors, translating abstract ideas into something we can see, taste, touch.

Here I think of something I have noticed about Harry Kaufman as I have followed him through four assignments. He always is hired to turn around distressed companies, and he always has had to move to a new locale when he took on a new assignment. So, as we envision his concrete circumstances, he is subjected to upheaval wherever he goes. And, since he is a creative leader, he does not scramble to get everything back into a comfortable order and routine. The directors hire him to stir their company up, to induce change and discomfort, break habits and patterns, and tear down old walls of bureaucratic and hierarchic sclerosis, and that's what he does, usually with a high degree of success.

When he arrives on the scene, not only does Harry do what he has been hired to do, churn up the company; since he is a creative leader, he also churns up his own life. He doesn't stop at just moving to a new place. That is not enough. That would only be a metaphor for the decision to make a commitment to the effort. He also creates a metaphor for the work he is doing once he is on the scene and is fully engaged. He renovates his new homes. In every new place in which Harry has accepted a new assignment, he has either built a house from scratch or has bought a condominium, gutted it, and rebuilt it to his and his wife's specifications.

In doing this, I believe he creates around himself a manageable, directed, more constrained image, metaphor, for the big, unpredictable, collaborative, potentially chaotic situation into which his work has transported him.

I am not sure that Harry agrees with this depiction of his propensity for renovation. He thinks it is just natural to do that kind of thing when you move to a new place. But even this response, I believe, supports my contention that we create metaphors so naturally, they are completely transparent to our conscious minds—we just don't give the whole process a second thought. We don't even realize we are creating metaphors in order to help us make sense of the large-scale endeavors we engage in.

How often do we take an abstract idea and express it in a linguistic metaphor that makes the experience more immediate, physical, and concrete bodily? Many complex, abstract mathematical ideas boil down to simple metaphors that express things we can see around us every day: equivalence or dependence or a chain of linked events, amount of greater or lesser, etc. What other abstract ideas do we have that depend on metaphors to be meaningful?

METAPHORS IN ACTION

Think about the idea of time for instance. What could be more abstract than the idea of time? So, we make time into something else. How often do we say things like, "Time flies," so, it's a bird; or "Time is dragging," now, it's a lead weight; or "time passes," so now it's like a train moving down the tracks. These metaphors make our concrete experience of time palpably clear and compelling to ourselves and to others.

Time is an especially an important category for leaders whose energies are devoted to actually "drive" (a metaphor) the pace and experience of time by fostering changes that are desired instead of changes that "happen" in the "natural" course of events. In the case of experiencing time, there are (at least) three very important connotations to the metaphor. We make time into a possession, a cause of our feeling, and an area of space.

For instance, think about the metaphor, "having time." Here, time is viewed as a possession. In this metaphor, that object, time, is something, like a piece of property, that we "have" and which we can use in any way we wish. We envision that by possessing time, we have control over it. We perform actions that make us the masters of its moving, by shaping its direction, pace and its contents – the experiences others have in that span of time. It is a possession with which we do as we please. We all, therefore, want to "have" time. And when we don't, which is most of the time, we feel much less content or in control; or, when we "have" too much time on our hands, we also feel our control diminished – because, for some reason, there is nothing we can do with this time. It is like a farmer owning land that is filled with rocks – it's useless for his purposes.

Another way we create metaphors around time is to express how we feel in the process of living in time. When we say, "time is short," for instance, we are saying we feel some level of intensity about the experience. In this case, time is moving so fast that it seems "short," there is not much of it, there is little of it to grasp, it is closing in on us, it won't be in front of us for long. The metaphor carries with it a strong relationship in which we clearly depict ourselves in an anxious state vis a vis time.

The comedian Jerry Seinfeld makes clear that our use of metaphors of space in describing our relationship to time is strictly limited however. These are his thoughts about time metaphors: You can measure distance by time.
"How far away is that place?"
"About 20 minutes." But it doesn't work the other way.
"When do you get off work?"
"Around 3 miles." [2]

[2] Seinfeld (New York, 1998), p. 77.

METAPHORS OF PROSPECT

We can see how commonly we use metaphors to make sense of the large events and ideas that sprawl out before us and elude our grasp. But another level of using metaphor ties in directly with how creative leaders engage in the process of Moral Learning. These are what I call the "metaphors of prospect." They are metaphors that not only link our present experiences to the trove of metaphors from past experiences, but also link them to the futures we create for ourselves.

HOW WE FEEL ABOUT THE FUTURE

We use metaphors to envision our future all the time. Metaphors, in fact, are the primary way we do that. We use metaphors to talk about the feelings we have about the future. We say that something will happen "come hell or high water" when we are determined to make it happen; or when we are discouraged by the lack of possibilities when we say that something is as likely to happen as "a snowball in hell." Or we use them to predict an event that happens regularly, "like clockwork." Using metaphors we make plans and give structure to our actions as we move from day to day and prepare ourselves for an event to unfold actually as predicted, or not.

To leaders, these imagined futures portend more than the bare-bones possibility of something occurring. As we said above, the leader's vision begins with the experience of a disruption of the leader's sense of values, a discordance between how the world works at its best, versus what the leader sees occurring on the ground, in the present. We all feel discordances between the way the world is and the way our values would have it be. But leaders apply their cognitive, metaphor-creating abilities, in a particular way. The issue for the leader is not only "What is happening?" but "What difference can I make?" and "Am I the one to take this on?"

If creative leaders are thinking about a situation, they intend to change it. And creative leaders do not think about the situation abstractly, in terms of a game, as so many numbers, statistics, logistics, and pawns to be manipulated. The situation is taken personally, as a part of how the leader is living now. Not only do leaders use their cognitive ability for analysis, as intellectuals do, not only do they take the experience as a trigger for expression in various artistic forms, or as lessons to propagate through their teachings, they feel these occasions as personally transforming. They use these occasions to spur a vision of concretely different futures. Leaders relish these moments because in these times their creative energies flow, fully engaging them in what is possible and what they, with others, can do to bring it about.

CHANGING OURSELVES

Moral Imagination and its metaphorical methodology cuts two ways. As the leader is charting out a path for the endeavor that affects others, she is also, at the same time, shaping, challenging, and so charting a course of change for herself. Again, metaphors become the tool of choice.

Our work as mentors centers on this dimension of the leader's self-understanding. In our conversations, we probe our client's comprehensions of what is happening and listen carefully to the metaphors they use. We listen for the images they use to describe themselves in an endeavor or as part of the team. The metaphor is never right or wrong, but it tells us so much about how the person will respond and/or lead. Particularly fruitful are how feelings in a situation that concerns them evoke memories. These constitute vital metaphors we hold up as mirrors to our clients. Below I offer a couple of examples.

Recall Beth's experience, recounted in the introduction to part 2, of how, as a little girl of four, she was frustrated at being underestimated and underappreciated by an old-world, tyrannical, male-chauvinist grandfather. On this one day, when he chided Beth once too often about her predetermined gender-based limitations, she was wearing her favorite dress, made by her mother. All she remembers is the feeling of anger at that moment and that her response was to neither cry nor flee the scene, but to stand there and tear her dress—her favorite dress, made just for her by her mother. As a metaphor, the scene evokes feeling so defiant, of tearing off impediments—even alluring and cherished ones—in order to steel herself for a challenge.

Beth's career path fits the metaphor: she was determined not to let any of her past accomplishments, titles, positions, expectations stand in the way of taking on new challenges and learning. She saw herself as a person of courage and action as she imagined and summoned the emotions and bravery of that little girl standing up to her tyrannical grandfather. Her metaphor of tearing that dress laid out what became her leadership brand: never give in to artificial or self-created barriers.

Another recent client told me that her goal for personal growth was to be "bigger" in her role as a financial VP. "Bigger" was a metaphor that meant believing in herself more and being more outspoken among her peers. As she talked more, she recalled how her role in the family was to be the "good girl," the quiet one, sitting at the end of the table, while her sister acted out all her emotions, raised the ire or excitement, certainly commanded the attention of others at the table. She was the quiet one who didn't rock the boat.

I asked her how she felt in those times. "Ignored, alone, I didn't matter much," she answered.

"What was your response to those feelings?" I asked.

"I developed my own world, one that I was quite happy to be in, all by myself," she said.

"So do you want to be 'big' in meetings like your sister was at the dinner table?" I asked.

"No, that's not it. People that have coached me in the past just said that I should play 'bigger,' and it sounded good to me at the time."

"Well, what would you want for that little girl who is feeling alone and spinning off into her own world?"

"To feel connected, to feel that she mattered."

"So the metaphor is one of connecting, of being part of a two-way flow, of being recognized as a part of that flow?" I asked.

"More than I want to feel part of something, and be an important part."

So there we hit on a more appropriate metaphor. The right metaphor of prospect for her meant setting a completely different course. Instead of merely asserting herself more, she was going to take responsibility for creating a flow in a group that included her. She was going to think about how to embrace others' thoughts and concerns and then find a way to offer them something that would matter to them in pursuing their objectives. The metaphor was not one of just being "bigger"; it was one of embracing and engaging actively, openly, and expressing her vision.

By evoking important metaphors or by helping people to get to one that rings true to the fullest extent possible, these creative leaders can take initiative for their own development. They can think not about a list of traits that they have to exhibit, but rather about a scene, a picture that they either want to reenact or change in the context of the new situation. Their Moral Learning is their own because they tap their own metaphors as illuminated by their own, now activated Moral Imaginations.

METAPHORS OF ACTION: "SOURCE-PATH-GOAL"

When we are using metaphors to describe the actions that we are geared up to take, they take the form of what Johnson calls "Source—Path—Goal" metaphors. These are particularly useful for leaders, so we will pause and look at them in some detail.

The "Source" for creative leaders is their set of values, prodded into active prominence by the frustration and anger they experienced when confronting a reality that clashed with those values. The felt misfit between cherished values and a reality that falls short or even offends them acts as an impetus, an uprooting, that presents them with choices of response. The "Path" begins with the decision to lead and encompasses all the actions that endeavor entails. For the creative leader, the path takes the form of the vision.

The "Goal" for the creative leader does not reside in any list of operational objectives or quantifiable results. These managerial milestones serve to mark progress and to denote places and times when adjustments in the vision and/or strategy need to be made. But the leader's ultimate goal far exceeds those singular achievements or failures. A creative leader's goal encompasses the whole situation, the entire state of affairs and quality of life.

The creative leader's Source—Path—Goal schema weaves together all the pertinent metaphors that the leader is able to evoke in the moment of envisioning. The future, depicted in the vision, elaborated and activated in the leader's "Brand Speech," is heard by others as being world's real possibilities that can actually come about precisely because the metaphors ring true. The fact that the leader feels so impassioned, so alive as the vision is detailed and articulated, impels the whole endeavor forward. Others get the bug; they feel the same excitement. A new endeavor is born.

Think of the great "visions" that have sustained us and nurtured us through the ages. Jesus spoke of teaching people to fish rather than giving them fish—a concrete image that makes the idea of "educating" people or giving them "added capability," power and simplicity. Or, "I have been to the mountain top." In this image, we can all grasp how Martin Luther King Jr. struggled to gain clarity about our situation and then saw it, at last, from the highest vantage point, and saw it whole. All of this was said in a few words with which we all can unlock the power of the vision in ourselves.

The compelling vision comes alive in our forward-looking psyches, in our Source—Path—Goal metaphor schemes. The more compelling the metaphors, the richer are the connections. And the richer the metaphor, the more possibilities are opened to decisions that offer real change and possibility for the participants. The metaphors need not be grand or grandiose. "Teaching them to fish" is not a metaphor of great flourish, but it is so real, so accessible, so basic a skill, that it resonates with possibility for learning, teaching, helping, and growth of the spirit.

We portray situations, delineate character, formulate problems, and mold events. When we act, we engage in various forms of creative imagining: we compose situations, build relationships, harmonize diverse interests, balance competing values and goods, design institutional practices, and orchestrate interpersonal relations.

EMBODIED FUTURES

A metaphorical rendering of an endeavor's path into the future distinguishes the vision from the strategic plan. Metaphors differ from abstract, disembodied thoughts precisely in their ability to move the mind, heart, and soul of a person from out of the merely conceivable and interesting into the specific and potentially real. Creative leaders use metaphors to bridge this gap by:

➤ *Using them to define the whole that the endeavor addresses (see chapter 6): Is this a vision that includes a few, the community, the world?*

➤ *Demonstrating the vision's importance: If we do this, what do we gain; if we do not do it, what have we lost?*

➤ *Dissolving absolutes and showing relationships—constraining, equalizing, and/or liberating.*

➤ *Identifying the place, locale, level at which change can happen: Does this depend on us, or do we have to engage more? Who or what institution is this a concern for?*

➤ *Linking the vision to other familiar, institutionalized and habituated actions and ideas: Are we espousing liberal or conservative ideals, or principles tantamount to defining our humanity?*

➤ *Depicting how actions are connected in linear chains of events, or expanding concentric circles, or cascading chain reactions.*

➤ *Revealing what had been hidden, or hiding what is best left unsaid.*

Over time, these metaphors (reinforced by repetition and/or social convention) crystallize into beliefs and then into abstract, philosophical, or mathematical concepts. But these concepts and beliefs come later. We don't immediately quantify our experiences or conceptualize them. We don't immediately analyze them down into constituent parts or discrete perceptions. For creative leaders, metaphors act as markers at which people gather to chart, together, their next foray into the unknown.

CHAPTER NINE

Decision: Dialogue and Narrative

[The following is an excerpt from a commentary about Aaron Feuerstein, owner of Malden Mills. After his factory burned down in late 1995, Feuerstein kept all his employees on the payroll as the factory was.]

IN FACT, IT SEEMS PRETTY CLEAR THAT

SOME PEOPLE CALL FEUERSTEIN A SAINT

BECAUSE THEY DON'T QUITE HAVE THE

COURAGE TO CALL HIM A FOOL . . .

. . . CUSTOMER RETENTION AT MALDEN MILLS

RUNS ROUGHLY 95%, WHICH IS WORLD CLASS.

EMPLOYEE RETENTION RUNS ABOUT 95%,

WHICH IS PRODIGIOUS . . . AS FOR PRODUCTIVITY,

FROM 1982 TO 1995, REVENUES IN CONSTANT

DOLLARS MORE THAN TRIPLED WHILE THE WORK

FORCE BARELY DOUBLED. COMPARE THAT WITH AN

OVERALL PRODUCTIVITY INCREASE FOR THE U.S.

OF A LITTLE BETTER THAN 1% PER YEAR.

—THOMAS TEAL[1]

[1] *Fortune* (November 11, 1996).

Surveying the components of the third arch, the Arch of the Leader's Ethic, we turn our attention to the spire representing the Social Self. The Decision extends the import of what were the People Skills in the Effectiveness Arch and Culture in the Vision and Organization Arch. Decision includes the leaders' actions that bring the organization to a point of taking one path rather than another, or taking no action at all.

A musician performs his art by taking the stage and playing an instrument. Leaders perform by making decisions. These decisions create contexts (symbolized by the space within the arch) in which actions, aspirations, and great emotional energies converge, forming a collaboration. As the musician's performance transforms hearing how a piece of music should sound into an experience for the audience, the creative leader's decision transforms values, practical insights, people skills, vision, and organizational skills into distinctive experiences for all those who enter the endeavor.

Leaders make all kinds of decisions: They make decisions to take us to the mountain top in order to find a whole new way of living; they make decisions on the spot to determine which road to take, which person to hire and fire. And they make these decisions for themselves and for others. We can't look at all of the myriad kinds of decisions that leaders make.[2]

In this chapter, we consider creative leaders' decisions that envision new directions and options: a new product for a company, a new direction for a service, a new vision about how a community can grow

---

[2] So, for example, we aren't looking at the instantaneous responses that firefighters or tactical commanders or even line managers make in the face of imminent, changing circumstances. These are the kinds of momentary, on the spot, on-demand decisions that seek optimal results and outcomes out of the given circumstances—and these circumstances are often very dire. Often those decisions are crucial, determining the life-or-death initiatives, organizations, and, in the most extreme cases, individual lives (human and other lives). But for all their criticality, we will not focus on these kinds of decisions here. I do recommend that readers turn to Gary Klein's *Sources of Power* for a detailed discussion of decisions made under duress.

and thrive in a sustainable way. These decisions, while often made quickly and sometimes in the heat of the moment (as our example will show), emanate from sources deep in the psyches of these leaders. They may be made in response to immediate circumstances, but they reflect experiences, attitudes, and values that reach back into the long histories of these people's lives.

As we said in our discussion of the leader's vision, the leader's values spur the demand for a new possibility, and the felt need to engage in an effort to change things and, in so doing, to take whatever risks are involved. So the kinds of decisions we consider here envision no single goal, objective, or outcome frames "success." Creative leaders define success in much more fluid but personally more demanding ways. The decisions are judged on the level and quality of Moral Learning that can be brought to bear, moment by moment by the endeavor, and the quality of the Moral Imagination that the situation demands if the leader and all others involved in the endeavor are to succeed.

To illustrate, I will use as an example an actual decision that was made by a seasoned, experienced, and unexpectedly daring business leader, Aaron Feuerstein, the seventy-two-ycar-old (at the time) owner of Malden Mills, in Lawrence, Massachusetts. On December 11, 1995, the factory that had been in his family for ninety years burned to the ground. While rebuilding and modernizing the factory, he paid all his employees their full salary and benefits. In so doing, we glimpse not only a vividly creative decision in the making, but we also see how Moral Imagination and Moral Learning are brought into play.

I feel compelled, for some reason, to use the historically true and widely publicized decision made by this gentleman who is cited in the epigraph at the beginning of this chapter. I have to admit, this decision had a big impact on my thinking. I was living in Massachusetts at the time, and the story was front-page news for days. The decision was startling in its boldness and its unconventionality. It struck me as a decision none of my clients—even the ones I held in greatest esteem— would have made. And I found myself, asking over and over again how it could have been made at all.

As the epigram makes clear, Feuerstein was not universally lauded for the decision. How could he be? His decision flew in the face of every hard-headed, by the numbers, rational teaching that our business executives receive about how to do business. In these circles, this was not a business decision; it was a humanitarian one, or a charitable one, or the decision made by an old fool who should have known better. Those who consider Feuerstein a fool do not appreciate the historical context in which the fire happened. Nor do they have appreciation for how Moral Imagination can lead one to new realms of decision making.

BACKGROUND

The Malden Mills factory has been located in the town of Lawrence, Massachusetts, since its founding by Feuerstein's grandfather in 1906. It manufactures the patented material, Polartec, used to line cold-weather clothing marketed by many well-known clothiers and outfitters.

By any standards, Lawrence can be described as an economically depressed city. Lawrence began its modern history as a typical nineteenth-century textile mill town that exploited cheap labor— including that of women and children. In 1912, Lawrence workers staged the famous Bread and Roses strike in which scores of people were arrested and hurt, and several were killed by clashes with police. Thus a crucial part of the town's tortured history recalls how Lawrence's factory owners (possibly including Feuerstein's grandfather) were once known for their harsh treatment of workers. Today Lawrence suffers in poverty, with no end in sight.

The 1995 fire completely destroyed the Malden Mills factory. Feuerstein faced nothing less than a moral dilemma in deciding what to do. He had every business option open to him: He could have closed the factory and relocated it to a place where wages are lower; he could have taken the insurance money and run; he could have rebuilt the factory and reopened in Lawrence; he could have temporarily laid off the workers and let them draw unemployment. Those are all completely reasonable business decisions, justifiable according to any number of managerial criteria: cost/benefit, pragmatic analysis, good business sense, etc. or any combination of them. But he did none of these. Instead, he decided to continue paying his 1,300 employees full wages and health benefits while the rebuilding went on. This effort cost him $1.5 million. Not a paltry sum.

Some commentators have accused him of risking the very survival of his business with a lot of grandstanding magnanimity that served no purpose but self-advertisement. There's a suggestion that real businessmen, responsible owners, would never pay any employee a dime more than they had to, and that no factory owner could possibly have done what Feuerstein did unless he was touched by God—or just touched, period. One business school professor has pointedly instructed his students not to look to Aaron Feuerstein as a model for business decision making. He may be right.

Indeed, as of this writing, Malden Mills is emerging out of bankruptcy.[3] I am sure Feuerstein has heard all the "I told you so's" he can stand to hear. However, he maintains, in the press anyway, that it

[3] In a press release dated June 3, 2002, Malden Mills announced that it was outsourcing some of its production to mills in China in order to cut expenses and enable it to emerge from bankruptcy. While no current domestic jobs are being affected, this is hardly the decision an idealistic fool would make.

was not the decision about retaining employees that forced him into bankruptcy in the first place, but rather his decision to rebuild the factory as a completely state-of-the-art facility. Maybe Feuerstein decided that since he needed to modernize (in order to keep the factory in the United States and remain competitive), he would spread out the cost of doing so to some employees (that he did have to terminate), but also vendors, suppliers, and even customers would bear some of the burden, in the form of having to take terms consistent with a bankruptcy settlement. Maybe this was just an unforeseen result or maybe it was intentional. Maybe his family's involvement in the 1912 strike figured into his decision. In contrast to the way his own ancestors treated their workers in 1912, no employee of Malden Mills in 1995 would go to bed anxious about their livelihoods and the well-being of their families. Maybe he was a fool, or maybe he was a fool like a fox. We'll never know.

So still, we are left with lots of questions: What drove him to that decision? Some kind of moral obligation? Foresight that envisioned bankruptcy from the beginning? Impulse? And is this really a decision worthy of what we are calling creative leading? Was this decision based on moral imagination and does it reflect moral learning? Or, why isn't this just tomfoolery as the conventional wisdom maintains?

IMAGINING THE DECISION

To probe these questions, I have crafted an imaginary dialogue. It takes place between Mr. Feuerstein and his chief operating officer (COO), the executive in charge of the business's productivity and efficiency. Other dialogues are implied, but are not depicted. To make our points, we have added, in italics, accounts of the psychic processing that underlies the words we attribute to the characters. By means of these commentaries, we intend to contrast the kind of Moral Imagination that Mr. Feuerstein applied to the principle-based "reasoning" used by the COO, representing the conventional business wisdom. We then will follow this little skit with further commentary that illuminates the quality and progression of the creative leader's decision-making process.

> *Early in the morning hours, the telephone rings in Aaron Feuerstein's bedroom, rousing him and his wife from their sleep. It is his chief operating officer, the number two person in the company, calling.*

COO: Mr. Feuerstein, sir, sorry to wake you, but I have to inform you that there's a horrible tragedy going on. The factory is on fire. They say they can't control it and won't be able to save the factory. We're facing a total loss.

AF: Anyone hurt?

COO: No, sir.

AF: Where are you now?

COO: I'm calling from my car, sir. I thought I'd better get going and get down there right away, as soon as I got the call from the fire department. I'll be at the factory in about ten minutes.

AF: Well, I'm on my way too.

COO: Yes. I think that's best. The press will be there in force, I am sure. We do have to consider what to do from here. What will we tell the workers? The media? I hate to press you, sir, but I think we should consider some options. Metaphor: It's war out there, and we've got to control the field.

AF: Of course. I agree. I'll get there as soon as I can.

COO: Great, sir. I'll see you there.

> *As AF dresses, he tells his wife what happened. They don't say much, but as he leaves, AF and his wife exchange a knowing glance. "You'll know what to do," her expression seems to say.*

216

As he drives to the scene, many images, feelings, recollections cascade through his mind. He remembers stories from his grandfather about the horrible days of the Bread and Roses strike. He remembers how, as a boy, he made a vow that if he owned the factory he wouldn't behave that way. His feelings are racing with scenes of the factory in ruins, workers anxious. The family legacy hangs on a perilous precipice.

AF arrives at a chaotic scene: one of fire, fire fighters and their equipment—noisy diesel-powered trucks, ladders, hoses; lights—bright white, flashing yellow, red, blue; the media and all its gear—cameras, lights of their own, cords and recorders; pungent and acidic smells in the low-hanging smoke plus scores of the company's employees milling around. AF is cool, affably working his way through the crowds and anxious workers. "We're sorry, sir," they say. "Don't worry," he tells his employees. "We trust you, sir," some reply. The reporters swarm him for a statement. He asks for their patience as he extricates himself from the media that is mobbing him to find the COO. They make their way to AF's car, climb inside, and have this conversation:

AF: I'm ready. What are the options?

Dialogue is opened. Remember, however, many parts of the dialogue have already gone on in his head and, although mostly in silence, with his wife. He is now asking the COO to give him some options he can measure and weigh rationally, along with the other things on his mind.

COO: Well, sir, the first is to shutter the company and collect the insurance.

Principle: Cost/benefit in the face of continuing risk, take the secure money.

217

AF: Well, yes, and why would I do that?

    Metaphor of his life, at its end, as a monument to futility, collides with embodying a value of life as an ongoing effort, and sometimes a struggle with pain and adversity.

COO: Well, sir, you aren't getting any younger, and business is risky. Why not give your family security now while you can enjoy it?

    Utilitarianism for the family: most benefit to them.

AF: That's an option.

    Images collide—one image: he is old, a withering tree; another image: he is a vibrant and productive animal fulfilling its role.

    But what if I'm not ready to hang it up yet?

    An image of his family's security collides with an image of his workers' pain.

COO: I see how you feel, and I don't think anyone would want you to retire either, sir. But what about moving the factory to Mexico and capitalize on the cheap labor there?

    Feeling anxious because he clearly hasn't hit the mark, he looks for another principle. Try another cost/benefit approach.

AF: That's a possibility.

    A negative feeling stirs as an image of the factory as a money machine that just processes people and things to produce profits collides with images of all the people and families he has come to know in the factory.

So I should do this to make more money?

    A memory of the Bread and Roses strike and how badly his industry, including his grandfather, treated employees comes to mind. He remembers his vow that he would have behave differently if given the chance.

What about the workers who have been so loyal to us? Remember that in the last three years, we have tripled our production and profits and because of their efforts have only had to double the workforce. Can we do that in Mexico?

COO: Well, I don't know, sir.

Anxious because he knows he still is missing something. What is it? But look how well our competitors are doing in Mexico and Asia.

Principle: Pragmatism. But then I suppose you have a duty to the community as well.

Principle: Duty.

AF: How much better would we do abroad? How loyal would these people be to us, to our family, to our community?

Metaphor: Family. Are we going to forget what these employees of ours have done for us?

Metaphor: Life is reciprocity.

COO: Well, sir, it sounds like you have made up your mind. You are going to rebuild. So will we furlough the workers and allow them to collect unemployment?

Principle: Cost/benefit. Save as much money as possible. Minimize the expense while revenues are down.

A clue. Ah-hah. The "family business" model. We MBAs know what a knotty mess that kind of thing can be. Go slow here.

AF: We could do that.

Image of business as a means to generate personal wealth through others' labors collides with business as a means to collaborate and create incomes and wealth for all involved. What if we paid them their full salaries and benefits while we rebuilt. What would that cost us?

COO: *(Startled. Shocked, actually.)* Sir? That would cost millions.

AF: Probably about $1.5 million. How much profit have we made this year?

COO: Probably about twice that.

AF: That's profit, right? That these people made that profit possible, right?

Using his own cost/benefit principle:

If we put people on unemployment and we lost, say, half of them, how much would it cost to hire and retrain the new people? How sure would we be that they would be as productive as our current people are? How long would it take us to get fully up to speed? How much would all that cost?

COO: Well, I don't know, sir?

AF: But we'd be up and running in no time if everyone stayed on, wouldn't we? And we'd eliminate unnecessary turnover for the near term at least, wouldn't we? And think of the publicity we'd get. How about that cost/benefit analysis?

An image of happy workers. A feeling of solidarity of analysis and of continuity with a vow kept. A feeling of resolution of all the salient and important factors plants deep roots and gives a sense of resolve.

COO: Well, sir, I guess your mind's made up. Should I prepare the announcement?

AF: No, I'll do it myself. Summon the media and our employees over here. Put the employees on the inside of the circle, and have the media on the periphery. I'm ready to go.

COO: Yes, sir.

Feeling completely overwhelmed by a whole new concept of labor relations, for which he has only his first image and experience. What now, he wonders. He doesn't see how the numbers can be made to work. Well, maybe bankruptcy won't be the worst thing in the world. With that thought he consoles himself.

MORAL IMAGINATION:
THE CONTENT OF A DECISION[4]

As the realization of what was happening took shape, the Feuerstein character works through a deluge of remembrances, images, vows that resonated through his whole life. In the glance between him and his wife, all of these dynamics of his Moral Imagination were activated and called to the fore. He would not be making a decision in the dark solitude of his own mind. The energies and sources of his Moral Learning are alive and active.

It is easy enough for us to imagine how, when he was young, stories were shared among his peers about the Lawrence strike and their parents' roles. He may have gone to school with children of strikers that were hurt and children of mill owners and managers who perpetrated the abuses. He may have sat around the dinner table and heard stories, morality tales, about what was suffered in and learned from the brutal Bread and Roses strike.

[4] So, while this dialogue is completely imaginary, I believe it is a quite feasible one. We can easily envision a young "idealist" arguing with a wizened, hard-nosed, businessperson. Here, the septuagenarian sounds like the idealist. But even those appearances are deceiving. Feuerstein is no idealist. He believes in downsizing when necessary and has made many a "hard" personnel decision in his time. He knows how New England was emptied of its textile manufacturing industry as one company after another relocated, first in the south of the United States, then in Mexico and the Orient, in pursuit of cheap labor. He knows that his competitors have a tremendous payroll advantage over him and he has to be ever more mindful of his costs (variable labor costs included) if he is to keep his company solvent.

On the other hand, to some, the decision is neither idealistic nor foolish. There are business pundits out there who dare to argue that short-term profit is not necessarily the best way to achieve long-term business growth. In *Built to Last*, Collins and Porras point out how in 1991 the pharmaceutical giant Merck developed and then gave away (that's for free) the drug Mectizan that cured the disease called "river blindness" in Africa. Then, from the annals of business history, we might remember that Henry Ford not only decreased the price of the Model T 58 percent from 1908 to 1916, but also established the $5 per day wage for his workers—a pay rate twice that of the going rate at the time. Now, who would accuse Henry Ford (with his brutal crushing of labor's attempts to organize, not to mention his rabid anti-Semitism) of being a mushy idealist? In that tradition, Aaron Feuerstein can also be considered a hardheaded businessman, driving the profitability of his company.

It is thus also easy to picture the young Feuerstein making a promise to himself, "If I ever own the mill, I won't do that to my workers." We can imagine how he may have recalled, with pain and embarrassment, how many times in his long business career he had to compromise his principles and lay people off when revenues suffered; or how he may have recalled how he had felt diminished in making that decision—the logical one. These images remain vivid and active. We can see a man, truly successful (on the backs of his employees), nearing the end of his proprietorship, wanting to get back to that vow he made long ago.

The metaphors evoked by characters depicted here are vivid and compelling to him: the metaphor of the business as a family, immersed in living human relationships, in the community, in the long and stressed history of the community; the metaphor of the protector in times of crisis rises to envelop his own feelings as the enormity of the tragedy sinks in. Images from his life surge forward: the regrets expressed about past decisions; pride in being acknowledged as a "pillar" (another metaphor) that keeps the community healthy (another metaphor). The energies rise up through the spires of the arches—Self-Awareness and People Skills (the great human drama, especially), Practical Insight into the possibilities onto which the crisis opens, feeding his state of resolve on the issue.

We arrive at our view of these great, or strange, decisions by remembering our major premise about how we live: we are immersed in our worlds, with all our senses, reflexes, and responses tied to sustaining ourselves, our loved ones, and our species amid the changes and challenges that the world puts to us. As humans, however, we are not tied to every nuance of the world as it is given to us. We have an immense capacity to grasp our experience, reflect on it, and then work with the information we receive.

Mr. Feuerstein didn't "distance" himself from the people with whom he worked side by side for so many years. As he made the decision, he remained immersed in those relationships, connected and intertwined. And when that tapestry of interconnectedness was torn apart by a new, violent, and renting event, he rewove it out of the same material that had worked so well for so long.

MORAL LEARNING: VALUES VERSUS PRINCIPLES

First, let's look at what occurred in our depiction of arriving at a decision through a metaphorical, image-engendering process versus one relying on abstract principle.

Our character, the COO, acts from "rational principles" which reliably bring to the fore the most important and necessary criteria for making standard business decisions: costs and revenue. As a result of this catastrophe, the COO's standard thinking goes, Malden Mills has no means to produce revenue; therefore, the syllogism continues, reduce costs to as close to zero as possible.

Who could dispute that logic? If you accept the premise that the most glaringly draining variable cost to the business is labor, and when you have no revenues those costs must be cut to a minimum in order to keep the company in the black, what else is there to think about? Right? The COO in our depiction feels bad about this conclusion; still, he ultimately feels—if that is the right word—that this sad and wrenching conclusion is, according to this logic, the only right, reasonable, and eminently justifiable one to make. Frankly, wouldn't you fire a COO (especially a COO) that didn't start from this premise and arrive at this conclusion? The employees probably wouldn't expect a different conclusion either.

Abstract, deductive logic works that way: an outcome is desired; these are justifications that we can use to explain what we are doing—the steps to get there; do it. Deductive logic demands internal consistency. One step follows from the preceding step; the conclusion is foretold in the premise. These conclusions assume that there are only certain results that are desirable, elevating these principles to the level of sanctioned acceptance (and institutionalized to the level of an economic professional's imperative) they operate in the same way that values do. They crystallize conclusions about the way the world is and constrain our choices, pointing to a particular action.

But, as we have said repeatedly in our discussions so far, creative leading is not a matter of adhering to abstract principles. Rather, a decision is triggered when the leader's values are activated. Using our imaginary Aaron Feuerstein, we showed how the decision emanated from his recollecting and activating all the experiences out of which he formed a sense of himself as a leader, and not merely as a manager of a production facility. Acting on the basis of his values, in other words, he engendered a completely different response.

"Principles" lack the compelling qualities that enable values to act as sources of action. While abstract principles are set in stone—cold, imposing, domineering ("Profit is the goal, so cut costs.")—Moral Learning can always be touched by experiences, doubts, and surprises. By definition, acting on rational principles and their logical execution is supposed to pull us out of the flow of life. In contrast to this, acting on *Moral Learning impels us into that flow*. Acting on the basis of Moral Learning means we are entering that torrent, not stepping on to the safe and stationary banks.

We have to admit, and I think we all know, that the dangers of doing this are legion. For one, working out of Moral Learning has the potential to put us in conflict with the status quo. And because of this, we have to admit that leading in its purest, most creative form is, to use an extreme word, subversive. Leading changes things, right before our eyes, discomforting the comfortable. But then, creative leaders aren't brought to the fore to manage things, to keep processes under control, to make bosses happy. They are called upon, or they rise to their own call, to bring about change.

And so it is with Aaron Feuerstein; he subverts the conventional wisdom by applying his values to sustain what he believes are the most important principles of business: creating wealth for everyone in the enterprise, and not just the owners.

And that means doing so even when tragedy strikes.

Using Moral Learning rather than proven, logically validated rational principles greatly decreases the likelihood of outright success. We take on risks by doing so that are much larger than those prescribed by proven principles. Rational principles limit our thinking to those regimes of reality over which we are confident we have control. Not so with Moral Learning. It propels us into just those areas of our lives in which we forego control. Feuerstein's Moral Learning trades control for a connection to a moral imperative. And in so doing he enters a vast realm of risk that is not governed by the rational, sensible, and comforting laws of cost/benefit analysis. This is dangerous territory. And, indeed, bankruptcy did result.

And finally, making a decision on the basis of Moral Learning in this way neutralizes our ability to even measure success. We'll talk more about this factor later. But let's acknowledge, right away, Feuerstein and those like him forego the luxury of having clear measures of whether or not their decisions were "right." Even as Malden Mills emerges out of bankruptcy, can it be said that the decision about keeping on the employees was "right"? He forfeits the ability to make that claim because he did

225

not make the decision on the basis of criteria that are amenable to measure. How do we measure the forces that history, tradition, responsibility, and/or moral learning have on us? We don't, of course.

But that is not to say we have to throw up our hands and say, "Well, that's old Aaron for you. You never know what to expect from that guy." Creative leaders' decisions aren't arbitrary—even if they seem that way. Instead of appealing to quantitatively abstract measurements, the creative leader's decisions are anchored by their significance in transforming and shaping other people's lives. *The criteria that mark the success or failure of the creative leader's decisions are found in the qualities of the experiences of those who are engaged in making the decision (in the crafting of the narrative) and then by the experiences of those who are affected by the decision's aftermath.* Thus, the success or failure of the decision is spelled out in the terms elicited in the dialogues that generate the decision and in the narratives that are collaboratively woven so as to anticipate what may happen as the decision's actions spin out in real time.

Therefore, to complete our discussion, we now have to turn to dialogue and narrative and see how they constitute critical components of the creative leader's decision making.

DIALOGUE

NO, IT IS NOT LONELY AT THE TOP

Every once in a while, when leaders face emergencies or situations requiring immediate choices, they have to act alone. All leaders encounter these situations, and the best among them do make pretty good decisions most of the time. As Klein points out in *Sources of Power*, deep experience within a domain—a profession, business discipline, or area of expertise—contributes to an ability to recognize many factors in a situation that can be connected into a decision to go right or left, to act or desist, etc. These decisions are often life-saving or endeavor-saving and the beneficiaries of these decisions react with great appreciation when the decisions really help. I think of Rudolf Giuliani here, as he won the hearts of Americans struck numb and paralyzed by the attacks on September 11, 2001. This able administrator and politician stepped into true leading in the moments following the attack by making sound decisions and displaying calm empathy and understanding.

But despite the dominance of the omnipresent and fallacious image of the lonely leader, striding out front, walking down the deserted main street at high noon, bravely going to meet his fate, the great decisions are most typically made in the context of advice. They are made in the midst of *dialogue*. Actually many creative leaders have to work hard to get some time alone. Certainly the creative decisions that we envision here are not made in isolation. Happily, some of the good books on creative decision making point this out. For instance, in *Creative Destruction*, Foster and Kaplan describe the elaborate, time-extended program by which Johnson and Johnson conducted many "conversations" about the company's future in order to arrive at conclusions about new directions. Many people were involved, over a long period of time. These writers aren't exactly "touchy feely" authors who are advocating that alternative lifestyles be introduced into the corporation.

In another (rare) excellent book on business change, Jim Collins writes in *Good to Great* about how effective leaders first bring in excellent talent and then engage them actively in an ongoing appraisal of the company's situation, and then draw up a plan. *The decision emerges out of a process of respectful, though sometimes harsh and argumentative, dialogue.*

The process need not be neat or collegial. An effective executive team, whose members are truly leaders, does not comprise wimps or people who go along to get along. These are all people who enjoy putting their ideas out there, and they are all used to having something of what they envision be acted upon. So discord is likely, to put it politely.

Harry Kaufman follows a similar course in his creative leading. He is the first to admit that he is not creative on his own. He feels he is at his best when high quality people bring ideas to him. Alternatively, he will initiate conversations by walking around; he will go out into the field to find out what people are thinking that can act as a spur to ideas. There are several ways that he generates and participates in dialogue around his decisions.

One of his direct reports told me how surprised she was initially at this characteristic of his leading in the context of his staff meetings. "He doesn't say a lot," she explained. "He listens and lets the conversations, or arguments go on for quite a while. If it degenerates or starts to repeat, or when people lock into positions, he'll stop it, otherwise he lets it go on. It took me a while to realize that this is how he wins buy-in. He lets people talk it through, and he is counting on someone stepping up to take responsibility. Then he'll repeat to this person what the expectations are for fulfilling that responsibility. Now I think that process is really good. But as I said, it had me wondering for quite a while."

SUCCESS OR FAILURE: THE NARRATIVE

I can hear the skeptics: "Dialogue? Conversations? What kinds of decisions are made with these? I am the leader here. I make the decisions. We don't have the time or money for anything soft here."

Yes, many of our leaders assume they must behave this way. We are saying, of course, that while that driving efficiency and cost-effectiveness will get the job done, it won't be the most advantageous way to create followers who can build lasting, viable, and vital organizations. And, we are saying, the best way to arrive at creative decisions is to use methods such as metaphor-generating dialogue. We certainly agree that the leader drives the dialogue toward arriving at the decision that will accomplish what the situation requires.

What really makes a decision "hard," enabling it to act like the backbone of an organization's intentions, is, first, that it emanates from an indisputably important story in people's lives; and, second, that it cuts new paths of understanding and aspiration, creating new stories as the effort unfolds. People want this story to unfold to a productive outcome. They bear down and make their efforts into a force to be reckoned with.

That's what's hard—not the statistics that cite the residual quantities of already aggregated activities have occurred long ago. Unless the so-called facts and figures are backed with human stories, giving these decisions meaning, prospect, and vital importance, the so-called hard decisions will dissipate like air. And so, we conclude this section on what makes leaders great by linking decisions with the capacity to cause metaphors, dialogue, and decisions to yield and combine into compelling stories and narratives.

CREATIVE-LEADING DECISION MAKING

The endeavor begins with a story—the story of the values that the leader brings to the situation; and it proceeds by adding to it, or amending it, according to the stories that are generated as the collaboration has an effect on the world. These narratives create vital milestones and signposts of success long before results are distilled into numbers. The engine of the endeavor is fueled by the energies expressed in the stories of the engagement the effort inspires.

Maybe Aaron Feuerstein's decision wasn't perfect, but the unfolding of the actual story—the bankruptcy included—encompassed everyone that had contact and an interest in the company. His initial offering of generosity invited (in a curious sort of way) vendors and customers to join in, to offer their own generosity so that the company and the values it now represents could continue on with their participation as well. The decision expanded the compass and reach of the life of the company far beyond that of the employees, the local community, or certainly beyond the mere facts of its revenues and costs.

Before we move on, though, let's take a bit of a more detailed look at this aspect of the leader's experience—that of using narrative to lay out the course of the decision.

THE INITIAL STORY

Leaders enter into the decision-making arena—the arch—fully imbued with and invested in a story. This is the story of their Values, embodied in Self-Trust and expressed as their Leader Brand, portrayed in the vision. "This situation," the leader's story goes, "does not accord with the values that I, and presumably you, feel need to be in evidence." The leader declares and depicts those values. "I have a dream," Martin Luther King Jr. said. "A government for the people . . . ," Lincoln declared. "Every employee of this company shall be cared for," Aaron Feuerstein said.

At the outset, the story will seem to be appropriate and fitting, not just according to an abstract rubric, but according to how the endeavor envisions that story being fulfilled. It is the story that seems real, being loaded with emotion and value-based qualities and poignant metaphors. The criteria for the endeavor's success are already embedded in the values which the leaders and followers deem as being worthy and important, and on which they, to a greater or lesser extent, stake their lives.

Going back to our imaginary Aaron Feuerstein, he made a decision based on years of dialogue about his responsibilities to the company, the employees, the customers, and the community. When his wife looked at him as he walked out the door with a look that said, "I know you'll do the right thing," all those dialogues, stories and narratives in which Feuerstein had participated were brought to the fore. In this gaze of hers are contained the accounts of past experiences that make the endeavor compelling and the values conflict that makes it necessary and the glimmers of prospect that make the endeavor enticing. The decision he arrived at through this process is not a philosophical or objectively "scientific" truth. He arrives at a decision by actualizing a narrative of his values.

The narrative is focused at the outset by the leader's vision, that is, by the concern that important values be fulfilled by the endeavor's actions. It is the leader's initial story that brings him to the precipice of offering what we call "creative" or foolish visions or ideas. But the leader's intent, at this point is not just to move ahead, but instead, the intent is to look again at the situation in order to discern what else is possible.

ACTIVATING THE STORY: THE ORGANIZATION

The story moves out of the mere statement of the vision and into the moments of activating the vision through the organization. The organizational story, as you recall, comprises the outline of the Signature Behavior that the endeavor wants to put into effect. It comprises a Mission, Values, Strategy, and a commitment to a Culture that will bring about the Signature Behavior as something significant and singular in the world.

And so, *the narrative comes to take on the role of a script in which participants have parts to play; they all have their roles and responsibilities to play out.* In this way, their expectations are primed to bring about a specific result, a success that they can clearly identify as they proceed in their actions day to day. These organizational stories enable each and every participant a chance to see whether or not the endeavor is accomplishing its intentions with each encounter, each reaction, and each engagement. They don't have to wait for the weekly or monthly report. They know.

THE NEW STORY

When that point of setting out into action is reached, the initial story and the organizational story lose their crystallized form. They are put into play amid the active forces of the world they engage. And, as we all know, rarely, if ever, do things go as planned. Hardly ever does a decision get made that can realistically count on the actions it envisions progressing through a clear, unobstructed, or "empty" terrain, one that simply welcomes the effort.

The realistic decision envisions a meandering path, an effort that requires slogging through the thickets of earthly domains, competitors, traditions, regulations, and market conditions, to name a few of the obstacles along the way that fill the terrain on which the endeavor operates. *The great decisions make their way forward, fully honoring the complexity and emotional loading of the situation.* They keep people engaged and capable, while testing and expanding them. Then these step-by-step actions and modifications produce a result, at some point, in which everyone's effort counted.

This next narrative, the one that sets out the path on which the endeavor will move, helps leaders and followers alike gain a firm sense of whether or not they are on the right track. Rather than just ask the question—are these the results that we want?—i.e., rather than just call for managerial criteria, those in the endeavor get to ask whether or not this is the experience they want their efforts to create for all those affected by those efforts.

By crafting succeeding narratives of the path that all in the endeavor are on, everyone fully realizes whether or not they are slogging through the "right jungle." They know what the terrain is supposed to look like, they know, because they have discussed it, what it is likely to feel like. When things don't go quite the way they expected, they get to ask questions, not only about result, but about the story itself. The narratives provide the means by which everyone stays in the experiences as the collaboration unwinds envisioned possibilities and generates new realities.

Maybe Aaron Feuerstein knew that his decision included a stay in the jungle of bankruptcy, or maybe he didn't. *But his decision enabled everyone associated with him to take part in the story that would unfold, and feel that, as they slogged through the jungle, they all were part of a story in which they played a vital role.* They weren't merely statistics in an insurance reckoning, nor were they children paternally protected from the storm. A commitment had been offered, and, in taking it up, in accepting the terms of that commitment, they now had to make this new company work. He kept employees on the payroll, thereby giving everyone who associated with the company—employees, managers, vendors, customers, lenders—an opportunity to write a different kind of story about what a business organization could do in a crisis.

That's the invitation of the creative leader: "Come with me, beyond the metrics, into a story of our own creating." In deciding that the time to come to act, the leader moves the collaboration into another story or, more accurately, through a succession of stories—ones that actualize the vision. The point of telling these stories is to fully engage others in an imagining of their own. That's why Harry lets conversations go on and even allows the temperatures in the room to rise a bit. The point of the conversation is not to "make nice" or even to "reach consensus," but rather *create stories that open people's lives to possibilities that then translate into commitments and responsibility.*

The story isn't even about tasks and delegation; it's about who these people are—people who will be needed to translate the vision into reality. From this weaving of many narratives, in the telling and advocating of these stories, no concreteness is lost to analysis or abstraction. They deal with hard, recalcitrant realities, time, relationships—allies, competitors, habituated customers, employees, etc.

PART FOUR

The Leader's Ethic

INTRODUCTION

Matt was absorbed in his book, comfortably sitting with a pot of tea and a scone, waiting for Beth, in an outdoor café. The late spring morning sun beamed through the chill of the night, but the day's heat had not yet taken hold. They hadn't seen each other for nearly a year. A week earlier, Beth had called Matt and wanted to tell him some important news, "In person," she said, "It has to be in person."

Beth arrived. "Am I late?" She grabbed a chair with energy and authority.

"No. I decided to come early and do some reading."

Beth rapidly and silently unloaded the contents of a bag she had carried in with her onto the table. Out came a sketchbook, a folder, then another folder. "I bet you're curious," she said, as she settled in, and took a self-consciously deep and noisy breath—in and then out.

"To say the least," Matt replied.

"I am ready to get back into it," she said. "Into leading. And I have a few ideas I want to run by you."

"Congratulations. Or do you have to go back to work?"

"You can congratulate me. This is strictly a voluntary thing. The kids are old enough so they wouldn't mind. Chuck [her husband] works at home and wouldn't mind being there when the kids get home from school—in case I have to work late or something. He'd actually like me to get out of the house, frankly."

"First, congratulations, then. Now, tell me, what happened?" "It's funny, isn't it, how things break when you are ready for them to. I had been thinking about going back into it ever since Chuck left the firm and started his own accounting practice. I did talk to a few people, but mostly just thought about it. Then, out of the blue I got a call from Howard, you remember him, the CEO at Telecom—the place where we started working together. Oh, that's right. You're still friends with Howard, aren't you? He's running an investment company now, you know that, don't you?"

236

Matt acknowledged that he was still in contact with Howard. *"Yes, I know. He has me working with a company his firm has a large stake in."*

"Wait a minute," Beth grinned. *"Did you . . . ?"*

"No. I didn't do anything. Howard does ask about you, and I have kept him informed, but I . . ."

"Oh. So you know about this situation he's asked me to consider?"

"No, Beth. Really, you'll have to tell me."

"It's right here in town, a merger between two of the companies in which his firm is the major investor. He put the deal together, and he wants to bring me in as the new CEO. I don't know if I want to do it. Mergers are nightmares, especially between two entrenched technical companies and cultures. And, as you know, I've already been burned by rampaging engineers! But the point is, this has me thinking about getting back into it."

"For . . . ?" Matt quizzed.

"To get this leading thing right this time."

"Can we talk about leading and then come back to the offer?"

"Sure," Beth said. *"Leading is what I really wanted to talk to you about anyway—to thank you and to tell you how things have changed in that regard for me."*

"I'm all ears," Matt said, gesturing as though giving her the stage.

"Here's the story. When I started at Zee-Tech, I had only gone through part of the process. I only thought of my father and what he stood for. The other side, that I hadn't gotten to yet, was my mother. The fact that we were still estranged, or at least not really talking to each other, should have been some kind of a signal, don't you think? Obviously, I still didn't get it."

"I often wondered what was going on with your mother," Matt commented. *"You hardly ever mentioned her in our conversations, and as I recall, you went for years at a time without visiting her."*

"That's right. I jumped from my grandfather's goading to my father's idealism, but that was all in my head. My estrangement with my mom held a

key for me that I wasn't aware of, or certainly didn't even consider being an issue back then. Do you remember that conversation we had when I cried?"

"Which one?" Matt teased.

"Was I that bad?" Beth retorted.

"Hardly," Matt assured her.

"I mean the one where you asked me, 'You know what your father stood for, but what are your values?' When you asked that question, I realized how hollow I felt. It came in like a cold wind that I didn't know what mattered to me. All I knew was how to do things. That question just stuck with me for ages. I think that was the first time I cried."

"Oh, that time," Matt laughed and was relieved when Beth did too.

"Well, let me tell you what happened," Beth was more excited than Matt had ever seen her. "A year ago now—has it been that long?—I was playing with my youngest, Janine. She loves to draw. Just for the fun of it, completely spontaneously, without thinking for a moment, I asked her to pose for me and let me draw her. The drawing was terrible, but doing it brought back a flood of memories.

"I remembered how I was so artistic as a kid. I drew, painted, and even wrote poems. My mom is an artist. She paints, landscapes mostly, and a gallery in her hometown has sold her paintings for years. She actually lives on that income from her art, since Dad's insurance paid off the house. She lives modestly and happily. Well, anyway, she and I were very close when I as a little girl, and she was convinced that I would be an artist like her. Even better than her, she thought. So did I.

"Then, suddenly, and I don't remember why, in my sophomore year in college, something inside me snapped. I decided I had to 'get serious,'" Beth drew quotation marks in the air. "Suddenly, I dropped all my art courses, became a business major, got an MBA, and never looked back."

"What was your mother's reaction to the change?" Matt asked.

"I never knew, until recently. I never said a word to her. She never asked me about it. But I think it created a wall between us. And, I have come to realize, it created a wall within me."

"What do you mean?"

"By 'getting serious' I meant cutting myself off from that free-flowing exploration of the world and one's self that art demanded. It's just that. I cut it all off. I don't know what scared me. Maybe it was my grandfather's voice, and I needed to answer it in as sure and as measurable a way as I could; or maybe I didn't like what I saw when I experienced myself. Maybe I saw the failure my grandfather said I would be. I don't know. It was probably all of that, and more.

"Business school was perfect. It had rules, procedures, principles, and methods. It was creative too, that's for sure. And, as I learned, knowing all those things doesn't guarantee success. But it felt safer than being an artist. Also, and this was a big thing, my father was in business, rising through the ranks at the time. That was an exciting, understandable, logical image to me. So it may have seemed that I could defy my grandfather in a safe, recognizable, measurable way."

"So," Matt interjected, *"If you don't mind my speculating here, you seem to be saying that your breakthrough of a few years ago, that led you to Zee-Tech, wasn't a complete breakthrough at all, it was more like a fulfillment of one part of your life—your life as a business person."*

"I never thought of it like that, but it fits," Beth said. *"What I did realize, in this revelation,"* she continued, *"is how much of my life I had cut off in order to pursue my success. And then I realized this—and this is where you come in: all this stuff you had been telling me about self-trust and moral learning, I finally got it. I finally understood what you were trying to tell me. The way I thought about it was how could I have self-trust if I cut off, blocked out of my memory and self-awareness, such a huge chunk of who I am. I am creative and I can envision scenes and compose them into images that people relate to. Isn't that vision?*

"And I thought, how can I engage in moral learning and offer my self as a person who learns from life when I had stopped learning anything but the next managerial skill or technological innovation or bit of market data? I wasn't able to reach others because I had put so much of myself out of reach. And what was even worse, I had to protect myself from having this past, this discarded life, discovered. I had to be the professional manager to a tee, so I wouldn't realize how much I had dismembered the artist and playful girl I once had been."

There was a long pause, each looking at the other searchingly and somewhat tentatively. "That's some revelation," Matt said—just to break the silence and connect with his own speechlessness. The feeling he had from hearing how Beth made this connection was overwhelming. It just doesn't happen often, in Matt's experience as a mentor, that a true breakthrough happens, and someone really gets to the core of this endeavor of creative leading.

"And there's more! I've been doing some thinking, Matt. Are you ready?" Beth asked. "Here's why I know I am really ready to go back in. For one thing, my mother and I talked about that time, in detail, over several months. She told me how incredulous she was and how hurt she was that I had stopped 'being her daughter,' as she put it. She consoled herself with the idea that I was still valuing what Dad's life was all about. Now we talk all the time. She comes and visits and stays for weeks at a time. She draws with the kids, and I draw with them. And we all talk about it and learn. And we are brutal . . . then we laugh!

"Look," she opened the sketchbook she had brought, "these are some of my latest pencil sketches." They were simple and dramatic landscapes and portraits of her family.

"For another thing, and this is where the leading comes in, I now see myself as someone who learns. As someone who sees things with care and then learns from what is happening. I don't need to impose my vision anymore, I *can share it—like I do my artwork—and learn from the dialogue. That's what you were trying to get me to do at Zee-Tech. Frankly, I thought that was all bull, all 'soft stuff' and 'touchy feely.' Now I see that it was what needed to be done.*

"And finally, I am ready to lead because I will never give up the excitement of being with my family and growing and learning—about them, about art, about people in general—again. It's amazing what a life of leading a family will teach you. The management knowledge and technique is vital, it has a key and prominent place in business. But now I am ready to lead; I am ready to 'affect people,' as you would always say. I get up in the morning, really early, and I sketch. Then we all eat breakfast together. Then, after that, I could take on an assignment and accomplish something. I am ready. Or, more like it, I am ready to find out how ready I am. I figure, if you affect the lives of your children, why not the lives of employees or followers? Right?

"What are you laughing at?" *she asked.*

"Mentoring is so slow," *Matt laughed.*

THE KEYSTONE OF THE ARCH OF THE LEADER'S ETHIC: "ATTENTIVE RESPONSIBILITY"

Beth has learned to see creative leading in the context of her whole life. In a way, she has reached that milestone marked by the very first words of our definition of creative leading: this is a life commitment. Those who enter into this endeavor shape the entirety of their lives so as to accommodate as much of creative leading as they choose to partake. "Attentive Responsibility" names the ethic, the direction and intention of the life decisions that leaders are called upon to make.

The ethic we envision encompasses the leader's whole life. It is an ethic adopted by someone who has firmly, finally, and completely committed that life to creative leading. No one who has not made such a commitment would be even mildly interested in adopting such an ethic. From the description we have just given of this ethic, it is clearly beyond the pale of most of us to dedicate our lives in such a way. But to lead greatly requires nothing less than such a commitment.

The intent of adopting this ethic is that it prescribes a way of living that is up to accommodate the strenuous and difficult challenges of leading greatly. Since great creative leading requires nourishing and nurturing the energies that sustain Moral Learning, Moral Imagination, and Decision Making, the creative leader's sustenance takes on a form of a disciplined practice.

By applying the term "practice," we point to *a focused engagement of one's experience that improves certain skills while honing and strengthening certain feelings so they can endure throughout the challenges, disappointments, exaltation, and even boredom that great leading entails.* These activities thus act as metaphors for creative leading itself, strengthening the means of renewing and deepening insight, drive, empathy, and self-awareness. And finally, we mean a refreshing and energizing activity that sustains the leader as she encompasses larger worlds and engages issues of wider scope.

They engender the quality of experience that is called "Flow" by the psychologist Mihaly Csikszentmihalyi. "Flow" names the fourth spire, the spire of Vitality in the Arch of the Leader's Ethic.

Attentive Responsibility

BEING FINELY AWARE AND RICHLY RESPONSIBLE . . .

BEING A PERSON ON WHOM NOTHING IS LOST.

BEING RESPONSIBLY COMMITTED TO THE WORLD

OF VALUE . . . THE PERCEIVING AGENT CAN BE

COUNTED ON TO INVESTIGATE AND SCRUTINIZE

THE NATURE OF EACH ITEM AND EACH SITUATION,

TO RESPOND TO WHAT IS THERE BEFORE HER WITH

FULL SENSITIVITY AND IMAGINATIVE VIGOR, NOT

TO FALL SHORT OF WHAT IS THERE TO BE SEEN

AND FELT BECAUSE OF EVASIVENESS, SCIENTIFIC

ABSTRACTNESS OR A LIFE OF SIMPLIFICATION.

. . . A PERSON WHOM WE COULD TRUST TO DESCRIBE

A COMPLEX SITUATION WITH FULL CONCRETENESS

OF DETAIL AND EMOTIONAL SHADING, MISSING

NOTHING OF PRACTICAL RELEVANCE.

—MARTHA NUSSBAUM[1]

[1] *Love's Knowledge* (New York, 1990), p. 84.

THE CREATIVE LEADER'S WORLDVIEW

The picture of creative leading we have offered may not appeal to you. After all, what are we offering? Discomfort extended and anxieties magnified; a world once familiar is now seemingly, somehow, not measuring up to our professed values. Then, after enduring all of this, and after putting in arduous emotional and physical effort, we suggest the endeavor may not yield many of the outcomes desired. So all we can say for the life of creative leading is that once entered into, it only assures that no particular outcomes can be guaranteed, and that whatever is envisioned will probably not come to fruition just as it is envisioned; and if it does, the consequences from that fulfillment will yield many surprises—both good and bad. "What kind of a life is that?" you may ask. And with good reason.

So why would anyone choose this life? We have said that there is one main reason: creative leading is charged with vitality, energized by the excitement of change and opportunity each and every day. *People who enter into it, or stumble upon it, stay in it to feel alive.* That their lives have "meaning" as a result is almost beside the point. When Harry Kaufman can't envision possibilities, create followers, use organizational resources to ignite aspiration, he will move on—no matter what the cost—to take charge of an organization in which he can do those things. Brian Thomas doesn't even particularly relish the role; and he often finds his personal preferences for solitude, meditation, or bicycling in conflict with the amount of time and energy he has to expend in leading. Still, he just gets up in the morning and leads, because he cannot deny that when he is leading he feels alive.

But even for these committed leaders, the stresses are enervating, the anxieties are exhausting, and the failures are hurtful. And for those who stay in the role, its demands do seep out of the confines of the endeavor and end up penetrating into all aspects of their lives. This is no nine-to-five endeavor. When Moral Learning upsets one's bearings and assumptions about life, husbands, wives, friends, faiths and beliefs can be swept into the vortex. Everything looks different to the creative leader who works in the throes of this dynamic. This aspect of creative leading is exhausting even to those who are most abundantly endowed with vigorous, freely flowing cascades of energy—as are Harry and Brian. Thus we often find that the best of these leaders need an answer to this question: "Now that I have chosen this life, how do I sustain myself in it?"

Leaders, even seasoned ones, who dare undertake ever more difficult challenges, often find that this choice of life role, with its Moral Learning and constant testing of values, habits, and assumptions, generates far more enervating and disturbing demands than they ever imagined. To succeed at these more difficult challenges, even the most "natural" of leaders find they have to develop new practices in order to support the strenuous efforts they are putting out while inspiring success. This discovery often comes as a surprise or manifests itself in surprising ways.

HARRY KAUFMAN

For most of the ten years I have known him, Harry Kaufman seemed immune to the need to rethink his life in light of greater leadership challenges. After seeing him calmly and energetically succeed in one setting after another, each more challenging than the one before, without the slightest ruffling of his steady demeanor, I came to the conclusion that he was just remarkable in this regard. For him, my conclusion assumed, leading people to make companies great was completely satisfying, focusing, educational and spiritually nourishing for him. A few years ago, however, even the indomitable Harry Kaufman hit a wall. Up to that point, hard times never resulted from the stresses of leading itself. Then he took the post of president and CEO of Wireless Corp (a fictitious name) in Toronto.

In that position, Harry's learning went beyond that of being effective. In our terminology, he entered the third arch, in which Moral Learning takes place. He entered the third arch the moment he made the decision to go to Canada alone, without his family. The decision to live separately was difficult, but not wanting to pull their teenage children out of their familiar high school, Harry and his wife thought it made sense. After all, Harry's work had required long separations before, they rationalized, and this time Harry was only a two-hour plane ride away. So he and his wife reasoned that this separation would be manageable.

To keep his marriage on track, Harry called home often, at least every night; and he went home every other weekend and had his wife and children up to Toronto as often as possible. But under the pressures of a crucible-like turnaround effort that took more than two years, Harry's resilience waned. The phone calls only went so far in making the stresses of his life clear to his family, and his absence only demonstrated how little support he was providing them. He felt guilty, and they felt abandoned and angry at him. While he remained loyal to his wife and family, he felt intensely lonely. While he appreciated their forbearance, he was apprehensive about whether he belonged in that family any more.

Harry's absence was hurtful to everyone. Harry would try to get comfortable with the idea by citing his twelve—and fourteen-hour days. "It's better that I am away so that they know I won't be home, instead of having to explain why I can't be home for dinner every day," he rationalized. Another story Harry told himself was how success here would provide financial security and stability for the family, long into the future, maybe for generations. So when this was done, the story went, he could really be there for everyone. Another rationalization. As far as his wife was concerned, neither of these stories washed. She felt that not only was he missing out on her support, but he was depriving the kids of his influence and love while he missed their growing up.

The whole situation was exacting a terrible toll on the family. Harry felt he was in a tight bind of his own making, and true to the process of Moral Learning, his life decisions about being a leader started to feel strangely inappropriate all of a sudden; the life he had carved for himself felt disappointingly pointless: the exact opposite of what he had wanted for himself and his family. For the first time, I heard Harry say out loud that his need to lead large companies was driving him away from the things that mattered most.

As the job wore on and extended into several years, Harry began to put the experience he was having in a new perspective: he realized he could not lead as effectively when he was solely preoccupied with a turnaround effort at the expense of having a rich personal and family life. His Moral Learning consisted of finding out for himself that the family had a much more important role in his life than he had previously acknowledged. To be effective, he had to be a whole person, in touch with family and loved ones, with children that were growing and becoming adults and with a wife that was supremely caring and acutely alert to the values that ultimately guided his leading. The daily grind of leading turnarounds did not supply enough intrinsic nourishment to assure that wholeness. So what came into view for Harry in this crucible was that creative leading entailed creating a whole life structure and did not just consist of taking care of the company's business.

BRIAN THOMAS

Brian's Moral Learning has been completely different. From the moment I started working with him, Brian was always working on developing a rich path of self-development and balance. For him, the question was not "How do I support and sustain my leadership?" but "Do I really want this leadership role in my life?" In Brian's self-reflection, leading came upon him almost accidentally. He was a researcher, a scientist, and a creative force who always pushed new ideas. Then suddenly, a corporation bought one of his ideas and asked him to lead the company that would convert his science into a viable commercial product, and there he was, leading, not just a research team, but a whole company. Throughout this experience, and beyond it, into his next endeavors, he demanded that he be able to connect his ongoing search for a life with purpose and meaning to his leading, so that his leading more clearly reflected this level of quality of life, not vice versa. He used self-development life practices (meditation, spiritual study, philanthropic work, jogging, playing with his children) as his standard, rather than as chores to be fit into the crevices of his busy life.

So, whereas Harry had to come to a realization that leading wasn't sufficient, that other aspects of his life provided important balance that lent credence and breadth to his leading, Brian continually tested whether or not the endeavor of leading was worthy of his time and effort. "Can you lead a company and not be an asshole?" was a question he asked persistently early in our work. He tested this endeavor against the standards of his meditation. The corporate model he was being asked to establish, and that was absorbing his technology, didn't seem to measure up and never did measure up to the messages that emerged from his practice. He left that first company, after it was firmly established (and it is still going strong today under different managers) to strike out into a situation in which he had more influence on creating a company culture more to his liking.

Even this new endeavor, however, came under his scrutiny. "Aren't we just acting like everyone else? How am I different from an Enron CEO?" he has been heard to ask these days. His practices of meditation, exercise, and reading told him that having an integrated life was what made it all worthwhile. He wanted to lead his company to a Signature Behavior that would also be balanced and integrated. He wanted the company to represent something that ethically and technologically is closer to the sound, spirit-enriching, ecologically sustainable images that are supported by his practices.

DISCOVERING A DEEPER NEED

The stories of Beth, Harry, and Brian instruct us that no matter what the starting point, and no matter what the specifics of the demands are, *leading ultimately draws on the energies generated from a full sense of life, not merely out of success at executing the tasks of the job.* Accordingly, as the leading challenges become greater, so do we make greater demands on our stores of energy. Harry and Brian found out that their wells could indeed run dry.

To lead greatly and inspire success at a high level, under difficult circumstances, it is not sufficient to draw on accumulated expertise in the mechanics of organizing, motivating, or even inspiring. We return to one of our originating themes: One cannot merely cherry pick solutions from a catalogue of the leader's techniques. Instead, creative leaders draw upon the full range of the life experiences that energize them. Drawing on these experiences (in one's act of recollection and self-awareness), spontaneously or in concerted reflection, engender the appropriate and compelling metaphors, analogies, allegories that offer a full picture of the situation. Leaders create organizations by evoking metaphors and ideas from a full pallet of life experiences, their own and others', into focused dialogues that are eventually woven into a coherent narrative. Only in doing so does a creative leader activate a field in which the activities of many people congeal into a focused, purposeful, and collaborative organizational endeavor and thus merit the evaluation of being great.

Developing and learning leaders are often surprised to discover how their whole lives are called into play. Often I have heard young managers say that up until entering consciously upon this leader's path they had worked hard to keep their personal lives and professional lives separate. They are startled when they find how doing the right things, according to the book of managerial science, isn't enough. They (those who choose to stay on the path of leading) see that only by bringing their whole lives into play do they offer themselves or others a chance to succeed.

To do that, leaders provide a structure to the recollections of their pasts, becoming consciously self-aware, as we discussed at the outset of the book. And then, when living forward, they consciously use their energies in a way that dignifies, nurtures, and sustains their ability to engage in Moral Learning and Moral Imagination and guide a vision into actuality. In other words, they adopt what we call an "ethic."

A LEADER'S ETHIC?

Just as artists, athletes, musicians, or shopkeepers arrange their lives in ways that meet the demands of their occupations, so ever much more must leaders shape their lives to meet the strident demands of their calling.

All of us shape our lives to meet the demands of what we do for a living, or, for that matter, what we do for fun. We go to bed early to be ready for work the next day; we participate in or abstain from certain activities in order to be true to our relationships; some of us work out or control our diets so as to be physically fit for just our daily activities. We do this under a rubric, that of being good, or faithful, or true or honest. We have names for these paths on which we trek, such as professional, spiritual, of that of just being a "regular" guy or gal.

These ways of giving *structure* to our lives constitute our *"ethic."* Each of us probably has several ethics that we call upon in different situations. We have a "work ethic," a "personal ethic," and some of us have a "spiritual ethic." All of these name ways, we thread together the things we do into "themes" that give us a sense of continuity and identity. By structuring our lives in these ways, we also assign to certain activities a level of priority and importance. Thus the creative leader too needs an "ethic." Maybe she needs an ethic even more than others, given the strenuous and tension-laden responsibilities these people take on as the activity that is most important in their lives.

NOT A "HABIT"

In defining what I mean by the "structure" supplied by an "ethic," I see three main characteristics. These characteristics are made clear by contrasting a "structure" that underpins an "ethic" to the compulsive behaviors we surrender to under the guise of "feeding our habits."

First, remember how structure was created in the context of discussing the organization? There, the driving energy of attractors (spires and keystone) and the repetition of actions they specified for their actualization (the activities that transpired within the arch) created a robust structure capable of supporting and sustaining an organization's unique Signature Behavior. Similarly, the structure we envision as underpinning an ethic *requires focusing, guiding, concentrating energies. Habits, in contrast, merely absorb the energies our bodies generate.* They are done mindlessly, just soaking up those peripheral, unguided energies that idleness, boredom, or compulsion make available.

Secondly, this structure has intentional and "consequential" ramifications; that is, the structure supports and enables something else. Habits do not have this ability. In an ethic, *the structure sustains and nourishes the disparate functions of the individual's mind, body, emotions, and spirit.* They combine into the dynamic psyche of a creative leader. Needless to say, habits do not support or enable anything else. They just suck energy away, acting as sinks or parasites of the precious energies our bodies release.

One final characteristic of an ethic—*expending the tremendous amount of energy necessary to generate a dynamic structure—tires us out eventually.* However, if you have ever noticed, when you are done with a conscious, structured, intentional activity, you often feel refreshed and energized. That is what the cognitive psychologist Mihaly Csikszentmihalyi calls "Flow."[2] This is an optimal state of experiencing in which our minds and bodies are becoming more capable. Habits leave no such euphoric aftereffect of feeling energized. In the course of playing out our habits, we are just expending energy, sending it off into space, uselessly expended. Habits such as nail biting, compulsions such as useless shopping, or excess eating, addictions such as smoking or even pointless TV watching all fall under these rubrics of uselessly expending our precious life energies.

---

[2] We will discuss Flow as being the fourth spire of the Arch of the Leader's Ethic in the next chapter. This is a digression from our normal sequence, as we are going to look at the keystone of this arch first.

So, to be clear, when we are talking about structures that underpin and express an ethic, we are not talking about habits in which we allow ourselves to waste away. Our ethic enlivens us and makes us more capable, even as we burn up calories and expose ourselves to dangers and/or anxieties.

FROM ATTITUDE TO ETHIC

When I live according to an ethic, I make certain conscious demands on myself. These demands first arise in my *attitude*. A person arranges perceptions, bodily sensations and orientations, opinions and feelings so as to be able to act in a certain way. And then this attitude is put into practice by behaving in certain ways, by undertaking certain actions. Then, to close the circle, I assure that I include these attitudes and actions in my life, to the exclusion of some others. I put constraints on my life so as to have that life take on an identity, clarity, and intentionality in my interchanges with others. This is like putting my thumb over the end of a garden hose; by constraining the water's flow, I concentrate its energies, enabling the water to take on structure. Because of this structure, the water shoots farther out of the hose, providing useful energy that I can use to clear the debris off of a surface.

Concentrating my energies enables me to use them for purposes of my own choosing. As a creative leader, I create collaborative endeavors, multiplying and concentrating even more energy toward a chosen purpose. Thus, as with our example of the hose, this concentration of energy provides a structure that has an effect on something else: it enables others to see and benefit from creative leading. It inspires others, creates followers, focuses collaboration, and accomplishes new things in the world.

ATTENTIVE RESPONSIBILITY

To do this, creative leaders live out a particular ethic that I call "Attentive Responsibility." In becoming creative leaders, people embark not only on adventurous endeavors in their professional lives, but they accept the need to shape their lives so as to support that arduous role. *"Attentive Responsibility" names a unique blend of mental and emotional orientations that enable creative leaders to set out on, undertake and complete their strenuous journeys.* It is not an ethic needed by managers or people not engaged in bringing a vision into a tangible, organized entity. It isn't a disposition that is necessary in order to get things done, or to merely follow or give orders. Attentive Responsibility names an ethic specifically appropriate for attaining and sustaining creative leading. It prescribes a certain quality of living that only becomes necessary when Moral Learning and Moral Imagination are actively engaged in creating large-scale collaborative endeavors that intend to bring about concrete material, social and global changes in people's daily lives

ATTENTIVE RESPONSIBILITY AND THE ARCH

As we have said, the Arch of the Leader's Ethic depicts the energies of a creative leader's deep inner life, the life that occurs at such a depth that it underpins and enables the Skills of Character or embodiment of organizational attractors that were depicted in the prior two arches.

When Moral Learning and Moral Imagination are activated, the leader experiences a rush of intensely focused energy. Even though these forces are mostly invisible and hidden during the earlier stages of the leader's sojourn on the path (and are not named as being components of the earlier arches), these forces are active, compelling the leader's decisions, intentions, and aspirations.[3] Accordingly, just as Self-Trust represented the integration of the leader's Skills of Character that were directed at being effective, *Attentive Responsibility names the means by which the leader integrates his life ethic.* You might say that Attentive Responsibility names the driving force by means of which creative leaders lead themselves.

Since Attentive Responsibility is the keystone of the new arch we have been creating since the beginning of part 3, it gathers to it the energies we have defined as Moral Learning (its testing of values), Moral Imagination (generating metaphors of possibility), Flow (as we described above and will again in chapter 11, an invigorating, restorative, learning structuring of mind and body around chosen activities) and Decision (elevated, purposive, comprehending and compassionate weaving of decision).

WHAT DOES ATTENTIVE RESPONSIBILITY LOOK LIKE?

ATTENTIVE

Creative leaders fully immerse themselves in what they do. When they speak to you, you feel like you are the only person in the room and are all that matters to this person. That's the good news. On the other hand, they may be neither the best company on a long trip in the car nor great companions on vacation. Harry is virtual terror on vacations. He can be sullen, testy, or, when at his best, on his mobile phone back to the office. Creative leaders crave leading.

---

[3] Freud had his unconscious, for instance, his "id." In our work and in the field of self-organizing systems, there are the dynamic, preconscious, interlaced workings of our conscious psyches.

Back on the job, they are also emotionally open to what is going on in their endeavors. After all, their whole stance in their actions begins with the fact that their quiet and repose has been disturbed by certain aspects of that world falling short of what they value. Creative leaders are not hostile or angry because of this dissonance, but they are attentive to all the salient characteristics to all the factors and influences at play. All of them are registered and taken into account.

Martha Nussbaum, our muse, expresses this aspect of Attentive Responsibility beautifully when she talks about this way of life that we see as poignantly descriptive of how creative leaders look and behave: A person who lives according to this way of life, she says,

> ... burrows down into the depths
> of the particular, finding images and connections
> that will permit us to see it more truly,
> describe it more richly;
> by combining this burrowing
> with a horizontal drawing of connections,
> so that every horizontal link contributes to the
> depth of our view of the particular, and every
> new depth crease new horizontal links ...

> [She acts] like ... a spider sitting in the middle of its web,
> able to feel and respond to any tug in any part of the
> complicated structure. It advances its understanding of life
> and of itself, ... by hovering in thought and imagination
> around the enigmatic complexities of the seen particular ...
> seated in the middle of its web of connections, responsive
> to the pull of each separate thread.[4]

[4] *Fragility of Goodness* (New York, 1986), p. 69.

RESPONSIBLE

Then, unlike mystics, prophets or artists who adopt more solitary transforming roles, creative leaders feel irrevocably compelled to organize with others in response to the dissonance they feel. They do not meditate on the dissonance or proclaim its evil or translate it into an expressive form. Instead, they envision a process of organizational transition from what exists now to what they feel able to bring about.

They don't seek to impose an ideal, but to actualize values: her own values, the world's irrepressible values, and, probably, some combination of the two. Thus their ethic impels an attitude of *responsibility, of being full witness to what occurs as the process unfolds, all the while maintaining the openness to be affected, changed and educated by what occurs.*

LEARNING

Attentive Responsibility succeeds to the extent that engagement, vividness of experience, and vitality are generated for all involved, and it fails to the extent that only power is exercised, only the envisioned result ensues.

Continuing the Nussbaum quote started above,

The image of learning expressed in this style . . . stresses responsiveness and an attention to complexity; it discourages the search for the simple, and above all, for the reductive. It suggests to us that the world of practical choice is articulated, but never exhausted . . . ; that the correct choice . . . is, first and foremost, a matter of keenness and flexibility of perception, rather than of conformity to a set of simplifying principles.[5]

[5] Ibid., p. 69.

Brian never sees his work in terms of accomplishments. Sometimes I wish he would. Frankly, he and other creative leaders are reluctant to acknowledge accomplishment at all. Yes, this or that was done, but these leaders are never satisfied; they are always envisioning what comes next. But that is not because something is done and accomplished; it is rather that something has been done, and other things, which also need to be done and are vital and important, are not suited to this restless, relentless questioning and interrogating mindset of the creative leader.

FINELY AWARE, RICHLY RESPONSIBLE

The epigram at the beginning of this chapter contains phrases that give a sense of what Attentive Responsibility looks like.

Start with the most important and definitive of those phrases. "Finely aware and richly responsible." I love those words. They are taken from Henry James, the nineteenth-century American novelist (and brother of philosopher and psychologist William James). The phrase implies both "being a person on whom nothing is lost" and being committed "to the fine possibilities of the actual," a "civic use of the imagination." What could be more tantalizingly clear? I am going to pay attention, and I am going to respond in a way such that something of consequence to my community and myself ensues. I will live today, so as "to be counted on to investigate and scrutinize the nature of each item and each situation, to respond to what is there before [me] with full sensitivity and imaginative vigor, not to fall short of what is there to be seen and felt because of evasiveness, scientific abstractness or a life of simplification."

SELF TRUST CHARACTERISTICS	ATTENTIVE RESPONSIBILITY CHARACTERISTICS
A psychological, physical state that orients the leader toward the current situation.	A consciously developed attitude that constrains behaviors and guides choices in a way that benefits creative leading.
Resolve that one must proceed into the situation as it is given.	Realistic, grounded, unqualified determination to fully comprehend, appreciate and understand the situation, as a basis for the endeavor's collaborative action.
Recollection of one's experiences, values, knowledge.	Taking recollection into developing new comprehensions, or refreshing and enlarging older ones, opening to the feelings and emotions that are engendered, allowing a new realization of self and other to take shape.
Acceptance of one's comprehension.	Acceptance of what the situation teaches and demands, using the new insights gained.
Worthy of one's actions and those of others.	Determination that one's appreciation of the situation, skills of insight and realization, and compassion for all beings and aspects of the situation will guide actions so as to fulfill the promise presented and not unnecessarily cause unwarranted harm.

EXEMPLARS OF ATTENTIVE RESPONSIBILITY

Another way to picture Attentive Responsibility is to consider exemplars of the ethic. While throughout I have made it clear that creative leaders are all around us, leading our businesses and community organizations, participating in and sometimes rising above or being crushed by political office, there are a few creative leaders that we can study in greater depth. From this study we can glean those characteristics that exemplify the kind of ethic we are talking about. This is often easier to do than trying to pick out characteristics in a living, contemporary figure or friend.

LINCOLN

For Lincoln, nothing could be clearer than his ethic of challenging study in the context of continual Moral Learning. While he declined to talk much about his early life, a story from the sad "annals of the poor," he says, new studies make it clear that from his earliest days, he pursued a course of self-education that was startling in its breadth and scope. He felt an early calling to lead, and so he developed habits of reading and studying to fulfill that calling. He read the Bible, Shakespeare, American and world history, and taught himself the law. His father thought Abe was lazy. With good reason. Lincoln often shunned his proper part in the family's farm work, and instead would go off and read under a tree. Some of his peers thought him strange because he didn't cuss, womanize, drink, smoke or fight (unless provoked). He studied instead.

Studying is a far cry from leading a country through the most costly and savage war the country has ever experienced. But Lincoln's ethic of study created for him a structure of hard work, constant challenge to his moral *status quo*, and provided a worldly perspective, all of which contributed to supporting and enabling the leadership that took us through our second revolution, as one writer put it, and launched the US into its modern phase of development and success.

MANDELA

We have already commented on how this extraordinary man maintained his Leader Brand throughout his twenty-year imprisonment. Now we can say that the way he conducted himself throughout that period exemplified Attentive Responsibility.

His conduct exemplified Attentive Responsibility because he used his imprisonment as an occasion neither for disengagement with the conditions of his people nor for absolving himself of responsibility for the nature of the revolution in its progress forward. Instead he used the occasion to deepen and solidify his ethic of multiracialism, showing it to be appropriate, strong and viable under even the worst circumstances. To do this required a tremendous effort of structuring life patterns under circumstances that would seem to cancel their relevance. But these patterns mattered to him. He completely understood his life as that of being a creative leader, and that meant, under any circumstances maintaining a life that would do the cause proud.

GANDHI

For Gandhi, leading was a very personal life-shaping and life-giving matter. Gandhi made constant Moral Learning his personal hallmark and he made acting out the tenets of his deeply adhered to his spiritual practice as his primary method of leading. Before major decisions as to whether or not to engage in a "Satyagraha" – an act of non-violent civil disobedience – he would meditate and fast. His intent was to await a sign from God as to what his course of action had to be.

I think it is legitimate to take Gandhi at his word and see his actions as eliciting a sign from God, and I think it is equally legitimate to see these actions as an act of a more secular idea of Attentive Responsibility. In that interpretation, fasting and the ascetic way of life Gandhi led constituted an effort to concentrate all his energies on a period of strict moral learning. These periods of prayer and fasting were times when all other concerns were put aside, when all the external accoutrements of life were completely devalued in an effort to be able to make a clear, clean and unambiguous life commitment to the demands of leading.

THE REST OF US: WHAT CAN WE EXPECT?

So what can we expect from living according to the mandates of this ethic? We can expect, at best, the great and the sad, and a lot of variation in between. As for the great: Attentive Responsibility spurs and underpins a life of Moral Learning, engenders more encompassing and inclusive visions of our human lives, and enables leaders to feel capable of taking possibilities into becoming living realities whether these be products, services, or whole new social forms. As for the sad: even enduring the most terrible suffering in no way guarantees the success of any particular leading endeavor. Gandhi's fasting and other self-mortifying feats were completely unable to forestall the partition of colonial India into Hindu and Muslim nations. Lincoln's dream of racial accommodation has only begun to be realized, more than 140 years after his assassination. South Africa is far from successful in providing for the health and well-being of its entire people, as Mandela dreamed.

In between the extremes, we have the myriad small successes and failures that everyday leaders offer us in all aspects of our lives. It is in the sum of these, and especially from the efforts of those who work on making their creative leading greater for everyone they affect, that we can envision a better life emerging for us all.

Attentive Responsibility is an ethic we have seen in the likes of our towering exemplars, cited throughout this narrative; and we have seen it in so many of the people we have worked with daily in their everyday, mundane, and uncelebrated position. We have seen them cultivate its practices in their lives despite the opposition, despite the disappointments, despite their loneliness. It is to those practices that we now turn.

CHAPTER ELEVEN

Practice

THE NOTION THAT EACH ONE OF US HAS

AN ORIGINAL WAY OF BEING HUMAN ENTAILS

THAT EACH OF US HAS TO DISCOVER WHAT IT

IS TO BE OURSELVES. BUT THE DISCOVERY CAN'T

BE MADE BY CONSULTING PREEXISTING MODELS,

HYPOTHESES. SO IT CAN BE MADE ONLY BY

ARTICULATING IT AFRESH. WE DISCOVER WHAT

WE HAVE IT IN US TO BE BY BECOMING THAT MODE

OF LIFE, BY GIVING EXPRESSION IN OUR SPEECH

AND ACTION TO WHAT IS ORIGINAL IN US.

—CHARLES TAYLOR[1]

[1] *The Ethics of Authenticity* (Cambridge, MA, 1991), p. 61.

The inner lives of *great* creative leaders revolve around Moral Learning, Moral Imagination, Decision, and, as we will see, around the psychic state of Flow. None of these states are easy, and they are often disruptive of comfort and tranquility. Because the dissonance of these states arouses their visions and focuses their attention, leaders neither fall back on pillars of stability nor rest content in the quiet of the *status quo.* Yet, surprise! This is the very disruption that gives leaders a tremendous rush, making them feel alive. Even so, as they grapple with tests of values and envisioning new possibilities, creative leaders might also picture themselves floating or swimming like fish, immersed and suspended in a vast sea, never touching down on solid ground. As a result, creative leaders sometimes need help in seeing the ocean floor below or the terrestrial shores lying beyond.

These leaders, after all, are limited, humble, earth-bound, flesh-and-blood humans, who need a sense of place, a platform from which to launch their energies. Since leaders are never content to merely criticize or to sit back and act the part of the know-it-all cynic, they need a positive, firm, affirming dimension to their lives. Attentive Responsibility, as their self-actualized ethic, provides that *terra firma* on which, and within which, leaders can put down their feet and plod ahead, one step at a time. By anchoring themselves in a place, within a domain (a space marked out by the arch, to use our metaphor) that is at once familiar and in need of changes, leaders find out that the world becomes more vivid, valued, respected, and even revered.

This reverence centers the experience of Attentive Responsibility. It anchors leaders in their worlds of values, concerns, and devotions, propelling them into deep engagements with all dimensions of their lives. Young leaders are often surprised at how this happens. "I have always tried to keep my professional life separate from my personal life," they say. "Now I find out it isn't possible." We will look at some of the ways in which Attentive Responsibility breaks through this barrier.

First, we will look at how Attentive Responsibility pulls their "private" lives into the same dynamic that guides creative leading. Here we see leaders enjoying certain play or recreational activities that they keep separate and private, holding them away from their professional roles. Though they pursue their enjoyments privately, these leaders approach these activities with the same gusto and attentiveness they do their leading. By doing these things, creative leaders accomplish several objectives: they keep themselves in shape for their professional exertions; they enrich their stores of metaphors for comprehending what they are doing; and they create "spaces," metaphorically speaking, in which new and fresh insights can arise, nurturing their creative leading.

Then we will see how these practices firm up and toughen leaders' psychic boundaries. Practices that support creative leading train their psyches to recognize, welcome, and amplify the principle experience of Attentive Responsibility. This experience called "Flow" (the fourth spire on the Arch of the Leader's Ethic) encourages detachment and, most of all, joy, fortifying their psychic boundaries against degrading feelings such as discouragement, fear, and anger.

FROM ATTENTIVE RESPONSIBILITY TO A PRACTICE

In the course of exercising Moral Learning and Moral Imagination, creative leaders pry their psyches open to the demands of dialogue, to the intrigue of others' suggestions, as well as to the nagging pull of their own problems and fears. Leaders not only listen, offering their earnest attention, but they also take all this information to heart, letting it matter, letting it work its way through their own psyches in order to dismantle old mental constructs, and, in the process, exciting their Moral Learning and Moral Imaginations. This "habit of learning" (seemingly an oxymoron I know) becomes such a life-shaping lure for these leaders that they actually seek out or replicate these disrupting but energizing and joyful behaviors throughout their lives.

These are strenuous efforts. If you have ever gone through a time of anxiety or disruption, when your psyche, your body, your senses are on high alert, you know what I mean.

An hour of emotional upheaval can feel like a day, and physically, such upheavals can take a toll equal to running a marathon. So, as you can imagine, Attentive Responsibility demands that leaders keep themselves intellectually, emotionally, and physically fit.

While athletes train for the big game or the big bout, leaders train for facing every day of their leading lives. Training for Attentive Responsibility entails getting body and psyche in proper readiness for the exertion to come. Leaders' situations differ a bit from those of the athletes', however. First, athletes train for the specific meet, bout or game immediately ahead. Second, the athlete can leave the life and the drudgery of the training regimen behind. I think of how the superb drama *Raging Bull* portrayed the professional boxer Jake Lamotta piling on the weight, puffing up like a doughboy, once his need to remain in fighting trim passed.

Leaders' training, in contrast, pertains not just to an upcoming event, but to an ongoing stream of life. The training goes on continually. And, of course, leaders are not likely to be able to leave their pursuits, the way athletes retire from the game. Some leaders manage to retire from one position or another, but many just keep leading in whatever they do. So, for both these reasons, we call the leaders' efforts at being prepared, primed and fit for her ethic, not as training, but as constituting a *"practice": an activity or set of activities the leader engages in regularly, continuously, conscientiously, with the intent of sharpening, vitalizing, and nourishing their leading.*

CONSTITUENTS OF A PRACTICE

The chief objection we get when we urge leaders to establish a practice is this: "I am too busy. I don't have the time." Sound familiar? Are you saying that to yourself right now? Rest assured, I don't have any pat answers I use to shame leaders into adopting a practice. Nature, however, provides some tried-and-true antidotes to the age-old plea of not having the time: being injured in a car crash gets people's attention; experiencing a divorce is a worthy signal; having a heart attack changes perspectives on how to spend one's time. Hopefully, the conversations we have anticipate nature's call, forestalling the need for her level of action.

So, while we don't prescribe any specific practice for leaders, there are characteristics we recommend to be present in practices that support Attentive Responsibility.

HEALTH

Any practice should encourage good health. *For many leaders, there is no sense in talking to them about anything else,* since this basic element is often missing. The fact is, you can't lead if you aren't here among us, the living.

CHALLENGING LEARNING

A practice that sustains and nurtures creative leading is more than a collection of actions done in order to let off steam. It is not just a matter of going out to spend some time at a movie or hitting through a bucket of golf balls at the local driving range. The practitioner seeks nothing less than an activity that fosters the ability to overcome a physical limitation, change a mental habit, reshape an attitude, and reconfigure a perspective on their lives and/or on their world. Many activities can fit this requirement. *What counts is the intent to learn from this activity.*

For example, reading can be appropriate for a practice. "Leisure" reading (romance novels, Ludlum mysteries, or typical business or "how to" books), however, would not qualify as constituting a practice. Appropriate books need not be difficult to read (although some are), but they do need to offer the *prospect of transformation*, of seeing things anew and with fresh eyes. Reading is an appropriate practice when it offers challenging learning. Of course, this book falls into this category!

Titles of some of the books that we recommend are included in the bibliography of this volume and some are also listed on our website (www.archofleadership.com: go to "Resources").

They include high-quality leader biographies, books that help us be current with state-of-the-art, paradigm-creating science, novels that touch on complex human issues and/or paint characters in all of their rich and ambiguous detail. For some, reading Shakespeare or other fine authors has many benefits, giving one a sense of the majesty of the human drama as well as providing a lexicon of the language in which vision and tragedy are spoken. And reading Shakespearean works can alert us to the ever-present dangers that lurk within the leading endeavor.

Still, however, reading becomes a practice only if challenging reading is done regularly, with a means to capture and use what it is that is being presented. One of our clients really wanted to be able to better inspire her people by being clear and forceful, not bureaucratic and managerial, in her communications with them. She realized that her lunch hours were often absorbed into the crush of the day and didn't have to be. So she marked out the time to leave the office and go to a beautiful nearby park to read Shakespeare and write in a journal. As of this writing, she has kept up that practice for nearly two years.

DISCIPLINE

Creative leaders are rarely overnight wonders who instantly turn failures and limitations to glorious successes. Our leaders are patient weavers of step-by-step changes, each building on, or correcting, what has gone before, preserving even as they create change. Expecting instant gratification keeps most people from leading successfully (and keeps many more from following successfully). *Since creative leading entails evoking and producing something new, a patient, evolutionary sense of progress needs to be cultivated.*

And at no stage of the process will success be completely evident, nor will what actually transpires be predictable. The discipline of creative leading demands Attentive Responsibility in order to see what is really happening while the endeavor is still in its unfinished stages. From stage to stage, leaders resolve how to proceed, producing the next result and next evaluation and the next resolve to proceed, based on careful attention. Thus the practice will pose challenges and will engender feelings alternating between inadequacy and satisfaction. By specifically and intentionally applying focus, enduring rigorous repetition and submitting to continual self-evaluation, the practitioner will eventually surmount these internal obstacles. The whole experience, from the inadequacy of one's present skill, through the tedious efforts at changing the limitation, to finally seeing progress, is part and parcel of the effort an appropriate practice will support.

A RHYTHMIC, RITUALISTIC COMPONENT

This may seem to be a strange requirement. What does rhythm have to do with leading? Just this: As it moves toward completion, a project goes through cycles, ups and downs, completions and new beginnings. There is a pace to the endeavor. And a leader can sense when a project is gaining or losing momentum. There is, in other words, a rhythm to the movement in the changes.

Attentive Responsibility enables creative leaders to see not only how certain changes are transpiring; it fosters the ability to discern the patterns of those changes. Out of these patterns the possibilities for what comes next will emerge. Rhythm can be thought of as a *structure of motion.* As we have described, patterns in motion create dynamic structures capable of supporting and enabling larger structures. *The rhythm of the endeavor translates the energy being exerted by coordinated collaborators into a resilience capable of withstanding opposition and contention. A practice with a rhythmic component trains a leader's perception in detecting patterns in motion.* Physical activities, music, breath and heart-oriented practices, all have these characteristics.

Emotional patterns also come into play in these practices. A practice of improving one's golf game involves concentration, frustration, and depletion of energy, breakthroughs, and a sense of accomplishment. So does practicing guitar. So, whether the cycle is momentary, daily, or seasonal, the activity should demonstrate a sense of completeness and wholeness. Also, a practice with a rhythmic component will give the leader a complete sense of his own emotional cycles, its order and content, so that this will be familiar in the actual endeavor.

DEEP ROOTS IN ONE'S LIFE

Practices don't have to be activities that are completely foreign. If a person has been an active athlete all his life, a sitting meditation practice would probably not resonate; on the other hand, a person who has been contemplative and/or artistic would possibly find taking up competitive ice hockey intimidating. If the athletic client wanted to work in a more meditative approach to his life, yoga or tai chi or aikido would offer a good transition.

Often, a creative practice is simply a matter of rethinking the kinds of things one already does.

Many of the people I mentor had loved artistic pursuits (writing, painting, piano, photography, drama) in their youth, but sadly left them behind as they "got serious" about their careers and "became adults." They believed these things to be somehow not "grown up," so they went back to school to get their MBAs. Of course, they brought to that pursuit the same kind of discipline, intensity, and focus that they once applied to their art, paradoxically, and so diminished the range of skill, critical thought, and emotional balance they applied to their leading. They became effective managers, by emphasizing rational process and technical proficiency, at the

273

expense of developing the more "artistic" and expressive skills involved in inspiring others.

I always urge these people to retrieve their lost arts, and to now use them as practices that encourage attentive responsibility. One client of ours recalled how he was on a track to become a concert pianist, but gave it up to go into business. "Do you miss playing the piano?" I asked. "Very much," he said, "but," in the typical plaint, "I am so busy now . . ." I just sat and looked at him, completely silent for a while. "So . . . ?" I asked. "Right," he answered. A week later, he went out and bought himself a piano.

AN INFINITE HORIZON

A practice is not about achieving a grand goal. There may be small, incremental milestones, marking progress along the way, but not grand goals. The practitioner learns that even getting to Carnegie Hall is only a part of the whole experience. It is great to have a short-term goal that can focus attention and spur the need to practice more. But when the performance is over, the practice remains.

I teach meditation to some clients. I make clear that the worst thing a novice can do is have a goal, such as to release tension, to attain some kind of enlightenment. *The idea of the practice is to do the practice. The practice itself creates the imperative that it must be done, just because it's time to do it and for no other reason.* To employ a cliché here, the journey is the point. This mirrors the creative leader's role. A practice sharpens Skills of Character, keeping a leader fresh and vital. The idea is not to channel and constrain the possibilities offered in the practice in advance, but to let the practice work its magic on you. The great creative leading will eventually follow.

A SENSE OF COMMUNITY

I don't think a monk's ethic would be one of Attentive Responsibility. The monk's ethic may be one of attention and mindfulness, but its purpose is to achieve some kind of salvation for himself, not take responsibility for the outcome of direct actions with and on others. The monk can more easily go off to the mountaintop for a life of solitude than he could reenter the mundane world, as did Jesus or the Buddha, and become a leader.

So a suitable practice for sustaining Attentive Responsibility encompasses an appreciation of a community. The aim of the practice itself may not be to change the community. Participating in it, being a member, may be sufficient. A practice within a community means not only doing it with other people; rather, it also means doing it with the intent to bring the practice to other seekers (not proselytizing, but in being welcoming, receptive, and generous to those who are similarly engaged or can otherwise benefit from the activity). One learns and develops one's character and psychic resilience, therefore, not only for one's own benefit, but also for the benefit of others.

A TEACHER

Accomplished, creative leaders use everyone and everything they experience as teachers and mentors. Many maintain extended or even life-long relationships with those whom they have chosen as their mentors. Having a practice with a teacher, at some time in their lives, and/or having a practice with a mentor as they go on through life, makes this receptivity to learning easier and more enjoyable.

The teacher takes us out of the realm of the hobby and opens up realms of the practice to what we are ready to learn, whether we ourselves know that or not. A teacher keeps the lines of learning open and focuses on the things we don't want to have to learn. And in that regard, in the relationship with the teacher, conversations about change and learning take place as a matter of course. These conversations are remembered as key experiences for the leader as he or she moves the endeavor toward decision and resolve.

MENTORING: THE ULTIMATE PRACTICE

Of all the practices of Attentive Responsibility one can undertake, one is necessary: mentoring. *Mentoring is that distinctive human endeavor in which some take it upon themselves to closely attend to the growth and development of others, and take responsibility for seeing them succeed at a higher level of human accomplishment and maturity.*

Mentoring is necessary for two reasons: first, there is no other way for leaders to be recognized and developed than by another, more experienced leader; and secondly, mentoring happens only by means of Attentive Responsibility.

Recognizing potential leaders is no easy task. The history of Silicon Valley is peppered with the stories of ambitious and capable entrepreneurial engineers who, not recognized by their bosses (some of whom may have even been leaders), started their own companies. Or, how many executives have tapped a potential successor only to find that the prospect acts imperiously with others or just talks a good game? The disappointments are legion, and "getting it right" seems so much a matter of luck. Some people rise through the din of everyday business noise and demonstrate how well they lead. But just as often, the call to lead comes in subtle ways. By themselves, the prospects may not even recognize that the drive to lead is taking shape in their lives.

Just think of what would happen if a young prospect said to the company's hard-driving, results-oriented CEO, "Sometimes I feel like I should be doing more." To an executive who is counting on this prospect to come through with critical sales or product performance, this plaint sounds wishy-washy, not what you'd call inspiring of confidence. I once hired a CEO, whom we'll name Collin, to evaluate and nurture a prospect named Susan.

His assessment of her as a potential leader was right on target. One could easily be taken in by Susan's charm. Her quick wit shows up as she offers a cutting line here and there, and she misses no opportunity to inject her humor into a situation. But this same charm and caring quality aroused suspicions in the CEO and some of her peers. Susan herself quips that she is the beneficiary of the women's movement, i.e., her male bosses looking for a woman to promote into visible positions to show how progressive they are. In fact, Collin felt Susan took good care of her people, and she was a great performer, a real "charmer," in meetings; but he wondered if she wasn't "soft," whether she had that extra edge, to drive people over the top to success.

Early in the course of our conversations, Susan exclaimed, "I'd never say this to Collin, but sometimes I just wonder, well, whether I shouldn't be doing more. And what bothers me is that I don't know what that is. It's nothing about the job, or the people or my boss. I have nothing to complain about. So what could it be? It's driving me crazy. Collin would think I was just being lazy for not seeing all that needed to be done. I see what needs to be done, but it's not the task list that makes me ask that question. It's more to do with me, shouldn't there be more of me involved in what is going on? My mother would say, 'Snap out of it. What's your problem?' That advice just doesn't help me right now."

Susan's question reflected her own impulse to bring even more to the situation than she had in the past. She felt highly anxious, filled with a sense of obligation and desire. What disturbed her only came from her internal sense that she was not reaching her potential for affecting her opportunities; it came from her internal sense that the situation was calling for something that she was capable of providing but was not yet providing. I felt, with all of these factors in play, that she could be on the brink, teetering on the edge of moving to a new level of engagement with her world. What she said next, however, affirmed to me a desire (at least, if not the ability) to lead.

"It's more of a quality thing," she said. "It's as though there are times in my work when I feel I should say things to people, or jump in to their problems in ways that I never felt before. But then I'll ignore the feeling, and go back to my job."

When executives ask, "Who are my potential leaders?" they look at all the people running around pleasing them, managing well, and getting things done. Most top executives are determined to drive results now, for this quarter's reports, to keep costs down, to keep people focused on their tasks. They don't look at the people who, quietly, with some struggle and loss of their bearings, are asking, "Shouldn't I be doing more?" Instead, they look for prospects in the blazing, vivid energies offered by their good managers.

This approach will disappoint. Some leaders, as we have said, just rise, like fine cream, to the top. But for many, leader qualities emerge slowly, almost imperceptibly, as they grow and mature. These people are most often discovered in conversations that require time, that develop patience, trust, and a sense that there is time in the future in which to work things through, things that don't have anything to do with results, but focus on the person herself. These patient conversations begin in the attitude of Attentive Responsibility, in which a leader listens not only to the words but also to their "underlying sonority," as one leader put it. The question, "Shouldn't I be doing more?" could be the plaint of an unimaginative, but hard-driving worker who wants more to do—or, with a different underlying tone, could be a statement of soul-searching and the need for a catalyst, i.e., a mentor, in the long process of discovering oneself as a leader.

Attentive Responsibility detects these underlying sonorities and from them derives realizations about what is being asked or said in a situation. The attentive part hears the tones; the responsibility part knows whether or not to offer a mentoring relationship.

THE MENTORING RELATIONSHIP

What is the relationship we are envisioning here? Mentors aren't coaches who help leaders "perform" better, applying better managerial skills, or even give better speeches. One big difference between a mentor and a coach is this: *mentors are willing to let their protégés fail at those tasks.* Coaches, who are often the leader's direct supervisor, cannot afford failure and so coach their reports to succeed at any cost. Mentors, however, have the luxury of allowing failure. What they don't want as a result of such failures is for their charges to lose heart, or to forget the big picture, or to be too timid about what the leader is willing to risk. So a big difference between coaches and mentors is that mentors are not judges about the tasks of managerial proficiency; instead they are guides in the experience of the life of leading, including its inevitable, necessary, ubiquitous failures.

On the other side of the equation, mentors observe how often they have been unable to explain to a new leader what it will be like to see peoples' eyes light up as the challenge before them unfolds. A mentor can't express the awesome sense of responsibility one feels in that situation. A mentor can't explain the terrible pain at seeing a venture sputter or fail, or how unsatisfying merely winning is, in comparison to the thrill of continuing to lead ever greater challenges. The mentor simply puts people in the right situations, with the right frame of mind. Then it's up to the protégé.

The mentor just lets the protégé experience the full force of leading, guiding the protégé's perceptions and responses. The mentor might smile, giving the protégé a moment of recognition for being on the right course. Or the mentor might just provide the occasion for his protégé to keep talking about what is going on so the leader can think things through. The mentor might just say, "Well, give it a try." *But the smile, or the look of concern, tells his protégé that an experience is about to unfold.* That smile conveys Attentive Responsibility; it says, "I am paying attention, you are not alone; and in doing this, we are a part of something together."

Therein resides the magic in the mentoring relationship. So much is unspoken; not much is done in terms of direct exchange; yet attitudes, values and hopes are conveyed whole in the encounter. Not much is assured by the mentor, but the protégé experiences the sense of possibility rising in her, by having an affirming voice and expression offered to that leader alone.

Mentors have another special role to fulfill: they bring the news that no one else will ever convey. A client of ours, we'll call Ernest, comes to mind: a young executive who was thought to be (mostly by himself, but by others as well) the highest potential candidate for succeeding the founding president. I found him to indeed be an effective manager, hard driving and executive-like. He had a great sense of humor. During one of our sessions, I observed him in a different role, as his family, wife and two young daughters, came into the office. He was affectionate, animated, and full of joy at their entrance. They left, and we returned to the subject of his role in the company. His passion drained. The color in his face even paled. He looked down and started to talk about the objectives and the numbers. What a contrast.

"Are you always this way, when it comes to your role in the company?" I asked.

"What way?" Ernest responded, with some defensiveness creeping in.

"Dispassionate, by the numbers, calculating. That's the way I experience you, and that's what I feel from you whenever we discuss your role here. Seeing you with your family really drove it home for me, made it clear why I find our conversations, well, even a bit boring."

"You think I am that way? I am not that way."

"Well, I certainly see that you aren't such a cool, calculating character with your family; but as soon as they left and we got back to your role here, all that excitement went away, didn't it?" I asked.

"I guess it did."

"How do you expect to get people to rise up and perform with excitement and passion if you are a dry, execution-mongering executive?" I asked. "Is Hal [the founder] that way?"

"No, he's pretty emotional, which is a pain sometimes; but at other times it's great when he's excited."

Who else but a mentor would give Ernest the benefit of such an observation? His boss wouldn't. Ernest got things done without failure, with little or no supervision; Ernest was the very embodiment of my maxim, *"Managers are needed by their bosses; leaders are needed by their followers."* Why spoil a good thing? The people that report to Ernest obviously wouldn't say anything. His wife and family see a completely different person. Only a mentor could bring this kind of news. If Ernest wasn't a prospect for leading, his cool demeanor wouldn't be an issue. But if he is going to inspire success and take the company to growth and prosperity, if he is going to lead, it is an issue. Here is where taking responsibility comes to the fore in the mentoring relationship. *The mentor has to be willing to risk the hurt, the insult, even the parting of ways in order to bring to prominence the kinds of attitudes and orientations that go into creative leading.* If a person is going to have a chance at leading successfully, who else but a mentor can provide this kind of guide?

MENTORING AS ATTENTIVE RESPONSIBILITY

Mentoring, then, is concrete, interactive practice of Attentive Responsibility. These are some of the ways that make it so:

1. Attentive Responsibility helps leaders grow by pushing back barriers. Using the metaphor of the arch, the keystone of the leader's innermost psyche rises up and is then held aloft by the spires of Moral Learning and Moral Imagination, Decision and (as we will see) Flow. Mentoring first demands that the protégé be willing to push back the barriers, preconceptions, and ego defenses that limit growth as a leader. Mentors work with the protégé during these times, insisting that the barriers be pushed back and showing the protégé how to do it.
2. Attentive Responsibility allows oneself to hear different voices

in the context of dialogue, weaving a narrative of possible futures. Mentoring trains the protégé to allow those voices in and to do their work in fostering aspiration, possibility, and success.

3. Mentoring is offered selflessly, as is Attentive Responsibility. No one can insist that this ethic be adopted and entered into. No one can demand that one guide and channel one's attention to a world of passing events, many of which are difficult and painful. No one can demand that a person take responsibility. Mentoring is entered into selflessly, with no pretense of expectation of a personal benefit. The protégé might not even know mentoring is going on. And sometimes the mentor has to be so difficult that the protégé abandons the context of the relationship. All this must be done. One chooses to mentor a protégé in whom one recognizes a germ of something that needs cultivation in order to take root, no less flower. This germ is noticed in attention, and it is only nurtured by, for no reason, taking responsibility.

CULTIVATING "FLOW": THE ENGINE OF ATTENTIVE RESPONSIBILITY

Having a consistent practice over an extended period of time (or maybe for a lifetime) shapes lives by strengthening certain feelings while diminishing the impact of others. By acting out of the stance of Attentive Responsibility, leaders will develop the more welcoming, positive, and affirming emotions ("He never gets down," people say about some creative leaders) and will be more resistant to anger and discouragement. These constructive emotions have an infinitely greater chance of arising, when they are cultivated. The practice strengthens emotions that stabilize leaders' minds and hearts, allowing a quick recovery and a renewed resolve to get back into the fray.

Then, no matter what extreme adversities leaders face, no matter if they are temporarily off balance and agitated or disappointed, they have vibrant deep wells of psychic energies to draw on. Nurturing, sustaining, and replenishing those wells of energy are the motivations for adopting a practice. And the stream of those special energies, that contains the nutrients our psyches crave in order to grow, is generated in the special experience called "Flow." This seminal experience puts creative leaders in touch with two feelings that may not be available through any other means: "nothing special" and joy.

FLOW: THE FOURTH SPIRE

Flow is the name we give to the fourth spire, the spire of the "Vital Self," in the Arch of the Leader's Ethic. This spire expresses the leader's energy, quantitatively and qualitatively. In the first arch, we characterized this spire as representing Drive, referring to the abundant energy the leader displays and well as the kind of determination that leading requires. Here, at the third arch, where leaders become genuinely open to the world and its lessons, trials and riches, that energy becomes *"Flow"—the free exchange between the leader's personal energy and the universal energies available through engaging that wider world.*

Flow is the name given to a certain kind of learning experience. The experience takes the learner beyond new knowledge and new facts to new constellations and possibilities of living. In the Flow experience, I see myself doing something more competently, more confidently, and more successfully because I just, well, flow seamlessly, effortlessly, without any self-conscious control. The range of action in which I feel competent now encompasses and solidifies new behaviors that offer greater capability. These new capabilities enable me to participate in new levels of activity—benefiting more from them and being more challenged by them, and gaining more satisfaction from them than ever before.

You can see why Mihaly Csikszentmihalyi, who has studied the phenomenon, would call Flow an "optimal experience." He and his staff have documented that Flow is likely to occur when these three parameters are present: first, the experience mixes just the right amounts of challenge, interest, and potential for success; second, it has continual feedback mechanisms indicating progress or decline; and third, it goes on for just a certain amount of time so as not to be either physically or psychically exhausting. The experience, as you can see, definitely can fit any of the practices we have encouraged. Interestingly, Csikszentmihalyi's group found the experience more likely to occur at work than in leisure activities. I bet it does occur, however, in the "leisure" activities of kind we describe as practices.

THE FEELING OF FLOW

When in the Flow state, what is most important is the action itself and how my energies channel into that action. My psyche's feedback loop then "speaks" to me about what is happening. I get to see what I am doing as though it were "objectified" and made real. I may experience frustration or disappointment, even pain as I put myself through the paces of meeting the challenge, and yet, the last thing I want to do is stop. I want to go on, make the next pass successful, repeat the success a few times and ingrain it. I want not just the result to be real; I want what I can do, who I can be, this newly capable and successful practitioner, to be real.

In the context of a practice, Flow gives me a sense of release from trivia and enervating aggravation, and I cultivate the motor and mental skills that are necessary to take on the next level of challenge. In my meditation practice, for example, I pay attention over a long period of time to just one thing, the breath, a flower, a mantra, training my mind to guide attention and ever more easily enter the Flow state. As I am released from enervating and exhausting fragmentation, I am able to freely engage, with all of my being, into a chosen field of attention. A psychic state of release such as this allows me to restore my equilibrium, even in the heat of engagement. In this state, all my experiences are layered, organized, prioritized. Some difficulties fade away; they lose their power because one can invoke release. Even great pain can be transcended by guiding and firming up the stream of attention onto other dimensions of the experience. It is these dimensions that yield feedback in flow and joy in their coming to pass. All else is dross. And then, it is time to move on.

Flow is a highly desirable psychic state. Csikszentmihalyi hypothesizes that Flow is pleasurable because it is nature's way of attracting the mind to learning new behaviors that support survival and thriving. Through the experience of Flow, we grow psychically and overcome the strictures of genetic or cultural limitations. Our brains, indeed our whole psyches and bodies are reformed and reconfigured. Thus Flow enables humans to grow out of and beyond, or at least not be prisoners to, our chemical, genetic, genealogical, and environmental and/or our cultural inheritances. For many people seeking to break through the managerial barrier, Flow offers the prospect of success. Just because we started in our careers as efficiency-driving managers does not mean we cannot grow into inspiring leaders. We do not have to accept the premise, "I've always done it that way," or, "If it ain't broke, don't fix it." We can take ourselves to vastly new horizons.

HOOKED ON FLOW

For the best news of all, hear this: According to Csikszentmihalyi, people get "hooked" on having Flow in their lives. They seek out experiences in which Flow can happen. They are so hooked, if they are not learning in this way, their lives feel less satisfying. I think this is why leaders push themselves and their followers to new heights. It isn't ego, as it would appear to the uninitiated. Creative leaders need the experience of challenge and learning in order to feel alive. And so they crave the experience of Flow. Nature uses flow as the hook, the lure, the aphrodisiac that compels creative leaders to seek out those experiences, raise the bar, and put values to more sever and stringent tests.

Does this sound masochistic? To some, it would be. But to creative leaders, these challenges open to the possibility that beyond the short-term pain, down that path they know that real joy awaits.

"NOTHING SPECIAL"

Flow induces a paradoxical condition. I am able to experience things intensely, with focus and constancy, and also, beyond that, to also know that what is happening is "nothing special," and so add no extra feeling to what is happening.

Another word for this attitude is "detachment." I hesitate to use that word because it can be misinterpreted as meaning apathy or passivity. Actually, the word means nothing of the sort. It means that while I am fully engaged, sporadic surprises and inevitable discouragements don't take precedence over the fact that I am engaged in the situation to begin with. I like the term "nothing special" because it is an orientation in which *I do what I do no matter what happens as a result, and without any window dressing of expectations. It is just what I do, it's "nothing special."*

To explain this phenomenon, I will use a story told by Suzuki Roshi in his classic primer on Zen practice, *Zen Mind, Beginner's Mind*.[2] In a chapter entitled "Nothing Special," he talks about how visitors to his zendo, or monastery where monks practice Zen, comment on its peaceful, holy atmosphere. To these outsiders, the place has a special, additional atmosphere they call by these various names. But to the practitioners in the monastery there is no such feeling. The zendo is just the place where the monks eat, sleep, meditate, clean, and do other chores. To them, the monastery is just the venue in which they carry out the activities of their normal, daily lives as monks; to them, it is "nothing special."

Similarly, in the context of a practice, Flow becomes a normal, natural, assumed, unquestioned part of one's day. At a particular time, you just think, "It is time to . . ." do the practice. That's all. Why is that so important? Two reasons: First, it trains the mind to be more immune to moods or other disruptive temptations. If I am in a bad mood, everything just feels harder to do.

If I feel good, everything flows. But if I never even register these feelings, if I have no expectation or windup about them, I'll just start. Nothing special, it's just what I do.

[2] Suzuki, *Zen Mind, Beginner's Mind* (New York, 1987).

Second, the overly emotional leader flames out. She may excel at exciting and motivating her group in the short term, but on her bad days, she can be so down that the whole group is dragged down with her. The fewer the emotional ups and downs a leader presents, the more likely it is that the endeavor will endure. If you meet the objective, good—move on to the next. If you don't, keep working. In the context of a practice, it's no big deal; we're just learning.

JOY

Joy emanates from Flow. In Flow we experience being openly energized, wanting to more fully engage in the challenges we have set for ourselves.

Happiness—that state of being we all say we want—is a variant of joy. Happiness is expressed in many ways. Glee, having fun, comfort, and contentment are a few of the ways happiness is experienced in our lives. It derives from joy, but is more limited and situation-specific. Happiness fades quickly when the activity is terminated.

Paradoxically, one need not feel "happy," good, or even comfortable to be experiencing joy. *Joy defines a psychic state of being completely connected with what is happening, in a free flow between inner and outer experience.* I can be sad and in mourning about the death of a friend and yet, at the same time, even more, feel a sense of joy at what this person accomplished, contributed, and had the chance to experience in his lifetime. I can feel frustration at the lack of success my endeavor is having, and yet not want to do anything else because the joy of just being in the endeavor at all is so overwhelming.

A practice that supports Attentive Responsibility predisposes a leader to this kind of joy. Joy ends up being the predominant emotion of creative leading. Out of this attitude we differentiate between what is good in life and what is not; that we discern in the detail of our experiences what sustains us and what drains us; and it is against the standard of this experience that we realize the benefits from the stance of being "finely aware and richly responsible." If we are aware of the experiences that constitute what is good in life, we can be resilient against the adversity that inevitably will occur. We know how to move back toward what is affirming and positive. If we know the difference between the nurturing and the negating, we know when to completely let ourselves be immersed in life and when to hold back. And if we know the joy that comes from the labors required by Attentive Responsibility, we may be more willing to step into the next, more difficult, maybe impossible endeavor. That's the leader's experience of joy.

APPENDIX

THE ARCHES: COMPLETE

THE ARCH OF LEADERSHIP: COMPLETE

The scheme of three arches introduces irritating complexity into the narrative. Why the complexity? Please consider these factors:

FIRST, THE ENDEAVOR OF LEADING IS COMPLEX.
It involves a personal orientation to doing things in certain ways—viz., with people; it requires an ability to envision what has not yet happened; it requires an incredible amount (as well as a specific composition) of energy; it requires an ability to organize, empathize and enforce. And the list goes on.

THEN, THERE IS THE MATTER OF HOW PEOPLE GROW AND CHANGE IN THE COURSE OF THE EXPERIENCES OF LEADING.
When people grow their worlds not only look different as they progress through their lives, but they actually think differently about those worlds, calling upon additional and/or different psychic resources than they had in the past. At each stage of my life, I am in a place, a state of mind, a way of being that, for me, is "the way it is."

Thus each stage has to be taken on its own merits, as presenting a very competent, if not complete, sense of life. Each stage constitutes a place, a context, a specific organization of values and priorities. Since leaders define places and even whole worlds for people, we need to acknowledge each significant place in the leader's developing.

This volatile combination—the multifaceted dimensions of leading and the competence of each stage of the leader's development—results in the complexity of the scheme of three multicomponent arches. I see no alternative to this complexity. If we are trying to present a picture of leading that respects the character and depth of both the role itself, as well as the depth and courage of the people who decide to undertake it, we have to respect that complexity. As a mentor, my premise is always that there are no cookie cutter ways to help leaders.

THE COMPONENTS

Each arch contains these, and only these, elements: four spires, one keystone, and one interior space.

KEYSTONE

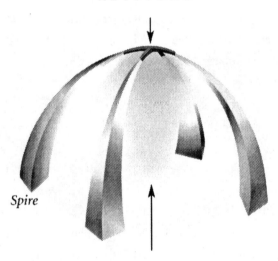

Spire

INNER SPACE

PSYCHICAL STATE

We have stated that the arch symbolizes the "mind set" or the "psychical state" of the leader. When people enter the arena in which leading is at issue, many feel like an actor setting foot on to the stage. They are not pretending to be something they are not; rather, they concentrate their minds and bodies in a very particular, singularly different way, from roles they take in their private, nonleading lives. As they leave their houses in the morning, the roles they took in their families are loosening their grips. As they drive to work, family issues may blend and collide with the issues of their organizations, but as they approach their offices, it is the organizational needs that press on their minds. When they walk into their respective buildings, they know that eyes are upon them, reading them for mood, energy level, focus of attention. They are being seen as leaders. Like it or not, the role of leading presses in on them.

The arch represents that psychical (standing for a vast range of intellectual, emotional, feeling, perceiving, and reflecting activities we carry on as active subjects) state that is required in order to fulfill that role as leader.

DEVELOPMENT

THREE DIFFERENT ARCHES signify how, as time goes by, anyone in the role of leading grows as new experiences and realizations take hold in their lives. At each arch, the psychical state in which leaders think and feel themselves to be living seems to be complete and whole. The next arch is not in view. However, when they are dwelling within the second and third arches, they always remember the psychical states that preceded them. Not only do they remember these states but, in the new setting, try to take the former states to new levels of competence, wholeness, and resilience.

The arches mark out the course of learning that leaders must undertake in order to fulfill their senses of themselves. And each arch envisions a more encompassing, challenging, and difficult set of learnings that creative leaders set for themselves.

ARCH III: ARCH OF LEADER'S ETHIC

ARCH II: ARCH OF VISION
AND ORGANIZATION

ARCH I ARCH OF EFFECTIVENESS

*There are three different arches, along the path,
signifying three stages of a leader's life.*

1. THE ARCH OF EFFECTIVENESS

KEYSTONE: SELF-TRUST

INTERIOR SPACE: LEADER BRAND

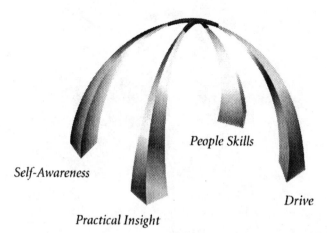

People Skills

Self-Awareness

Drive

Practical Insight

THE EFFECTIVENESS ARCH

This is the arch in which leaders first discover their "calling." They find they are able to influence people and accomplish large-scale projects. Here the learning is to turn away from technical and even managerial subject matter towards the person, the self (of the leader) to which people are responding so favorably. The person in this arch learns how to go from being surprised at how well people respond to their leading, to consciously—using the Skills of Character in the arch—creating followers. Thus a person, for the first time, *consciously decides* to set herself on the path of leading.

2. THE ARCH OF VISION AND ORGANIZATION

KEYSTONE: SIGNATURE BEHAVIOR

INTERIOR SPACE: PROCESS AND STRUCTURE

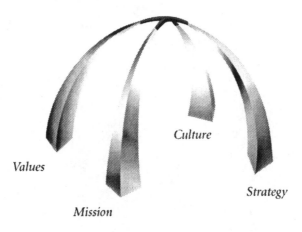

Culture

Values

Strategy

Mission

THE ARCH OF VISION AND ORGANIZATION

Here, a person who has already decided to lead—and to develop the leader's skills of character—takes that decision into the new learning space of leading to fulfill their own vision of the world. Since they are doing so as leaders, they must fulfill this *vision* by creating an organization. (Those in the other transforming roles—i.e., mystics, prophets, or artists—do not create organizations in order to express their felt need to generate change.)

Even though the names of the spires are typically considered concepts of organizational development (we call "attractors"), the leader is responsible for making these concepts come alive, be vital and compelling to the people in the endeavor. Thus, they are psychical dimensions of the leader in that he or she must learn how to portray and embody these concepts.

297

3. THE ARCH OF THE LEADER'S ETHIC

KEYSTONE: ATTENTIVE RESPONSIBILITY
INTERIOR SPACE: PRACTICE

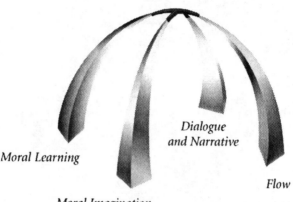

*Dialogue
and Narrative*

Moral Learning

Flow

Moral Imagination

THE ARCH OF THE LEADER'S ETHIC

In this final arch, leaders have fully decided that their *lives are to be lived as leaders—nothing else,* nothing less or more. This arch portrays a life of the leader's peculiar and special learning. The leader is no longer learning about how to do things or acquire skills, but how to be a learning person. There is continual contact and attention paid to the world, and the leader constantly grows and consciously guides changes in order to be more capable in the leading role.

The leader also learns and adopts life practices that enable him or her to sustain that life over the long haul, and thus be able to take on larger, more arduous, and long-term efforts.

With the completion of this arch, the leader flows seamlessly among and between all the skills, attractors, and practices that comprise the great role of leading.

THE SPIRES:

SPIRE	PURPOSE	ARCH	SKILL	IN
The Developing Self	The internal driving factors that result in a person deciding, acting and behaving in certain ways (and not others).	Effectiveness Vision Ethic	Self-Awareness Values Moral Learning	Ch. 2 Ch. 6 Ch. 7
Self-in-Action	The ability to discern in a situation the potential for novel approaches and solutions that have an important effect on how others are able to engage in their lives and world.	Effectiveness Vision Ethic	Practical Insight Mission Moral Imagination	Ch. 2 Ch. 6 Ch. 8
Social Self	The ability to relate to others in such a way as to appreciate their perspectives and to affect, modify or reinforce those perspectives such that they decide to collaborate in the endeavor.	Effectiveness Vision Ethic	People Skills Culture Decision: Dialogue and Narrative	Ch. 2 Ch. 6 Ch. 7
Vital Self	The energies that are available to expend in a coherent and forceful way, in the organizational context, so as to engender collaboration that produces worthy outcomes of change.	Effectiveness Vision Ethic	Drive Strategy Flow	Ch. 2 Ch. 6 Ch. 11

THE KEYSTONES:

ARCH	SKILL	DESCRIPTION	IN
Effectiveness	Self-Trust	The ability to accept the worthiness of decisions based on the recollection of Skills of Character and how they connect to the current situation. "Charisma" is the ability to call upon Self-Trust when interacting, deciding and acting with collaborators in the endeavor.	Ch. 2
Vision and Organization	Signature Behavior	The ability to establish a singular way into which all the organization's activities coalesce such that it can establish a clearly identifiable niche in (that is supported by) the environment, and can survive and even thrive as it conducts its actions.	Ch. 6
The Leader's Ethic	Attentive Responsibility	The orientation the leader takes to the world: paying close attention ("being finely aware") to the world, and taking responsibility for people's lives, as well as for what is seen, understood, appreciated, valued and in need of change.	Ch. 10, 11

THE INNER SPACES:

ARCH	SKILL	DESCRIPTION	IN
Effectiveness	*Leader Brand*	*The enduring expectations leaders set for their followers and how they allow themselves to be needed by those followers.*	*Ch. 2*
Vision and Organization	*Process/ Structure*	*The repeated, supported and constantly improved core activities that are necessary if the organization is to accomplish what its attractors (spires) and Signature Behavior intend.*	*Ch. 6*
The Leader's Ethic	*Practice*	*Activities that reinforce the kind of learning, imagination, stamina and attentiveness which creative leading requires.*	*Ch. 10, 11*

BIBLIOGRAPHY

BIBLIOGRAPHY

Best, Geoffrey. *Churchill: A Study in Greatness*. New York: Hambleton and London, 2001.

Burns, James McGregor. *Leadership*. New York: Harper Torchbooks, 1979.

Burns, James McGregor, and Susan Dunn. *The Three Roosevelts: Patrician Leaders Who Transformed America*. New York: Atlantic Monthly Press, 2001.

Collins, James. *Good to Great*. New York: Harper Business, 2001.

Collins, James C., and Jerry I. Porras. *Built to Last: Successful Habits of Visionary Companies*. New York: Harper Business, 1997.

Csikszentmihalyi, M. *Flow: The Psychology of Optimal Experience*. New York: Harper & Row Publishers, 1990.

_____. *The Evolving Self: A Psychology for the Third Millennium*. New York: Harper Collins Publishers, 1993.

Csikszentmihalyi, M., and Csikszentmihalyi, I. S., eds. *Optimal Experience: Psychological Studies of Flow in Consciousness*. New York: Cambridge University Press, 1988.

Damasio, Antonio. *The Feeling of What Happens: Body and Emotion in the Making of Consciousness*. New York: Harcourt Brace & Co., 1999.

_____. *Looking for Spinoza: Joy, Sorrow and the Feeling Brain*. New York: Harcourt, Inc., 2003.

Deacon, Terrence W. *The Symbolic Species: The Co-Evolution of Language and the Brain*. New York: W. W. Norton & Co., 1997.

Donald, David Herbert. *Lincoln*. London: Jonathan Cape, 1995.

Foster, R., and S. Kaplan. *Creative Destruction*. New York: Currency, 2001.

Frady, Marshall. *Martin Luther King Jr.* New York: Penguin Books, 2002.

Gardner, Howard. *Creating Minds*. New York: Basic Books, 1993.

_____. *Frames of Mind.* New York: Basic Books, 1993.

_____. *Leading Minds.* New York: Basic Books, 1995.

Goleman, Daniel. *Working with Emotional Intelligence.* New York: Bantam Books, 1998.

Graham, Katharine. *Personal History.* New York: Vintage Books, 1998.

Hegel, GWF. *Philosophy of History.* New York: Dover Publications, 1956.

Hegel, GWF, and A. V. Miller, tr. *Phenomenology of Spirit: The Science of the Experience of Consciousness.* New York: Oxford University Press, 1997.

_____. *The Science of Logic I, II.* Atlantic Highlands, NJ: Humanities Press International, Inc., 1989.

Holland, John H. *Emergence: From Chaos to Order.* Reading, MA: Addison-Wesley Publishing Co., 1998.

Jantsch, Erich. *The Self-Organizing Universe.* New York: Pergamon International Library, 1980.

Johnson, Mark. *Moral Imagination: Implications of Cognitive Science for Ethics.* Chicago: University of Chicago Press, 1993.

Kauffman, Stuart. *At Home in the Universe: The Search for the Laws of Self-Organization and Complexity.* New York: Oxford University Press, 1995.

_____. *Investigations.* New York: Oxford University Press, 2000.

Klein, Gary. *Sources of Power: How People Make Decisions.* Cambridge, MA: The MIT Press, 1998.

Kohut, Heinz. *Self Psychology and the Humanities.* New York: W. W. Norton & Co., 1988.

Lakoff, George. *Women, Fire and Dangerous Things: What Categories Reveal about the Mind.* Chicago: University of Chicago Press, 1987.

Lakoff, George, and Mark Johnson. *Metaphors We Live By.* Chicago: University of Chicago Press, 1980.

_____. *Philosophy in the Flesh: The Embodied Mind and Its Challenge to Western Thought*. New York: Basic Books, 1999.

Lehrer, Keith. *Self-Trust: A Study of Reason, Knowledge, and Autonomy*. Oxford: Clarendon Press, 1997.

Lewin, Roger. *Complexity: Life at the Edge of Chaos*. New York: Macmillan Publishing Company, 1992.

Lewin, Roger, and Birute Regine. *The Soul at Work: Embracing Complexity Science for Business Success*. New York: Simon & Shuster, 2000.

Margulis, Lynn. *Symbiotic Planet: A New View of Evolution*. New York: Basic Books, 1998.

Margulis, Lynn, and Dorion Sagan. *Microcosmos: Four Billion Years of Microbial Evolution*. Berkeley, CA: University of California Press, 1986.

Maturana, Humberto R., and Francisco J. Varela. *The Tree of Knowledge: The Biological Roots of Human Knowledge*. Boston: Shambhala, 1998.

Nunez, R., and Walter J. Freeman. *Reclaiming Cognition: The Primacy of Action, Intention and Emotion*. Bowling Green, OH: Imprint Academic, 1999.

Nussbaum, Martha C. *The Fragility of Goodness: Luck and Ethics in Greek Tragedy and Philosophy*. New York: Cambridge University Press, 1986.

_____. *Love's Knowledge: Essays on Philosophy and Literature*. New York: Oxford University Press, 1990.

_____. *The Therapy of Desire*. Princeton, NJ: Princeton University Press, 1996.

_____. *Upheavals of Thought: The Intelligence of Emotions*. New York: Cambridge University Press, 2001.

Prigogine, Ilya, and Isabelle Stengers. *Order Out of Chaos: Man's New Dialogue with Nature*. New York: Bantam, 1984.

Ray, Paul H., and Sherry Ruth Anderson. *The Cultural Creatives: How 50 Million People Are Changing the World*. New York: Harmony Books, 2000.

Samson, Anthony. *Mandela: The Authorized Biography*. New York: Knopf, 1999.

Seinfeld, Jerry. *Sein Language*. New York: Bantam Books, 1998.

Shenkman, Michael H. *The Strategic Heart: Using the New Science to Lead Growing Organizations*. Westport, CT: Greenwood Publishing Group, 1996.

—————. *Value and Strategy: Competing Successfully in the Nineties*. Westport, CT: Greenwood Publishing Group, 1993.

Spinosa, C., F. Flores, and H. L. Dreyfus. *Disclosing New Worlds: Entrepreneurship, Democratic Action and the Cultivation of Solidarity*. Cambridge, MA: The MIT Press, 1997.

Taylor, Charles. *The Ethics of Authenticity*. Cambridge, MA: Harvard University Press, 1991.

—————. *Sources of the Self: The Making of Modern Identity*. Cambridge, MA: Harvard University Press, 1989.

Thompson, William Irwin. *Coming into Being: Artifacts and Texts in the Evolution of Consciousness*. New York: St. Martin's Griffin, 1998.

Varela, Francisco J. *Ethical Know-How*. Stanford, CA: Stanford University Press, 1999.

Varela, Francisco J., Eva Thompson, and Eleanor Rosch. *The Embodied Mind: Cognitive Science and Human Experience*. Cambridge, MA: The MIT Press, 1999.

Waldrop, M. Mitchell. *Complexity: The Emerging Science at the Edge of Order and Chaos*. New York: Simon & Scheuster, 1992.

Wolfreys, Julian, ed. *The Derrida Reader: Writing Performances*. Lincoln, NE: University of Nebraska Press, 1998.

INDEX

Printed in the United States
51309LVS00002B/286